Every Mother's Nightmare

The Murder of James Bulger

Mark Thomas

iBooks
Habent Sua Fata Libelli

iBooks
1230 Park Avenue
New York, New York 10128
Tel: 212-427-7139
bricktower@aol.com • www.BrickTowerPress.com

Library of Congress Cataloging-in-Publication Data

Thomas, Mark.
Every Mother's Nightmare.
p. cm.
1. True Crime. 2. Non-Fiction—Crime, I. Title.

ISBN-13: 978-1-59687-478-7, Trade Paper

First iBooks printing, December 2005

Cover art by Kev Walker

Cover design by J. Vita

November 2011

Every Mother's Nightmare

The Murder of James Bulger

Mark Thomas

Every Mother's Nightmare

ACKNOWLEDGEMENTS

Researching and writing my first book on such a difficult and distressing subject was a daunting task. Without the help and support of many people directly involved with this harrowing case and the encouragement and advice of others who lent me their professional expertise in a number of areas it would have been an impossible one.

I must begin by recording my gratitude to Ralph and Denise Bulger and the many members of their large and closely-knit family who welcomed me into their homes and shared with me their recollections of the most terrible experience of their lives. In particular I would like to express my thanks to Ray and Deliah Matthews for their endless patience, hospitality and assistance. My thanks also to their solicitor, Sean Sexton.

As important to this book as the co-operation of the Bulger family was the help and access provided to me over a lengthy series of in-depth interviews by many officers from the Merseyside Police Force. Their willingness to take me beyond the professional details of their task and explore the emotional toll this crime took of all of them provided an invaluable, possibly unique insight into what this investigation was like for the human beings caught up in it.

My thanks then to Detective Superintendent Albert Kirby, the senior investigating officer to Detective Inspector Jim Fitzsimmons, police press officers Inspector Ray Simpson, Diane Halliwell and Wendy Johnson, Detective Inspector Andy McDiarmid, Detective Sergeants Phil Roberts, Jim Green and Andy Rushton, Detective Constables Dave Tanner and George Scott, PC Mandy Waller, photographic and technical support unit manager Ian Clague and his colleagues Colin Smith and Alan Williams.

Covering the case through my job as Merseyside staff reporter for Britain's national news agency, the Press Association, put me in a unique position to write this book. For that, and for giving me permission to pursue this project, I am deeply indebted to them. A special word of thanks to Peter Beal.

I would also like to thank Liverpool Walton Labour MP Peter Kilfoyle, solicitor Mr Rex Makin, Professor of Psychiatric Mental Health Nursing at the University of Pennsylvania School of Nursing Ann Burgess, Liverpool University lecturer in Forensic Clinical Psychology David Glasgow, Professor of Child and Adolescent Psychiatry at Liverpool University Jonathan Hill, Professor of Sociology at Liverpool University Ken Roberts, David Bamber, David Utting and his colleagues from the Family Policy Studies Centre, Crime Concern and NACRO, Graham Clegg, Father Michael O'Connell and Lynda Roughley. I extend a special word of thanks to Diane Power, the mother of the young boy almost abducted earlier on the day James was taken.

Finally, I would like to thank all those who have guided and helped me in the preparation of this book. Thanks, in particular, to my editor Catherine Hurley, to Sara Fisher, Peter Rubie and Lori Perkins, to Diane Bin, and to my wife Andrea, who was there for me in the dark moments when this whole project was almost too much to bear.

Note: The names of any children mentioned in the book, with the exception of Robert Thompson and Jon Venables, and the Bulger family, are fictitious.

Chapter One

James Bulger was a month short of his third birthday when two killers lured him away from his mother in a busy shopping mall, dragged him to a lonely railway embankment and murdered him. It was an unspeakably cruel death. The thought of anyone being evil enough to inflict such a fate on an innocent little child defies comprehension. Astonishingly, the killers in this case were both just ten years old.

James's devoted parents Ralph and Denise Bulger lived in Kirkby, an overspill town on the outskirts of Liverpool, in the north-west of England. Denise, twenty-five, had taken her only son on a shopping expedition to the nearby town of Bootle on the afternoon of Friday, 12 February 1993. She was queueing for meat in a busy butcher's shop in the Strand Shopping Centre, a sprawling modern mall in Stanley Road, Bootle town centre, when the toddler strayed from her side and was gone. Every mother knows that terrible moment. For seconds or minutes there is a frantic search. Usually the outcome is a tearful reunion with a mother much too relieved to be angry. For Denise that reunion would never come. For her, every mother's nightmare became a terrible reality.

Security cameras in the mall watched in discreet silence as James was led away by two boys. The blurred images the cameras captured of an effervescent toddler skipping along trustingly in the wake of two young boys with murder in their hearts were seared into the minds of a stunned nation in the days that followed. When police first released the pictures at news conferences on the Saturday and Sunday mornings, there remained strong hopes that the massive search that had been launched would have a happy ending. Those hopes were dashed on the Sunday afternoon, when the boy's tiny body was discovered, horribly mutilated, on a railway track in Walton, Liverpool.

Merseyside Police took less than four days to track down and arrest the two killers. One lived close to the murder scene in Walton, the other in nearby Norris Green. News of their arrest was withheld for twenty-four hours while detectives completed further important inquiries. On Friday, 9 February, the news that two boys aged ten had been arrested for the murder was broken by the officer in charge of the investigation, Detective Superintendent Albert Kirby.

The shockwaves from this crime reverberated rapidly throughout Great Britain and the world. Nobody could quite believe what had happened; nobody could understand why. The case threw into sharp focus the debate about an erosion of standards of behaviour that was nibbling at the very roots of British society. A generation was perceived to be running wild, without fear of punishment or any real sense of right or wrong. If children so young could be so wicked, who could begin to predict the atrocities the future adults of this lawless generation might inflict?

Many ordinary people in Britain had been experiencing a growing sense of unease about the way things were heading. Juvenile crime had outraged and shocked the nation before. This murder emphasized and underlined that feeling and did something more. The James Bulger case frightened people. If ever there was a moment to declare that enough was enough, it appeared that this poor child's death was to be the rallying point.

There had been child murders before, and dreadful crimes committed by children too, but this particular case seemed to strike a universal chord. A powerful element of the equation, I believe, was the impact of those security video pictures. They were so indistinct that the children involved could, with a little imagination, be anyone. Was there a parent anywhere who did not spot something of their own child, from past or recent recollection, in the scampering little infant on the screen? And what of the killers? Many parents of uncontrollable, naughty children must have looked hard at those little boys and searched their own souls to ask if they knew for sure that their sons were not capable of equally terrible crimes. Above all, though, there was the feeling of desperate helplessness those images instilled in everyone who has ever cared about a child. Knowing what was to befall that little boy, you instinctively wanted to reach out on to the screen and pull him back to safety. 'If only I had been there,' you found yourself thinking, 'somehow I would have stopped it'. Yet nobody did. Out of all the hundreds of shoppers milling around, preoccupied by their private cares and anxieties as they hunted the bargains that Friday afternoon, nobody noticed anything wrong. Would you or I have been any different?

I first became aware of James's disappearance late that Friday afternoon. Liverpool and the rest of Merseyside form part of the territory I cover as a reporter for the Press Association, Britain's national news agency. At first, none of us in the national media was unduly concerned by the incident. Children, even of James's tender years, go missing surprisingly often. They usually turn up safe and well within a few hours. By the Saturday, with no sign of the youngster and after the release of those video images, it became clear that something much more sinister was afoot. Still, through all the anxious appeals and searches of the nearby Leeds-Liverpool Canal by police divers, there remained the gut feeling that it would all turn out happily. After all, two young boys could plot mischief, but murder seemed outlandishly beyond the bounds of probability. More likely, as police were hoping, these were runaway boys living rough in the area who were keeping James with them in some derelict building.

Those hopes ended for me with a telephone call I received from a well-informed source on the Sunday afternoon. 'They've found him,' the caller told me.

'Alive?' I knew the answer I would receive from the tone of his voice. I just didn't want to believe it.

'No,' was the flat response.

Soon afterwards the police gave me official confirmation that a child's body had been found. I took the call on my mobile telephone as I was heading for the murder scene from my home on the far side of the River Mersey. By the time I arrived at the spot, a matter of 300 yards from Walton Lane Police Station, officers from the British Transport Police, a separate force responsible for policing Britain's railways, had cordoned it off. A long, bleak evening lay ahead before I was given the first official confirmation by Merseyside Police of what we all knew would be the case. The body had been identified as that of James, and he had been murdered.

You are supposed to be immune to most things as a news journalist. Like police officers, reporters try to develop an invisible second skin that enables them to detach themselves emotionally from heartbreaking situations and allows them to get on with their job. That is the theory. Late that night when I heard unofficial, off the record information that James had been tortured and mutilated, the mask slipped a little. While I had been out my wife had spent the early part of the evening playing with a neighbour's eighteen-month-old twin daughters. She knows me better than I know myself and could tell at once that something was troubling me. She pressed me until I told her what I had heard. She cried for an hour that night before we both slipped into a troubled sleep.

The next morning I awoke to the 7 a.m. news bulletin on Liverpool's independent radio station, Radio City. It carried the Bulger family's first reaction to the discovery of James's body. His paternal grandmother Helen Bulger who, like most of the large and close-knit family, also lived in Kirkby, had been listening to a radio phone-in show in the early hours of the morning and had felt moved to call in with her own response to the tragedy. The station was carrying a brief clip from the programme in its bulletins, but I rang their Liverpool newsroom and they played the full tape down the telephone to me. Mrs Bulger was quick to nip in the bud any suggestions that her daughter-in-law had been at fault, describing her as 'a very protective mother'.

'It has just devastated us all. I don't know how they could be so cruel,' she said. 'It is like a dream. I feel as if I am watching something happen to someone else. You see these cases but you don't know -there's no possible way you could know -the depth of feeling'.

She then made reference to a recent case in which a judge at Newport Crown Court in Gwent, South Wales, had caused national outrage by making a fifteen-year-old boy who had raped a schoolgirl of the same age the subject of a supervision order and telling him to pay his victim £500 so she could have 'a good holiday' to recover from her ordeal. (Britain's Attorney General Sir Nicholas Lyell subsequently appealed against this sentence and the young rapist was sentenced by the Court of Appeal to two years' youth custody. Ironically, the boy's sister then claimed that her brother was paying the price for public feeling against juvenile crime since the James Bulger case.)

Her voice breaking with bitter emotion, Mrs Bulger said, 'U they are children they should not be allowed to pay for a holiday for my son and daughter-in-law. They should be put away where something can be done to them. Even a child knows when it is doing wrong. That's what I think. Maybe a lot won't agree with me...'

Mrs Bulger said her protective sons had not allowed her to go to the police headquarters in Bootle, where her twenty-six-year-old son Ralph and his wife Denise had spent so much of their time since James had disappeared. Asked how the couple were feeling now, she paused for a moment and said in a trembling voice, 'Very bad ... very bad'. It was a deeply emotional interview. At times the radio presenter, Pete Price, sounded close to tears himself. Mrs Bulger saved her most poignant words for the last: 'We know he is dead but we still think we are going to get a hug off him. He was a bubbly little boy. He was beautiful'.

That morning I attended another news conference: at Bootie's Marsh Lane Police Station, now the headquarters of the murder investigation. After filing a story from there I took the five-minute walk to the Strand Shopping Centre. It was years since I had been there, and I was surprised to find that the drab, run-down precinct I recalled had been refurbished and improved into a typical light, airy modern shopping mall, complete with g1asse4 atriums, potted plants, escalators and top British high street stores like Marks and Spencer and Mothercare.

It was the school half-term holiday week, so I was expecting there to be lots of children milling about. There were very few. Mothers and fathers kept their children in their push-chairs or clutched tightly to their sides. That day, a few toddlers were on reins. These had been fashionable in the 1960s as a way of keeping wandering children in check, but were little used these days. That Monday morning the few shops that still stocked them in Bootle sold out, and found themselves with full order books. By the end of that week, almost every young child you saw was tottering about on the end of a length of sturdy nylon. They were attached to their mothers as surely as if by umbilical cords, and a sharp jerk on the rein ended any notions of striking off in the wrong direction. The children looked a little bewildered at this sudden constraint on their freedom to explore. Their mothers were grimly resolute, immune to all protests from their offspring. 'Nobody takes my baby,' was the message etched clearly in those faces.

In A. R. Tyms, the butcher's shop where Denise had been shopping when James had strayed from her side into the clutches of his killers, manager Paul Bennett, a forty-one-year-old father of two, said that Monday, 'There is a general quietness this morning, which there never is on a Monday. Parents are worried, and although it is half-term I haven't seen a lot of children in the Strand this morning. My staff and I all feel devastated that a thing like this could happen, and I think the general public feel the same. They are really sad for the parents of the baby, and that it could happen to someone so young. We've been here for twenty-two years and we've seen robberies and all kinds of things, but never anything like this'.

Michelle Lynch, twenty-six, rarely let her eyes stray from daughters Natalia, four, and Melissa, eighteen months, as she made her wary way through the mall. 'I just feel sorry for that poor family. They have gone through so much, with the disappearance and now this it's really awful,' she said. 'You can't watch kids twenty-four hours a day, and it's hard when you are getting your shopping in to keep an eye on them every moment'.

Sylvia Lythgoe was planning to get reins for her three-year-old daughter Rachel. 'I've been worrying about her all morning. It gets so busy here,' she told me. 'Even if it turns out that it is children who killed James, they should get treated exactly the same as an adult would be'.

Mr Yaser Kilani, twenty-two, said as he pushed his five-month-old son Kassim through the mall in his push-chair that he shopped there every day. 'I feel suddenly very vulnerable. It is a terrible thing to happen to a young child'.

Bus-driver Paul Devaney, thirty-five, and wife Lorraine, thirty-three, from Walton, were keeping an eagle eye on their daughters Amy, five, and Beth, eighteen months. 'Amy is on holiday from school and she is keeping a tight hold of Lorraine's hands or the pram. She isn't moving away from us at all because we aren't letting her,' said Me Devaney. 'Amy is petrified about what has happened. We've used the Strand for a few years and we were shopping here on Friday morning. We are on our guard all the time now. We feel so sorry for the parents. Someone must know these boys, but they aren't saying. They are the ones who need locking up as much as whoever did it'.

Police officers were mingling with the shoppers asking if they recalled anything suspicious from the Friday afternoon. A police poster appealing for information, with a picture of a chuckling James alongside fuzzy stills of the two killers taken from the indistinct video footage, had been pasted to one of the main entrance doors.

By the time I left the mall, someone had laid a bunch of carnations beneath the poster. A little card attached to the flowers read: 'To the family of James, from a well-wisher and mother, Deepest Sorrow'. It was to prove the spark for a remarkable outpouring of emotion, as the people of Merseyside opened their hearts in a quite astonishing fashion in the days ahead.

The wreaths, bunches of flowers and teddy bears multiplied daily until they formed a long, deep, fragrant mound stretching back from the entrance to the mall. The following Friday, a week after James disappeared, the flowers became the centre-piece for a simple ceremony conducted by the Reverend Chris Jones from the local St Matthew's Church. Shoppers observed a tearful minute's silence at 3.40 p.m., the moment James had vanished seven days earlier.

Two miles away there were similar scenes in Walton, as people queued to lay hundreds of floral tributes and children's toys on a grass bank on the corner of Cherry Lane, close to the spot where James's body had been found on the railway track. A message from a child with one teddy read: 'James, this is my bedtime bear. You can keep him now so you can have sweet dreams. Love, Katy'.

These masses of flowers brought back inescapable memories of the last time Liverpool had found itself the centre of international attention, following the Hillsborough disaster on 15 April 1989. In the days that followed queues that were often more than a mile long formed outside Liverpool Football Club's Anfield Stadium as football fans from Merseyside and all over Britain made what became a pilgrimage to lay flowers and pay their last respects to those who had died. First the 18-yard-deep penalty area around the goal filled with flowers. The tribute kept on growing until finally over half the pitch was covered in what was literally a sea of flowers. Their sweet, overpowering scent was everywhere as a memorial service was held in the stadium later. It was a heart-rending almost unbelievable sight, and something those of us who witnessed it will never forget.

When James Bulger died, Liverpool's naturally emotional, warm-hearted people responded in much the same way. Once again, they decided to say it with flowers. This public demonstration of shared grief was seized on as the focus for some of the largely unjustified criticism which descended on Liverpool in the wake of James's death. One of the more vindictive national newspaper reports in the media battle which engulfed Liverpool following the murder appeared under the headline 'Self-Pity City'. Maybe Liverpool people do have a tendency to wallow in their collective sorrow. Perhaps they do tend to be overly defensive when faced with criticism from outside. I will leave that particular debate to the social historians. As a man born in Liverpool who has lived and worked on Merseyside for most of his life I am perhaps too close to the issue to make a judgment.

What I can say for certain is that there was nothing crass or phoney about the outpouring of emotion that followed James's death. There was real shock, real anger, and a genuine sense of loss that was tangible to anyone with an ounce of common humanity.

The Hillsborough Family Support Group, a self-help group formed by families of the victims of that disaster, had a message of sympathy for James's parents published in the deaths columns of the Liverpool Echo, the city's evening newspaper. They were not alone. In the days following the discovery of his body the classified pages of the newspaper were swollen with a total of over a thousand tributes and messages of sympathy. As is the tradition on Merseyside, relatives and close friends of the Bulgers expressed their sorrow through the columns. The youngster's death had so affected the Merseyside community that hundreds of others added their messages. Regulars and staff at many Merseyside pubs, employees at dozens of firms, and members of clubs, trade unions and political groups were all moved to send their tributes. Denise and

Ralph published their own death notice for their son in the newspaper. It read: 'Bulger James Patrick, 12 February, 1993. Tragically, aged 2 years 11 months, darling son of Denise and Ralph'. The couple added details of the arrangements for their son's funeral mass and a request that, instead of flowers, anyone outside the family wishing to pay their respects should send a donation to Liverpool's Alder Hey Hospital, the largest children's hospital in Western Europe. .

The newspaper was anxious not to be seen to be profiting from the huge wave of emotion that had been channeled through its pages. On the day after the funeral it collected all the tributes together and published them again in a special twelve-page free supplement with a photograph of James and the message 'We will never forget you' on the front cover.

That first Monday as I wandered through the Strand Shopping Centre, several of the shops had already set up impromptu collections for the Bulger family. Various local pubs and groups had the same idea. Of course, money could not really help. Everyone was painfully aware of that. It all came back to that sense of helplessness. People felt they just had to do something. As donations started to trickle, and then flood, into Marsh Lane Police Station, it became clear that something had to be organized to deal properly with the thousands of pounds that were accumulating. On Friday, 26 February, the Mayor of Knowsley, the local authority that covers the Bulgers' home town of Kirkby, launched the James Bulger Memorial Appeal. Mike Reddington, a former Liverpool City Council senior official who was trust fund manager of the Hillsborough Appeal, became one of the trustees of the new fund. It was established with the twin aims of attempting to help the family to rebuild their lives and providing a lasting memorial to James which would be of benefit to young children.

Sean Sexton, the solicitor representing Denise and Ralph and acting as a buffer between them and the intense media attention, issued a statement on their behalf. 'The family is extremely grateful to everyone who has donated money

and is anxious that some good should come out of this terrible tragedy' he said. 'It is their ~ and the wish of community leaders in Knowsley that in addition to helping the family the money should be put to good use in the community'.

On the Friday night, even as the two boys who had killed James were being questioned by detectives, a candlelit memorial service was held at St Mary's Roman Catholic Church near his home in Northwood, Kirkby. Every pew was filled and many stood in the aisles. Loudspeakers relayed the service to others waiting outside in the bitter cold. In all, up to 1500 mourners attended, including some of James's aunts and uncles. Denise and Ralph were too deeply immersed in their grief to be able to face the hour-long service but Father Michael O'Connell the parish priest who had done so much to try to bring them comfort, extended their thanks to people throughout Merseyside, England and the world who had shown such support.

The spirit of ecumenicalism is strong on Merseyside, led by an Anglican Bishop and Roman Catholic Archbishop of Liverpool who have formed a close and inspiring partnership to work for the greater good of the region. This night it was left to the Reverend Bernard Schunemann, Anglican curate of nearby St Mark's Church of England Church, to speak of the evil that had befallen James. 'Tonight the whole of Northwood and, I think, the whole of Merseyside and the whole of England is very sad, and I think also we are very, very angry,' he said. 'The terrible death of James reminds us of the very real possibility of evil, evil in ourselves, evil in each one of us and evil, certainly, in young people. We must ask God for his grace for the light of Jesus to help us to overcome evil'.

It was a night of quiet emotion, of dignity and compassion. Weeping children and adults queued to light candles for James and place them on the altar, and later a huge queue formed to sign a book of condolence for the family.

The next afternoon at 3 p.m. over 35,000 football fans stood to observe a minute's silence for James before Liverpool FC's home match at Anfield against Ipswich

Town. A giant banner waved from the Spion Kop carried the simple message 'RIP JAMES'.

Just under four hours later, after three days of patient, gentle questioning, the two boys police were holding were at last formally charged with the abduction and murder of James Bulger. They were also charged with the attempted abduction of a second two-year-old boy from the same shopping mall earlier that fateful Friday.

Monday morning brought their first court appearance, and a very different kind of emotion on the streets of Bootle. Scuffles outside the courtroom led to arrests and a barrage of articles in the national papers condemning the people of Liverpool, as if they were all somehow responsible for the activities of a few.

There were those who showed more compassion and understanding. A group of mothers from the south of England were spurred by James's murder to form a protest organization called Mothers Against Murder and Aggression (MAMA). On Saturday, 27 February, some of them caught a coach to Liverpool where they joined several hundred local parents in a vigil as a gentle flurry of snow fell on the plateau outside Sl George's Hall, a masterpiece of neo-classical architecture in the centre of the city. Other members of the group held a simultaneous vigil outside St Paul's Cathedral in London. Both culminated in two minutes' silence in memory of James.

On the following Monday, Denise and Ralph said their last farewells to their son and laid him to rest in his small white coffin at Liverpool's Kirkdale Cemetery. The Requiem Mass funeral service in Kirkby was harrowing to witness, but thankfully it was the quiet, dignified occasion the couple had wanted. The anticipated thousands did not turn up outside the church, content to respect the family's wishes and watch the live television coverage of the ceremony in their homes. Both public and media respected their requests for privacy at the cemetery.

Two days later the two accused boys made their second appearance before the youth court, but now things were tangibly calming down. The crowds were smaller and the mood was more restrained. Media coverage of the previous week's events had clearly had a sobering effect on the lunatic fringe. The growing numbers of national and international camera crews hoping to report more baying lynch mobs went away disappointed.

It had been less than three weeks since James vanished, but to those of us who had been caught up in the maelstrom, it felt like a lifetime. Returning home from court that Wednesday, I felt mentally, physically and emotionally drained. There had been so much frantic activity, so much anger, so much -sadness. Only now was there time for quiet reflection, to try to make some sense of it all.

At the funeral, Father O'Connell said James's death had touched the world. I had no doubt that he was right in that. Even Prime Minister John Major, making his first important trip to visit recently elected US President, Bill Clinton, had found that the burning question from American journalists had not been the threat of a trade war or the future of the special relationship between the two countries but the James Bulger case and Britain's crime problem.

At home James's death brought the problem of juvenile crime to the top of the national agenda. In the weeks that followed the killing a series of other crimes by young offenders were prominently reported. The theme of society's apparent helplessness in the face of adolescent recidivism arose time and again. The police could catch youngsters and bring them before a court but the judicial system had no remedy that would prevent them from absconding and re-offending, sometimes within hours of their court appearances. Some of these little hard cases were openly laughing at the impotence of the law. They were untouchable and they knew it. There was a callousness about them that angered and disturbed. They showed no evident remorse for those they hurt. Conscience was not a factor in their deliberations. They knew they could do more or less as they pleased and nothing very bad could befall them as a result. That was enough.

There is of course something especially shocking about child malefactors, seeing such a loss of innocence so early, but as a journalist I regularly find myself recording new examples of the growing brutality of many sections of British society. The old and the weak are seen as easy prey by people who seem to have no conscience about the results of their selfish actions for their victims. A few pennies or pounds are enough to tempt these thugs to levels of violence that frequently destroy the lives of their frail and vulnerable victims.

Perhaps I am one more victim of what sociologists identify as the 'golden age' syndrome, where each generation perceives society to be getting worse than it was in their own youth. But to me, life on the streets of Britain in the 1990s seems harsher and more aggressive than I can recall it being in my own teens twenty years or so ago. People have less patience with each other. Latent anger seems quicker to erupt into abuse or violence. Politeness is ignored, courtesy sneered at. I know many others share this view, rightly or wrongly. I also know, quite categorically, that we have come to accept more extreme forms of crime than was the case a few years ago. When I entered journalism, and through my early years in the job, almost any murder case outside the most straightforward domestic incident would guarantee national news coverage. Today a murder has to be 'different' in some way to merit more than a passing mention outside the local media.

It is not a pleasant environment to raise children in, even with the benefits of a strong family structure. That kind of supportive background is something that most of us took for granted not so long ago. Today it is in danger of becoming the exception rather than the rule.

A lot of children today have a pretty awful start in life. More often than ever before, they may have only one parent who has to struggle hard to make ends meet, let alone devote quality time to teaching children to be good citizens. Sitting a child in front of the television to keep him quiet is an understandable but potentially damaging option for many a harassed parent. The diet of violent videos to which many children are exposed at home at an age that no censor would dream of permitting in a cinema could hardly give our children worse role models. In some depressed areas soaring unemployment leaves all but the brightest and most talented children with no realistic hope of a decent, well-paid or rewarding job to look forward to. Meanwhile they are shown glamorous television images of lifestyles they can never hope to attain. Small wonder, perhaps, that many of these children see no reason to conform to the rules of a society that offers them nothing but the prospect of a bread-line life of meagre state handouts. If they see something they want, they will reach out and take it.

But does any of this offer an excuse for murder? The margins of right and wrong have been blurred for many such children, but not eradicated entirely. A little boy, however badly guided and educated, knows he is doing wrong when he pilfers sweets from the corner shop. How much more must this be true of the crime of killing another human being?

A child must surely realize as well as an adult the pain and suffering he is inflicting on another. It is hard to imagine how any child, however sorely misguided, could justify to himself an act of such unmitigated wickedness as what happened to James. Deprivation is no excuse for evil. Nor does it begin to explain how a child could turn so bad, so early.

The stark fact remains that two ten-year-old boys committed this terrible act. We can explore the facts of this case in detail and we can try to understand why it happened, but it is a case that refuses to be pigeon-holed. We look for convenient reasons when something as dreadful as this happens because something inside us finds it reassuring to be able to explain it away. Two young, presumably deeply disturbed products of an alienated, desperate generation reached into a safer, more familiar world of love and care and snatched away a child from its protection for their own dark and terrible motives. I believe this act to be so extreme that it stands alone.

Current trends in society may have helped pave the way for it but it is not part of any trend. It is a shocking, nightmarish aberration. The elements that led to it are complex. Some of them we can really only guess at. There are no neat answers.

Chapter Two

Eileen Matthews sat back in her armchair, smiling indulgently as her tiny granddaughter Antonia capered about at her feet. The child, just two yean old, chuckled to herself as she littered the carpet with her toys, her eyes twinkling with mischief. Her Nan was seventy, white-haired and bespectacled, a frail woman with a careworn face. Eileen, twice-widowed mother of thirteen children, had seen many happy times, but also much hardship and more than her share of sorrow. She had been there for the christenings, the weddings and, God help her, more than enough funerals.

She was the axis around which her family revolved. Her neat, beautifully kept terraced home in Scoter Road, Kirkby, was the headquarters, the meeting place and the foundation rock upon which her close-knit family was built. Eileen was perhaps not quite the traditional matriarch. She was too softly spoken, too quiet for that formidable role. Her health was no longer good. She had battled back from the brink of death two winters earlier. Still, she remained strong inside. When one of her daughters proposed a shopping expedition to Birkenhead or Bootle, Eileen would brush aside the aches and pain, put on her mat and a brave face, and be ready for the off.

Eileen doted on her grandchildren. She would never return from one of her regular shopping outings empty-handed. There would always be a present for one or other of the toddlers who brought so much life and laughter to her hearth. In her bedroom, neatly wrapped, were a child's torch and a magic painting book. She had bought them on a shopping trip to Birkenhead, on the day her family was enveloped by tragedy on a scale bewildering even to this kindly woman who had seen so much. They were for her grandson James. Now, he would never receive them.

Eileen was born in the Walton area of Liverpool in 1923. It was a different place then. Times were hard, memories of the war to end all wars still fresh. But it was a time when communities thrived in those red-brick terraced streets. The corner shop and the local pub were the meeting places. Eileen and her family lived for much of her childhood in Drayton Road, over a chemist's shop. She remembered it fondly as a lovely little building, like a doll's house. Everyone knew each other in streets like those and a stranger would be instantly noticed. Nobody bothered much about locking doors. Children played outside without fear. Eileen remembered carefree days as a child playing on the grassy bank in Cherry Lane that was to become a shrine of flowers to her grandson, yards from the scene of his death. Coronation Street may be a modern-day fantasy of working-class northern life, but it has its roots in the reality of neighbourhoods like Walton in those days.

Eileen grew up through the Depression, married her first husband John Samuels, and gave him three children. He was killed in 1945 flying a Lancaster bomber over Germany in one of the final sorties of the Second World War. It was a sudden, brutal loss for a young mother with three children to support. Like many other war widows, Eileen surmounted her heartache for the sake of her children, and somehow carried on.

After the war she met and married Hugh Matthews. Like Eileen, Hugh had suffered badly in the war: he had been a prisoner-of-war in Germany for five years. The couple moved to a prefab in Peter Road, Walton, and from there, some thirty-seven years ago, to Scorer Road, Kirkby. Most of the sprawling overspill new town that is Kirkby today was still farms and open fields back then. The family was among the first to move in to the newly-built road. The couple had ten children together. Hugh, a fitter by trade, worked at various local factories, eventually retiring from A. C. Delco on Kirkby's industrial estate in his mid sixties. Skilled with his hands, he built up a comprehensive workshop of tools in a shed behind their home. His sons learned by his example, watching him work and lending a hand when they could. The Matthews family rarely need to turn to outside tradesmen for help. They decorate their houses, tile their floors, fit their own wardrobes, and make their own wrought-iron gates. It is part of their legacy from Hugh.

As the town of Kirkby grew, so did the Matthews family. Denise was born in 1967, the second youngest of the clan. Like her brothers and sisters, she went to Quarry Green Junior School, and then to Ruffwood Comprehensive School, a couple of minutes' walk from Scoter Road. Friendly and apparently outgoing, with an acid wit, Denise was a popular girl. She had her shy side, but concealed it with a warm smile and an acerbic line in humour.

Her idol as a teenager was Michael Jackson. Denise was dancing to one of his hits at the nightclub at Kirkby Town Football Club one evening in 1987 when a slimly built, young man called Ralph Bulger caught her eye.

'He just came over and asked me to dance,' Denise recalls. 'We hit it off from there. He often asked to take me out for a meal, but I would never go, so we used to go for a quiet drink together'.

'It took her years before she would eat in front of me,' smiles Ralph. 'She can be a little bit shy. We both are at first, getting to know people, but after that we are all right. I liked her right away'.

Ralph had lived in Kirkby all his life. One of six brothers and sisters, his parents Helen and James had moved out of the Scotland Road area of Liverpool and eventually to Kirkby over thirty years previously. It was a route followed by many families as the old communities of that area of the city, with their roots in Liverpool's once-thriving docks, were torn up by the planners and moved out.

Helen and James Bulger had four sons and two daughters. She calls Ralph 'my baby'. 'He was always laughing and joking. Everything out of his mouth was a joke,' she says.

With that humour as a bond between them, Denise and Ralph's relationship quickly blossomed and eventually Denise became pregnant. The couple were not married, but by now they had moved away from their parents and were sharing a tiny bedsit in Cherryfield Heights, Southdene, Kirkby. They were thrilled at the prospect of having a child, despite their cramped living conditions. The one major cloud on the horizon was Ralph's continuing inability, like many young men in the area, to find a job.

In the 1991 census 34 per-cent of men over sixteen in Kirkby were unemployed, a figure that rose to 44.9 per cent in the eighteen to twenty-four age group. Ralph tried hard to use the system and land a job. He enrolled on seventeen different training schemes, to no avail. 'I am a professional jobber, but I can't get a job!' he says with a grim smile. 'I've been on training schemes as everything from a plasterer to a re-upholsterer, bricklayer, landscape gardener and fork-lift truck driver. But there are just no jobs around here. It gets me down, but I try to keep myself busy'.

Tragedy was to overtake the couple for the first time when Denise gave birth to their daughter, Kirsty. The baby was stillborn. Ralph had been at her side during the birth. It was a devastating blow for them both. Nurses handed the baby to Denise to cuddle as soon as she was born. They took two photographs which they gave her to keep. Overwhelmed by grief himself, Ralph's first concern was for Denise, who was deeply distraught. He asked her to marry him that day, and Denise accepted.

They held a funeral service for Kirsty and buried her in a tiny wooden coffin. 'I'll never forget that day,' Helen Bulger says. 'When a woman loses a baby it is a terrible thing. I lost my second son Gerrard through a cot death at two and a half weeks. I can remember that as if it was yesterday. It just stays in your head. Denise was in a really bad way over Kirsty'.

The couple married at Prescot Registry Office on 16 September 1989, eighteen months after their engagement. It was Denise's twenty-second birthday. 'It means I only get one present, but it's a good one,' says Denise, her face lighting up with a rare, warm smile. The family celebrated the two events with a party at Eileen's house. Fortunately the loss of Kirsty had not affected Denise's ability to have children, and by now she was pregnant again with their second child. Her brother Ray recalls how anxious the family were about her this time. 'We were all concerned for this baby after what had happened to Kirsty. Denise was kept in hospital for two and a half weeks before James was born because of the previous stillbirth'.

Everything progressed normally, however, and in March 1990 Denise went into the maternity unit at Liverpool's Fazakerley Hospital. She gave birth to a baby son on the afternoon of Friday, 16 March 1990. Once again, Ralph was at her side. This rime they had a healthy blond-

haired child. Delighted, Ralph went to find a telephone. Grandfather
Hugh answered the call back at home in Scoter Road and shouted out
to the assembled family, 'It's a baby boy!'

'We were all thrilled,' recalls Ray Matthews. 'We went to the
hospital to see him that afternoon. I held him when he was just a couple
of hours old. He was just a little bundle -more sheet than anything else!
I unwrapped him to see his face fully. I thought he was very much like
Kirsty. He was an unbelievable baby'.

Denise and Ralph chose for their son the names James Patrick after
Ralph's father, who had died of cancer, aged fifty-seven, just before James
was born. Ralph's eldest brother was also called James Patrick. By a
remarkable coincidence grandmother Helen's father and father-in-law
had both also been christened with the two names. Helen smiles as she
remembers: 'When I was married the registrar saw the three James
Patricks on the marriage certificate and said, "They will think I was
drunk when I take this back to the office." '

From the start, Denise and Ralph were extremely protective of their
child. The tragic loss of Kirsty made the couple acutely aware of how
precious a gift a healthy baby was. Nothing was too much trouble for
James. The couple brought him home to their cramped bedsit and
showered him with attention.

Denise recalls: 'As a young baby James constantly cried. We walked
the floors with him all hours of the night. But after he was about four
months old we would hardly hear him cry. He would sleep through all
night after that and during the day we would hardly hear him crying.
As long as we were playing with him he was all right. He had blond hair.
He took after his Dad, who had blond hair as a baby.

'He started talking early. At about four months old he was saying
"Mum" -not properly at first, but I knew what he was saying. I got quite
a surprise the first time he did it. I told everyone but the trouble was he
would never say it in front of anyone else!

'He was about one when he started walking. He used to walk along
the furniture, holding on to it to support himself. Then one day he let
go. I screamed the first time he tried it! He would only take one step
and he would fall back down, but he kept trying again:

By then the couple had managed to get rehoused in a one-
bedroomed flat on the ground floor of Oak Towers in Northwood,

Kirkby, a few hundred yards from Scoter Road. It gave them a little more room to bring up their baby, and brought them closer to home. Denise would take James to her mother's house every day. He and Antonia, Denise's sister Sheila's daughter, were about the same age and grew up together, becoming firm friends. As she wistfully watches Antonia playing alone at Eileen's feet, Denise says, 'James used to be over here at his Nan's every day. He and Antonia would have their little arguments and fights but they got on great. If they fell out they would put their arms around each other afterwards and kiss each other.'

Brother Ray remembers James playing with Antonia and his own daughter Heather, also about the same age.

'Antonia was his best mend. They would run in and out and get up to mischief. Their favourite place was a little den under the dining-room table. They were very good chums. The children point to his picture now and say "James". With him being there one day and then taken away, there is a blank space there for them. We always talk about him when the children are there. We would never let them forget him, any more than we could forget him ourselves.

'He had quite a personality of his own. Every time I went into my Mum's he was there. You couldn't just tap him on the head. You would have to pick him up and cuddle him and hold him. He looked small for his age and he was cuddly. You wanted to hold him all the time. He was very lovable'.

The only little boy among several young girls in the family, James was often the centre of attention, and brought much-needed laughter to the family as it reeled from a series of tragedies in the first months of his life. Two of his namesakes, his grandfather and great-grandfather on Ralph's side, had both died in the same year.

His three surviving grandparents doted on James almost as much as his parents did. His grandfather Hugh, seventy-two, would delight in bending down to the chuckling child and letting him lift his glasses up off his nose. 'He thought the world of James,' smiles Eileen. 'At night he would take his glasses off in bed and say, "Where's James now?"'

Hugh was an old-fashioned man, not much given to modern concepts of equality. He never shopped. That was Eileen's job. The only time he would venture into a shop would be when he went to the newsagent's to buy a newspaper. But he took himself to a toyshop and found a cuddly toy dog puppet to buy as a gift for his grandson. James was that important to him.

A few days before James's first Christmas, Hugh told Eileen he was going to take a Sunday stroll down to Ray's house. Ray is another of the four members of the family who have homes in Scoter Road. Almost all-the others live only minutes away. Eileen's eyes mist over as she remembers: 'I was sitting here talking to Hugh and he turned round to watch TV, and then put his shoes and coat on and said he was going round to Raymond's for half an hour. As he left he shouted back: "I won't be long, Eileen". That was the last I saw of him alive. He disappeared out of my life as well, just like James'.

Ray says: 'At our house Dad could hardly speak. He couldn't get his breath. I had to run back down to my Mum's and telephone the ambulance'. Ray followed his father to Walton Hospital where he underwent emergency treatment for a heart attack. By that evening the crisis had passed and Hugh was holding court in his hospital bed, laughing and joking with Ray and his brother Paul. He seemed back to normal. 'A nurse told us there was no problem and he was as right as rain, and we left just after midnight,' Ray remembers. 'We got a call early on the Monday morning to say he had deteriorated. When I got to the hospital he had gone.

'Dad was always fit, and his death was very sudden. That Monday we were talking to the undertaker and then Mum had a massive heart attack. She was taken to the intensive care unit at Walton. They told us on the Monday evening that she wasn't going to come through. We were preparing ourselves for the worst. She was in intensive care for a week and had heart surgery. Then she started to come round. She's finer than all of us now, thank G04. It was a devastating time for the family. At the time we thought there was nothing we could go through that was worse than that...'

Children are strangely sensitive to adult distress, even when they may not fully understand what is going on around them. James Patrick Bulger must have felt the sadness around him in a world that for him was peopled by Mum and Dad and a constant procession of aunties, uncles and cousins. In his innocent way he helped brighten up a dark time.

James was a bright little boy, and as he began to toddle, his own personality developed rapidly. He sat and watched as Denise worked

their video-machine, playing her favourite Michael Jackson taps. Staring
at the television screen, the child was entranced by the star's strange
and wonderful dance moves. Before long, inevitably, he would climb to
his feet, move to the rhythm, and copy what he was seeing. He would
dance and turn, jerking his shoulders up and down just like Mum's idol.
Denise, Eileen, anyone else watching would be helpless with laughter.
He fed on that and increased the pace. It became his star turn. James
loved to make people laugh.

Denise's pale blue eyes shine with pride as she remembers the
merriment of those innocent moments. 'He had bags of energy. He
would· never sit still for five minutes. Even when he was eating his tea
if a Michael Jackson tape came on the video he would get up and start
dancing. I couldn't blame him. I would sooner watch Michael Jackson
than eat my cooking! He knew some of the words and he joined m. He
was all there for his age. It took me about four years to learn all the
words. James did the moves just like Michael. He was good at them! He
would always say, "Put Michael Jackson on". That's all you would get
out of him. He learned how to work the video-machine and he would
rewind it and play it over and over again. If you walked out of the room
for a minute he would rewind it and play it again'.

Eileen chuckles at the image in her mind. 'He would be dancing
and his arm would be going in and out -like Michael Jackson's. He would
be looking at me because I 'was laughing at him. He would do a little bit
more then, because he could see he was making me laugh. He always
used to make us laugh with his antics. He was a little showman'.

James's short life was spent surrounded by the warmth and
encouragement of his relatives. He grew confident in the company of
adults and older children. There were always children in and out of
Eileen's house. It was the kind of family environment that many of us
born in Liverpool thirty or more years ago look back on with affection.
Days at Grandmother's house with aunties and uncles to indulge you
and cousins to get up to mischief with gave you a sense of belonging.
You knew who you were because you were part of a family. If disaster
struck, there was a support system of generous and caring relatives. If
there was good news in the family, the celebration would be something
memorable. Families like this, all grouped around the same small
neighbourhood, have sadly become the exception rather than the rule,

as economic circumstances have seen old families spread themselves out around the country and the world, into neighbourhoods where people no longer know and trust each other and, in that chilling cliché that says so much about today's alienated society, people 'keep themselves to themselves'.

Kirkby has its areas like that, with lonely people living lives of quiet desperation. It also has pockets of community that are quite heartwarming in their closeness. A lot has been written and said about Kirkby over the years. It achieved an early notoriety when the BBC TV series Z Cars was set in "Newtown" a fictional Merseyside town said to be based loosely on Kirkby itself. The series, controversial in the 1960S though it looks tame enough now, portrayed crime and the associated problems of modern life in many major cities. It was an innovative and important piece of television drama, but had the unfortunate side-effect of helping to give Kirkby a bad name it has struggled to shake off ever since.

I first became directly involved with the town in 1976 when I covered it as a young district reporter for the Liverpool Echo. It certainly had its share of problems. The adult and juvenile sections of Kirkby Magistrates' Court provided a steady Row of copy: factory closures and industrial strife were commonplace, and the council tenants were in what seemed an almost constant state of war with hard-pressed Knowsley Borough Council over housing conditions which were in some cases unbelievably dreadful in buildings constructed just a few years before. Despite all that, there was something about the place and many of its people that you couldn't help but like and admire. The town had its share of 'scallies' -Liverpool's word for criminal tearaways -but it also had a lot of good, honest people struggled to keep their heads up and make the best of the hand life had dealt them...

Seventeen years later, Kirkby is still a town with a lot of problems but there are encouraging signs too. Joblessness remains a perennial problem, and factories still close. The deep and prolonged recession from which Britain was just beginning to emerge in 1993 was a jolt for most of the country, after the prosperous years of the 1980s, but had been just one more turn of the screw for the already ravaged local economies of towns like Kirkby. The last census revealed that Kirkby's population had dropped from 51,111 in 1981 to 43,341 in 1991.

But in 1989 the Labour council took a bold step to address the town's biggest single problem, the desperate state of much of its housing stock.

The visible impact of this policy can be seen in many parts of the town. Smart new housing cooperative developments rub shoulders with run-down maisonettes still awaiting their turn for improvement or demolition, giving a ray of hope to everyone on estates where prospects have been bleak for many years. Today the tower blocks that were such an eye-sore to those approaching the town have been pulled down and a £20 million project to redesign the urban Hampton Court Maze layout of the estates on more traditional lines is well advanced. Houses now have fronts with doors that lead through gardens on to streets. It sounds simple, doesn't it? The resulting information, however, is startling. Kirkby is at last on the way to becoming what it should always have been if the planners had got it right¬¬–a decent place to live.

That is important for people who no longer see themselves as exiles from the city centre of Liverpool, and want to belong to a town they can take pride in. 'Our perception is that the current generation are very much more Kirkby than Liverpool people,' said Rob Orme, assistant Housing Manager for the town. 'They regard Kirkby very much as their home rather than Liverpool'.

These people were particularly offended by Fleet Street writers who attacked the area with such venom in the wake of James's death. 'Alcatraz, one of them called it,' Ralph says, shaking his head in disgust. That kind of negative reporting rankles with people who regard Kirkby as home. They know better than anyone that the town needs more facilities and resources and there are still plenty of areas, notably in Northwood, that need major improvement. Above all, they know there is a desperate need for more jobs. There is crime too, particularly in some of the rougher areas, but it is mostly on a petty level and certainly not as bad as can be encountered in many inner-city areas throughout the country. Women, children and the elderly can walk Kirkby's streets in relative safety. Indeed, the latest crime figures for Kirkby were well below those for both Merseyside and the country as a whole. The town certainly did not need the kind of attack launched in some of the news feature articles, which almost seemed to be holding James's home town implicitly responsible for his fate.

James, you feel, would have made a go of things in Kirkby. With such a supportive, honest, caring extended family around him, he would never have lacked guidance. He was showing early signs of strong intelligence. 'He could count, he knew his ABCs and he was already learning how to read,' Denise says proudly. 'He had loads of books in the flat. He would pick the nearest one and sit for ages going ·through it with me. He would look at the pictures first and then he would say the words'. Uncles and aunts who dropped in on Denise and Ralph would find James climbing on to their knees with an Early Learning book, demanding that they went through it with him.

Nicola Bailey, the fiancée of James's Uncle Paul, says: 'You could see Denise had taught him well. He was like a five-year-old child, the way he spoke. He would count, and you could have a proper conversation with him. He had a really high-pitched, squeaky voice and he was a character. Seeing Antonia brings it all back. They were always together. They were little buddies'.

James was a gregarious little child. He and his parents were well liked by the other tenants in Oak Towers. In summer James would often sit on their ground-floor verandah, chatting to the other tenants or the caretaker as they cane in and out.

In the little flat James had his own special chair, a properly upholstered red armchair, made for him by his father in Hugh's workshop when Denise and Ralph were changing their own three-piece suite. 'He made it to measure, and it was the perfect size for James,' Uncle Ray remembers. 'Ralph is very good with his hands. He spent days making it. It was Jame's throne really – Prince James on his throne'.

Ray remembers taking James into the shed once to watch when he was working on some project or another. 'He was fascinated by the mess we had made. He played with the sawdust and shavings. We gave him a very small hammer and he would tap it on the work-bench thinking he was being good'.

At home James would pull out his special chair and sit in front of the television watching his favourite videos. 'As soon as I got up in the morning he would go and turn the telly on himself and he would sit in his chair in front of the fire until he got breakfast,' says Denise. Frosties were his favourite choice.

Ralph smiles. 'When I was sitting by the fire he would jump all over me. He used to batter me!'

A giggle from Denise. 'Only 'cause his mum told him to!'

Ralph is a man of few words these days, unrecognizable from the fun-loving, outgoing joker described by his worried family. Talking about James is particularly hard for him. Opening up like this, even for a few moments, is rare. 'He liked playing football, but he was too young to watch it in TV. He would hide behind things and jump out at me. He was in to all kinds of things. I used to push him up a hill near here and let him roll down on his go-kart. He loved that. James was the cracking little boy'. Ralph can't say any more. He stares at the wall, eyes haunted, lost in tormented thought.

One of James's favourite things would be hearing the whirl of the rotors of the Merseyside Police helicopter as it passed overhead. He would run to the window, point excitedly to the sky and shout, 'Helicopter. The police, the police!'

Ralph bought him a helicopter of his own for Christmas. It was a wonderful toy that wheeled around with Bashing lights and had a built-in speaker that said 'Stop or I'll shoot'. James adored it. He could talk of little else as he tucked into Christmas dinner, dressed in his smart new best outfit of dark green corduroy trousers and matching waistcoat. 'Everyone was telling him he looked like a snooker player, a little Jimmy White: Ray recalls. 'He thought he was the bee's knees'.

Ralph would make James laugh by playing with him with the dog puppet his grandfather had bought him. The father would touch the son with the puppet, and James would explode into gales of laughter.

At night James slept in his own little bed alongside Denise and Ralph's, snuggled up under a quilt covered in elephants and bubbles. He would take a toy torch with him. Ralph would reach out and hold his son's hand while he went to sleep. Sometimes the couple would wake in the night to find James had burrowed under their bedclothes to join them. After a few words of reassurance he would return to his own bed happily enough.

Everyone around the family has their own memories of James, things he would do that would make them laugh. 'Every time you looked at him he was doing something funny. If he saw he was making you laugh by doing something he would do it more: Denise says.

James found a kindred spirit for his sense of mischief in his Uncle Ronnie. Married to Denise's sister Rita, Ronnie Fulham was thirty-four, a giant of a man and an intimidating sight to a small child. He would take his false teeth out and pull a face at James. It frightened the child for a moment, but then Ronnie took him into the kitchen for a choice and everything was fine. James quickly got the measure of his uncle and realized that he was soft-hearted.

The little-boy soon plotted his revenge. Ronnie visited Ralph's flat and James came up close as if to kiss him hello. At the last moment James said 'Smell onions!' and breathed straight in his face. He had been chewing on onions and made sure that Ronnie got the full benefit.

Another day James was visiting Ronnie and Rita and spotted a new piece of furniture. He asked Ronnie, 'Is that your coffee table?'

'Yes, why?' Ronnie replied, leading with his chin.

'It's crap,' James responded, deadpan.

Rita Fulham shakes her head as she remembers the moment. 'We were all shocked but we couldn't stop laughing at him,' she smiles. Her four children now enjoy the fish tank that once adorned Denise and Ralph's Sat. It was James's but he-was so -fascinated with the fish that Denise, protective as ever, was scared he might pull it over on himself and gave the tank to Rita and Ronnie. .

'James was a normal two-year-old boy. He was great. He was sound as a pound and-just coming into his element,' says his Uncle Ron, real affection in his voice as he remembers his little sparring partner.

Grandma Eileen remembers how James developed his own version' of hide-and-seek. 'It started when he would kick the ball in them and if he got shouted at he would dart under the dining table. Once he started he would often hide under there. He would dive behind my armchair to hide from Denise sometimes. He was always on the go, always a happy little thing.

'He used to come and sit on the end of my chair with me. He would come up with me when I went up to bed early and Denise would come up and tell him to go downstairs. Now and again he would call 'me "Mother" because he heard the others call me that. He was a very happy little fellow. Everybody liked him. He liked getting a taxi. He used to say, "Taxi, Nana!" and we would get a taxi up to the Strand. He liked coming shopping, but mostly for the taxi ride with Denise and me. We would get a taxi even if we were only going to the local Co-op just to please James.

'He used to like singing and dancing with Antonia. They got on well together, the two of them. They had little fights now and again, but they got on well. They would be outside playing football in our back garden. I bought them both bikes for Christmas. I thought in the summer they could get out there in the garden on their bikes¬¬-but it wasn't to be'.

Eileen glances out at the garden. Her face clouds suddenly. 'We don't half miss him here. Things seem to have changed in the house now. I see Denise here all the time now and James not with her. All I have now are my own thoughts. James was my only baby grandson. The others have all grown up or are girls'.

Grandmother Helen, fifty-seven, remembers James coming to her aid when her asthma led to a coughing fit. 'Little James Patrick would bang me on the back and ask if I was all right,' she says.

'When Denise brought him to see me James would often make for the biscuit tin. I kept a big teddy bear here fat the children to play with. I looked after him on New Year's Eve and he was eating chicken. He went and sat on the teddy's knee and was feeding it to the teddy. Ralph would throw him right up to the ceiling playing with him, and James would love it. It would make me scream and say, "You'll drop him!" but James would shout, "Again, again."'

Helen's face starts to crumple. 'Our lives will never be the same again. Every time you sit and talk the conversation keeps coming round to James. You don't know you are doing it, half the time. Every time you see a little blond kid running by, your eyes are following him. People try to avoid you who have known you for years, because they don't know what to say to you'.

In the lounge of Ray Matthews's house in Scoter Road he presses a well-used video-tape into the machine and we sit back in armchairs to watch the screen as the tape starts. It is August 1992. Children run about laughing in the back garden of Ralph's sister Elaine's house. It is her daughter Stephanie's sixth birthday party. A chunkily set little boy with golden hair bounces vigorously up and down on a small trampoline, beaming at the camera.

The scene switches to Elaine's lounge. Children dance about, jigging furiously to the music. The golden-haired boy joins in with gusto, before bouncing on to a chair, his legs rolling up in the air as the other children giggle. Then the older children are singing 'Happy Birthday'. They finish the song and James Bulger suddenly shouts out 'Happy birthday to you'. It makes the other children chuckle. James was good at that.

Chapter Three

The boy sat sprawled across the front doorstep of his house, bored and indolent. 'Eh, mate, are you a reporter?' My suit had alerted his suspicions. The spiral-bound notebook ruled out a CID man.

I was ringing the doorbell at a neighbouring house for the second time. Nobody home. I turned to the boy resignedly and made the formal introductions. He was fourteen, dressed in the universal adolescent uniform of tee-shirt and jeans. His hair was cropped close to his head, his skin a pallid, sickly white. He looked scrawny and undernourished.

'Give us some money and I'll tell you a story about him'. His dull eyes shirred uneasily under my gaze as he spoke.

I thought for a moment. The kid could have done with a square meal, but somehow I didn't think that was what the money was for.

'Sorry, can't do that,' I said. 'If you want to talk to me, it's up to you. Otherwise...' I shrugged and started to turn away.

'I used to hang round with his big brother. Robert would tag on with us sometimes'.

I turned back to face him. We were a couple of doors away from the terraced house where ten-year-old accused child killer Robert Thompson had lived. It was boarded up now, a notorious place in an otherwise unremarkable little red-brick street.

'What kind of kid was he?'

'He was a dickhead. Give us four quid. Go 'ead'.

I shook my head. 'Sorry, I told you...'

Another lad, older, chipped in from the pavement. 'He was evil, that one. He used to draw pictures...evil things'.

'What sort of things?'

He looked at the ground sharply, studying the cracks in the pavement. 'Don't know. I didn't know him myself. It's what people say'. . . 'I saw him on telly, waving at the cameras on the night they found the body'. The first boy again, more forthcoming suddenly, feeding on the celebrity of having actually known the neighbourhood demon.

I recalled one of the clues a forensic psychologist suggested I might look for. 'Was he ever cruel to animals?'

'I saw him pull the heads off pigeons,' came the immediate response.

'Where did this happen?'

'In a bombed-out house round the corner. We used to be able to get in'.

'How did he catch them?'

'He got them out of their nests'.

'Baby pigeons, then?'

'Yeah'.

'How many times was this?'

'He done it a few times'.

'Did he say why?'

'No'.

'Did you ask him, or try to stop him?'

No answer now. Sullen, looking at his friend, then at the ground.

'Was there anything else that he did?'

The kid was tiring of the inquisition. There was no profit in it, and it seemed to be drifting uncomfortably close to home.

'No ... I don't know'. He brightened. 'You can look in the house. Go on, through the letter-box'.

'It stinks in there, stinks of meths,' his older friend advised.

It seemed a pointless exercise, but the two boys were watching me expectantly, so I walked a few yards along the road, up the steps, and lifted the letter-box. As I reached for the metal flap I could just make out the word 'BASTARD' written on it in faded graffiti. There was nothing to see inside. The boards on the windows meant it was pitch-black. I could just about discern the staircase.

'Look in the front room,' the boys urged. 'Through the boards'.

Going up to the front door was one thing, but this would have entailed climbing over the low wall and peering through gaps left in the boards. I shook my head. 'Thanks, lads. I've seen enough'.

They were already moving off down the road. I sighed, staring after them. They knew the Thompsons, I was sure of that. As for the rest, it is difficult to know in a case like this where facts end and lurid rumours begin. But there are some things about this unfortunate family that we know for certain.

Robert Thompson was born in Liverpool on 23 August 19882, the fifth of seven sons born to his mother Ann. She was married then and, according to one of Robert's elder brothers, the family were not unhappy. When Robert was two, his brother Arnold remembers his father buying a touring caravan. On holidays and at weekends in 1986 and 1987 they would go to a caravan camp in Southport. 'We all got on well. I got on well at school and liked it,' the brother recalls. At least in retrospect, it seems to him an almost idyllic time.

Then, on Sunday, 16 October 1988, their father left them quite suddenly. The bewildered brothers were to face another major shock within a week. The following Saturday they all went to their grandmother's home and returned to discover that their house had been burned down in an accidental fire. The family were then moved to a hostel in Toxteth, where they were to live for the next two months.

One of Arnold's brothers asked him whom he would rather live with and Arnold replied, 'My dad'. It was a mistake. His brother told their mother, who was to give him a hard time after that. Arnold saw his father only once more after he left them. Even the police have not been able to trace him. Ann turned to drink, and would go out regularly, leaving her six sons pretty much to their own devices. The eldest brother, then seventeen, was regularly left in charge, and would hit the other boys if they did anything wrong.

Eventually the family were rehoused in their red-brick terraced house in Walton. The street where they were to live for the next four years is narrow but quite busy, with locals using it as a handy 'short-cut' between two main roads. It is a curious, rather untidy mixture of pre-war terraced houses and little rows of small shops. Children run about the street on narrow pavements, dodging in and out among parked cars. .

With their-mother seeming to pay little attention, the boys began playing truant from school on a regular basis. The Thompsons gained minor notoriety in the area as a problem family, the boys unkempt and running wild, their mother hitting the bottle and looking much older than her thirty-odd years. Inevitably, they came to the attention of Liverpool City Council's social services department. The second eldest boy went into care in 1990, followed soon after by the eldest, who was put into a probation hostel.

Responsibility for the younger boys then fell largely on the shoulders of young Arnold. It was a duty he took seriously, doing the best he could to give guidance to the younger boys. One of them, just a year younger than Arnold, would go out at 8 a.m. and not come home until midnight. Arnold could do little to stop him and finally this boy too went into care. Arnold took Robert and his younger brother Simon to school, but Robert would still play truant, spending his days stealing from shops and getting up to mischief. Robert would also bully little Simon, a pleasant child trying his best at school, forcing him to play truant too. He was on the way to falling into the same bad habits as his elder brothers.

Meanwhile Ann had another baby, by a different father.

Arnold was still looking after the younger children, and still having trouble getting on with his mother. Finally, on 10 October 1992, things came to a head for Arnold in a confrontation in which, he said, his mother hit him with a cane. After three years of trying to hold the family together he had had enough. The boy went to visit a social worker and in November went into voluntary care. He could not stand it at home any more.

He did not return home much after that. The last time he saw Robert was when the boy was out 'minding' cars parked in the street by fans watching Everton's home match against Tottenham Hotspur at Goodison Park on the evening of 10 February 1993, two days before James was killed. A lot of children in the area supplement their pocket money offering to look after cars for fans watching Everton matches at Goodison and Liverpool games at nearby Anfield. Most supporters agree to the deal. Just who the kids are protecting the cars against is never clear, but it seems sensible to pay up.

Arnold told police he thought Robert was a normal enough boy. 'He isn't violent. In fact he is frightened of his own shadow. He hangs around the streets on his roller boots. Sometimes he tries to act big'.

Neighbours were no less astounded. In an area where school truancy and petty theft are a way of life for a lot of children, the Thompsons did not stick out as particularly terrible. If anything, their general good manners came as a welcome change from the attitude of some of the children in the area.

'They seemed very nice, especially the older boys,' one neighbour said. 'They were very polite when you saw them. I didn't know them well'.

The local butcher shrugged and said, 'They came in here sometimes. There are worse kids than them around here. I still can't believe Robert was involved'.

The family's next-door neighbour said the new baby had made a marked difference to Mrs Thompson's life. 'When they first moved here the mother was in the pub 'while the children were running mad, but the last two years they had been okay. I used to say hello to Mrs

Thompson and talk about her new baby. Since she had the baby it had made a difference to her.

'Robert seemed a nice little boy. He would let on to me in the street He would smash bottles and things like that, but no more than any other kid. What happened was a terrible shock. You don't think any boy would do that at that age'.

One neighbour, a mother of three, lived over the road and a few doors away from the Thompsons, and formed a dose friendship with Ann over the previous two or three years. Her children played regularly with the Thompsons. She puts much of the blame for the boys' problems at the door of the social services department. 'Ann wouldn't hit the kids if they were naughty, because of social services,' she said. 'She took too much notice of social5ervices. They would probably be all right if she gave them a good hiding now and then. If they did anything wrong she would take them round to the police station'. She tried to sort them out.

'Ann went through a bad patch for a while. She had just started getting herself sorted out over the last year' Of so and then' this happened. I feel for her. I' was totally shocked. I couldn't believe it. .

'Robert was' a' nice kid. He was no angel but he had a heart of gold. He used to pinch things off shops but it was things for his Mum and the baby. A lot of kids round here are into stealing from shops, anyway. He seemed a lovely child. You wouldn't believe he could do this if you knew him. 'He used to play with my kids and look after my little boy, who is seven. He was smashing with him. He wouldn't let anyone hit him. My little girl was his girlfriend. She is ten too. She liked Robert and she was very upset when he was arrested.

'All they used to do was hang around outside here and mind the cars when the matches were on. They would sit in the video shop waiting cartoons together. That's all they used to do. Robert was polite. He could be hard-faced if someone said something to him, but if you knew him well he was smashing with you. He was fine. It must be terrible for Ann, this. I haven't seen her since Robert was arrested.

'There was nothing anyone could say was really bad about the boys and nobody knew them better than me over the last few years. The one who put himself in care to get his own way, he was very good, that one. He was the only one who was doing well in school and top of the class'.

Jon Venables was another product of a broken home and an unhappy childhood. Jon lived in a nicer street than Robert, in a quiet residential back road off the leafy avenues of nearby Norris Green. Home was a terraced house, but with its own little front lawn behind a neatly trimmed hedge and a covered passageway alongside the front door leading to the rear garden. Jon was born on 13 August 1982, just ten days before Robert. He was the second of three children born to Susan and Neil Venables. His early years were marred by domestic strife, and Susan and Neil were divorced in 1985, when Jon was just three years old.

Both Jon's brother, who was three years older than him, and his sister, a year younger, were identified as having moderate learning difficulties. They both went to the same special school. By the age of nine the older child would have sudden bouts of tantrums. This is not unusual for children with learning difficulties, but was distressing for his mother and father. A social worker based at the special school arranged weekend respite fostering which seemed to help.

Jon was not the brightest of pupils, but was considered in the educationally normal range. Children can be especially cruel in situations like these, and Jon was given a difficult time by his contemporaries both in his home street and at school because his brother and sister were 'backward', He became a deeply unhappy young boy.

In September 1989, when Jon started attending a local junior school at the age of seven, teachers noted that he was displaying anti-social behaviour which was annoying but not particularly serious. In his second year at the school his behaviour grew worse and from January 1991 was causing serious concern. With his mother's consent Jon was referred to the school's psychology service, which made a report in May that year referring to his bizarre behaviour and the need to modify it. The possibility that he was hyperactive was also discussed.

Jon's class teacher at the time recalled that after the Christmas break his behaviour became very strange. She told police: 'He would sit on his chair and hold his desk with his hands and rock backwards and forwards and start moaning and making strange noises'.

The exasperated teacher would move him to sit next to her, but he would then fiddle with objects on her desk and knock them to the floor. Sometimes he would-bang his head on the furniture until it must have hurt. He would cry and complain that other children were picking on him outside class.

The teacher felt sure Jon was capable of doing more at school, though he would not do any book work and was a 'low achiever'. She invited Mrs Venables into school to discuss his behaviour, who said she was having trouble with him at home and he was being abusive to her. Mrs Venables said Jon wanted to be in the special needs school with his brother and sister.

That March, the teacher would not let Jon go on a weekend trip with other children because she could not take responsibility for his behaviour. The social worker helping the Venables family offered to go with them on the trip to look after Jon, but the school refused. After that Jon's behaviour deteriorated. He would go round the room revolving along the walls, pulling off pictures and displays. He would lie inside a group of desks, lodging himself so that his teacher had trouble moving him. Occasionally he cut himself deliberately with scissors, or cut holes in his socks. He would stick paper over his face and grab anything near him to throw across the room at other children. Once, when he was made to stand outside because of his behaviour, he simply started throwing things down the corridor. On another occasion he suspended himself upside-down like a bat on coat-pegs. Parents of other children came in to complain about the disruption to their children's education that Jon was causing with his attention-seeking.

Matters came to a head when he attacked another boy in class, with a 12-inch ruler. He stood behind the other boy trying to choke him with the ruler. 'I don't know how far Jon would have gone but the other boy was going red in the face,' the teacher told police. 'It took quite an effort for myself and another woman who was in the class at the time to get Jon off'.

Jon was suspended from school and, though he was never formally expelled, a decision was taken to move him to another school. For the teacher it was a major relief. 'In the fourteen years I have been teaching I have never come across a boy like Jon. During the period I had responsibility for him he caused me some anxiety. It was so stressful trying to contain him,' she said. 'I always felt that although Jon knew it was wrong to misbehave as he often did he carried on anyway so as to seek attention'.

Mrs Venables and the social worker approached a junior school in Walton in June 1991 and asked if Jon could attend as there had been problems at his previous school. The headmistress agreed to take him on condition that he behaved himself and agreed to go in an age group a year lower than his own. He started at his new school that autumn term.

Jon Venables's new school was the same one Robert Thompson had been attending since September 1989. His elder brothers had been there before him in a sequence dating back to 1982. The headmistress had notified the social services about the bullying tactics each of the boys had applied to his immediate younger brother.

After the boys were charged, Detective Inspector Jim Fitzsimmons spent long hours interviewing teachers at the school and came away deeply impressed by the caring and professional approach of the staff there. The shock of having two of their pupils involved in such a dreadful incident as the killing of James Bulger had a profound effect on them. It was not a school where discipline had been lacking. Doors were locked for the security of the children, but also to make it difficult for them to get out during the school day. DI Fitzsimmons said: 'The headmistress was shocked and distraught when she realized it was her own pupils. We spoke at length about responsibilities and child behaviour. There were problems with these boys but not problems at such a level that you would predict anything on this scale. In fact violence wasn't an issue particularly. The frightening thing is that they were just two ordinary kids, no worse than many others, in fact a lot better than some of the other kids. What more can teachers do? They must realize they can only do so much and society has to do the rest'.

In September 1991 Robert and Jon were put into the same class for the first time. Like Jon, Robert was put into the class a year below his own age group. Perhaps it was this shared factor that first drew them together. Whatever the reason, a friendship was kindled between the to boys. Jon had no history of playing truant, but once he came under Robert's influence he too eventually caught on to the game.

Jon was still showing symptoms of maladjustment. He would pretend he had not heard instructions from his teacher to avoid work, walk around the classroom being disruptive, or collapse in a heap across his desk to show he did not want to do what he had been asked. His teacher, a fifty-three-year-old man with sixteen years' experience teaching maladjusted children at special schools in Yorkshire and Warwickshire, knew how to handle him. Jon was set a well-structured pattern of work and behaviour norms in the classroom, and he responded. In the less structured environment of the playground, however, he still had great difficulty behaving himself. A dinner lady recalled having to reprimand him several times for being a nuisance to other children. As punishment he would be told to stand against the wall for a time, as was standard with any child who misbehaved. But when he was first at the school Jon reacted to this form of punishment by butting the wall with his head, falling on to the ground and throwing his arms around. He stopped only when he failed to get any reaction from the playground supervisors.

Their teacher recalls that both Jon and Robert would often get into petty squabbles and fights outside the confines of the classroom. He remembers once stopping Jon fighting with a smaller, younger boy and asking him how he would feel if someone bigger than him fought him. Jon agreed that it was wrong to behave that way.

His analysis of Robert in particular is illuminating. He told Jim Fitzsimmons: 'Robert was a quiet, often shy little boy making the bullets for the others to shoot. That was basically him in the classroom but in the playground he was often in trouble'.

But if the two friends were hardly model pupils, it would be wrong to run away with the idea that Robert and Jon were notorious. 'They were no different from many other pupils in the school and were certainly not out on their own as trouble-makers or problem boys,' said the teacher.

At home, meanwhile, Neil Venables had not abandoned his parental responsibilities, unlike Robert's vanished father. Mr Venables was living nearby in Walton, and continued to involve himself with the children. As the couple attempted a reconciliation, Mr Venables would have the children to stay with him from Thursday to Sunday while they stayed the rest of the week with their mother. He would get up early when the children were with him and make sure he delivered them to their mother's house in time for Jon's brother and sister to be collected by the minibus that used to take them to their special needs school.

The same pattern of bullying that had marked the history of the Thompson family at the school was repeating itself with Robert and Simon, who was now in a lower class at the same school. Young Simon complained to his teacher that he did not like his brothers, and Robert in particular because he often picked on him and hit him.

Simon told her Robert often forced him to play truant and, if he refused, would hit him. Simon is a very pleasant little boy who tries his best in class. He also has a very quiet temperament,' she said.

In the school year that began in September 1992, Robert and Jon went into a new class, and Jon's old disruptive streak began to re-emerge. He also started going missing from school with Robert. That autumn term Jon was missing for fifty half-days, ten of them legitimately on holiday while Robert was missing for forty.

Their new teacher saw Robert as the motivator of any minor problems or truancy. Jon, she felt, was the, type of boy who would go along with that. It is an assessment other colleagues also tended to confirm.

'Jon caused me the most trouble in class with his behaviour,' she told police. 'He was not generally naughty in class but he was disruptive and awkward. Robert was fairly easy to handle in the classroom. I deliberately kept the boys well apart in the classroom, their desks being at either end of the classroom.

'In general, Jon would respond to my discipline but only for period. When in trouble with me Jon would hang his head and not look me in the eye. Robert was totally different. When challenged over discipline he would adopt a meek character and could cry tears as and when–or so it appeared to me–he wanted'.

She said she never saw the boys involved in violence at school. Jon was, at times disruptive and lazy in class. Robert was always ready to tell tales on those around him but would never admit to wrong-doing himself. 'He was a shrewd, streetwise child and very aware of what was going on around him. 'He was a slow learner but was no trouble in class. The only trouble I had from both boys was when they played truant together and this had repercussions'. But, like their previous teacher, she stressed: 'Jon and Robert were certainly no more trouble than many of the pupils I teach'.

The boys' head teacher told, DI Fitzsimmons that she found Jon to be 'odd', avoiding eye contact during conversation, showing very little emotion but turning on the tears as he wished. In the playground he often got into fights and had a short temper. Yet, significantly, she regarded Robert as without doubt the more dominant of the two boys.

She said Jon had an aggressive nature and other pupils would try to 'wind him up' because of his short temper. 'He was a more open boy who was much more likely to tell the truth than Robert Thompson. He was often involved in brawls in school and I spoke to him many times. I pointed out that it was wrong to hit another person and I am sure he knew what I was saying.

'Robert has never been a problem in class but he is a liar and is cunning. Even when we had evidence against him he would continue to lie'. She said Robert was not only a regular truant but influenced other boys to play truant with him. 'For a child of mine to truant from school he or she must plan it en route to school or be very determined to leave whilst the school is open'.

That determination was manifested by both boys in an incident on 26 November 1992 that led the school to take a firm line in dealing with their joint behaviour. The school caretaker was off sick that day, and for once the access door to the school was unmanned. Robert and Jon were overheard plotting to run off while the door was unoccupied, and that lunchtime took their chance and made off while nobody was watching. The incident led to a staff meeting at which it was decided that one boy would stay in his regular class while the other would go into a different teacher's class each day. They were not allowed out of the school at playtime. They were kept under separate supervision at breaks and lunchtimes, one on the ground floor and one upstairs, to prevent them running off. They were even supervised when they went to the toilet.

Their class teacher spoke to both boys and asked them if they realized playing truant affected their schoolwork, got them punishment, and made their parents and her unhappy because they had broken her trust. Robert started crying and promised he would never do it again and would try harder at his schoolwork. Jon made the same promises.

Their former teacher, whose disciplined approach had had such an impact on Jon, was also asked to speak to them about their truanting. 'Robert told me that whilst they were playing truant together Jon stole from shops, and Jon told me that whilst they were playing truant Robert stole from shops,' he told DI Fitzsimmons. 'Robert lied as naturally and easily as he breathed, and when he was found out to be lying he seemed unconcerned and most of the time made no comment. Jon lied easily but would become tearful when pressured. When found out he was more likely to tell the truth than Robert'.

Mrs Venables went into school to speak to the headmistress about Jon's truanting problem. She shouted at him in the headmistress's presence. Both women spoke firmly to Jon and explained to him clearly how wrong it was both to play truant and steal. Jon's father, who lived near the school, was told about the problem and started picking him up from school at the end of every day. By now the couple were moving closer to reconciliation, and were spending more time together.

On 3 December Mrs Thompson came into the school and reported that Robert had run off from home the night before. She told staff she had told Robert how wrong it was to run off, and that she had taken and hidden his shoes. She promised that in future she would collect him from school every day at 3.30.

When the following term began on 4 January it seemed that Jon at least was making an effort to keep his promise to behave better. Jon was absent for just six half-days that spring term, two of them covered by a note from his parents. Robert was, if anything, getting worse. He was to be absent on thirty-seven out of sixty possible half-days up to half-term.

One incident in particular that term carried a chilling overtone of what was to follow. At the end of January Simon's teacher was called to attend the manager's office at Bootle's Strand Shopping Centre. She arrived to be told that Simon, Robert's little brother, had been found wandering crying and distressed in the Strand. Simon told her Robert and another boy–not Jon–had taken him by the canal alongside the Strand and left him there. 'He was very upset,' she said. 'He said that Robert punched and kicked him in the legs and arms, and was often distressed about the way Robert treated him'.

On 4 February the headmistress met Robert's mother, with a social worker and an education welfare officer, and it was agreed that the only way Robert was going to make it to school was for Mrs Thompson to bring him in herself each day.

The headmistress spoke angrily with Robert. Simon was such an enthusiastic child in school but Robert's domination and bullying were making him miserable. 'I told Robert it was wrong to play truant, wrong to steal and wrong to bully'.

If this incident points to some kind of rehearsal for what Robert had in mind, one more detail in their class teachers' accounts to the police points starkly to the fact that Jon knew something was about to happen.

On Thursday, 11 February, the day before the two boys played truant on the final day of half-term and James met his fate, Jon was with a group he had selected himself, in a lesson involving constructing an electrical circuit to light a bulb using batteries. But the boy refused totally to interact with his group. 'Jon behaved the worst that he had ever behaved for a whole day whilst he was in my class,' his teacher recalled. 'He was excited and fidgety and appeared as if he couldn't contain himself. Robert was his normal self'.

She told Jon off and made him sit on the floor near the door. This restless, often difficult child behaved so poorly that day that the teacher remarked on it to other staff.

After the children had gone home she moved Jon's desk to the back of the class ready for the next day. Jon would never occupy that desk again. She had taught Robert Thompson and Jon Venables for the last time.

Chapter Four

James Bulger bounced out of bed bright and early on the morning of Friday, 12. February 1993. It was a cold winter's day. He pulled up his little red armchair and sat in front of the fire at the family's flat in Oak Towers, while Denise fetched him a bowl of his favourite Frosties cereal.

Ralph was getting himself ready to go to help Denise's brother Paul install fitted wardrobes in the bedroom of his new house at the far end of Scoter Road. Denise decided she would take James round to her mother's house. It was a routine start to an ordinary day in toddler James's life. When he was washed and dressed in warm clothes, topped by his long blue hooded anorak and track suit bottoms for protection against the chill outside, Denise and Ralph took him on the short walk to grandmother Eileen's house.

Ralph left James and Denise at Eileen's with a quick 'Ta-ra'. James stood at the front door and waved as his father walked briskly on down the road.

Eileen had gone to Birkenhead on a shopping expedition with her eldest daughter Joan, but you are never stuck for company for long at Scoter Road. Denise sat chatting with her sister Sheila as James played with his cousin and best friend Antonia. Ray Matthews arrived at about 11.30 a.m. and joined in the conversation with his two sisters and younger brother Gary.

At lunchtime, Paul's fiancée Nicola Bailey arrived at the house. Dark-haired Nicola, twenty-five, had known twenty-nine-year-old Paul Matthews for ten years, and the couple had lived together for eight of those. They were now engaged, and Nicola was already very much part of the family. That day, she was planning to go to T. J. Hughes's department store in the Strand Shopping Centre in Bootle to exchange some underwear she had bought which had not been suitable. With her she had the three-year-old daughter of John Matthews, another of Eileen's sons. Nicola was looking after the little girl for a few hours. She called at Scoter Road to see if Sheila wanted to go with her to the Strand, but Sheila had other plans.

Denise thought for a moment and looked at James. She had nothing else to do with her afternoon and the little boy's favourite treat was to go for a car ride. It seemed too good a chance to miss. 'I'll go with you for the ride,' she said.

Glad of the company, Nicola agreed. Denise suggested putting the pram in the car–James never went anywhere without his pram. Nicola shook her head. 'It isn't worth it. We won't be there that long,' she said.

They all bundled into Nicola's Ford Orion, James barely able to contain his excitement. Denise sat in the back of the car looking after the two children while Nicola drove. They set off just after 1 p.m., James standing on the seat beside his mother, waving for all he was worth at his Uncle Ray, who waved back from the lounge window until the car disappeared round the corner.

They arrived at the Strand at about 1:45 p.m., and parked in an open-air parking area alongside the multistorey car park adjacent to the shopping precinct. They took a shortcut through Woolworth's into the precinct and then made straight for T. J. Hughes's.

It was a busy Friday afternoon. Shoppers wrapped in thick overcoats against the bitter winter air outside bustled about getting their groceries for the weekend. Everyone was in a hurry, it seemed. A few children hanging around among the crowds drew barely a second glance. It was warm and dry in the airy avenues of the precinct, a regular haven against the cold for youngsters 'sagging' school. Shopkeepers and the police were aware of their nuisance value, because of their proclivity for shoplifting, but they would pass virtually unnoticed by the general public.

Somewhere in that crowd, meriting no particular attention, were two ten-year-old boys, Robert Thompson and Jon Venables. Their faces looked fresh and innocent. The occasional furtive glances and whispered conversations between them might have hinted at mischief to anyone with time enough to look but no one could have guessed at the evil that was in their hearts that day.

James Bulger was thrilled. He was used to being strapped in his pram on these shopping outings, Denise and her mother watching him like hawks. Today he could walk about free. Denise would call him back sharply if he drifted off more than a couple of yards from her side, but still, it was an uncommon degree of latitude, and he was revelling in it.

In T. J. Hughes's, Nicola explored the underwear department looking for the right size to change the clothes she had returned. The children started running in and out of the aisles, laughing and giggling. Then, suddenly, James lost his bearings and could not see Denise for a moment. 'Mum!' he shouted, and in a second Denise was at his side. She grabbed his hand and snapped, 'Don't run away!' more from relief than anger.

James felt hungry, and Denise and Nicola took the kids into a Sayers store and bought them sausage rolls. That calmed them down, and they walked about contentedly munching while the two women looked in a couple of other shops. They went into Marks and Spencer's food department to buy a few groceries, and James started running about again, Denise grabbing him to bring him back to her side. Nicola picked the two children up and planted them in her shopping trolley, facing each other. She started spinning them round and they laughed delightedly.

From there they had a look around Tesco's. By now James was starting to get fed up with Shopping. He kept telling Denise he wanted to go in the car again. He began running about and his mother was having trouble keeping hold of him. When she held his hand he would shout to her to let him go. Nicola went into a sweet shop and bought some Opal Fruits while Denise waited outside to keep an eye on James, who already had some sweets. The two children were running about together and at one point James tried to go on the escalator and screamed when Denise would not let him. He made such a fuss that a woman shopper came up to her and asked her what was wrong.

With the two children increasingly restless, it was clearly time to take them home. Nicola and Denise had one more port of call, a butcher's shop. Denise pointed out A. R. Tyms and said to Nicola, 'This is the butcher's Mum and I go to. The meat is cheap and it is very good. We'll go in there'.

Nicola said, 'Okay,' and the four walked through the door together. Nicola went to the cooked meat counter, while Denise and James went to the fresh meat counter to buy some chops for their tea. Denise did not want to be long in the shop. She had the correct change in her hand but the assistant brought the wrong chops and Denise pointed out it was another type she wanted. Nicola, meanwhile, was still getting served at the other counter. She glanced round and saw James standing by the doorway.

Denise was served with the chops she wanted. 'As I went to give her the money I turned around and James was gone,' she said. 'He had been standing right by me when I went in. I would never leave him outside when I was inside'.

She looked anxiously towards the little girl and asked her where James had gone. She said, 'I don't know'. Denise asked her again. 'He's gone through the door,' she replied.

'When she said that I panicked,' recalled Denise. She rushed out of the door and looked frantically about her. Shoppers milled about everywhere, but she could see no sign of James. Her heart thumping furiously, she went back into the shop and said, 'Nicola, where's James?'

Nicola told her, 'He's there'.

Denise, frantic now, half-shouted, 'He's not there!'

Nicola hurriedly paid for her meat and tried to reassure Denise. 'It's all right. He'll be there'.

Denise and Nicola dashed out of the shop again and began a desperate search. In the blur of confused activity that followed, Denise remembers somebody directing her to the ground-floor security office of the precinct.

'I just looked as far as I could see but there was no sign of him. I went straight to the security office then. It wasn't even five minutes after he had gone. I ran up to the top of the corridor and looked down the first aisle and couldn't see him. Then I asked someone in one of the shops who told me where the security office was, and I went straight there. I had lost Nicola. I ran from her. She was looking in different places too'.

Denise went to the security room with its monitor screens to survey the precinct, and told staff there that her son was missing. They announced it on the precinct tannoy system several times. Denise remembers thinking they should shut all the doors to the precinct until

James was found. She rushed back out into the precinct and began running round the shops trying to spot her son. 'I don't remember exactly what I did,' said Denise. 'I was just running all round the shops. I even went back to the balcony looking down on the car park to see if he had gone back to the car, but he wasn't there. A man and a woman were sitting on the wall and I asked if they had seen him but they said no. People kept coming up to me and telling me that James had been found, so I was backwards and forwards to the security office. But each time they said, 'No, he's not here'. I was going mad. You wouldn't believe the amount of people I asked if they had seen a little boy. They all said no. Someone must have seen him. Who can miss a little boy like that?'

Nicola, keeping a firm hand on her young charge, was also still hunting. Somehow in all the confusion she met up again with Denise and they decided to return to T. J. Hughes's. By now Denise was in tears. In the cold panic that had gripped her, she could not understand why she could not transmit her own sense of urgency to those around her. 'A lot of the security guards didn't even seem interested,' she said. 'A security man in one shop said, "I haven't seen him" and that was it. I gave him a mouthful and ran out of the shop. The girls in T.J.'s were helpful. They kept phoning back down to the security office for me'.

A kindly security officer in the department store came up to Denise and said, reassuringly, 'Come on, I'll take you back downstairs to the security office. Don't worry about it. He'll be in Woolworth's. We always find them in Woolies, playing with the toys. We've never lost one yet'.

Police Constable Mandy Waller was on patrol in her Panda car in Bootle, when a message came over her radio that a child was missing in the Strand. It was a relatively routine occurrence, but thirty-one-year-old Mandy, who was the nearest officer to the precinct, drove there directly and went to the security office. She found Denise and Nicola sitting there, drawn and anxious, with precinct manager Peter Williams.

The call came in at 4.22 p.m. and James had been missing for forty minutes. 'That was a long time for a child to be missing on the Strand: said Mandy. 'I informed the inspector of that by radio and he started coordinating an immediate search of the Strand. I got details off Denise of what James was wearing and those were circulated to the patrols. I went round the Strand with Denise covering where she had last seen James and where they had been, with the knowledge that she would have been able to spot him faster than I would. She was frantic and very worried. I was worried, too, because kids are normally found in fifteen minutes, but I had to keep calm and deal with the situation'.

Denise and Mandy went out to the taxi rank in busy Stanley Road, in front of the precinct, and asked the drivers to keep an eye out for James.

Security staff wanted details of how long Denise, Nicola and the children had been in the precinct. Nicola and the little girl, who by now had sensed that something was wrong and was crying and upset, made their way back to the car to check their arrival time on the pay and display ticket. As they took the shortcut back through Woolworths, Nicola spotted her brother Colin, shopping with a friend for Valentine's presents for the following Sunday.

They joined in the hunt, and later Denise and Mandy met up with Denise's brother-in-law Andy, who was also shopping in the Strand. He too joined the search.

Nicola and Denise met up again back in the security office. Suddenly there was a sound of glass smashing, and somebody outside screamed. Denise responded instinctively to the commotion; with the logic of raw panic. She looked at Mandy and said urgently, 'Someone's found him'.

Mandy Waller ran out of the office. A youth had smashed a window in the door of the Strand. 'I didn't want to get involved because of Denise, but I couldn't ignore it,' Mandy recalled. 'I started chasing him, but the

kid was on a pedal cycle. One of our patrol can continued the chase, and the kid was locked up for causing criminal damage'.

Denise, frustrated beyond words by what seemed to her the lack of urgency around her, said to Nicola, 'All they are thinking about is other things. They aren't taking it seriously'.

The gloom of a cold February night was already starting to descend. Denise, fighting to control the waves of panic that threatened to overwhelm her, told Nicola in a helpless voice, 'He's not in here. He's out there somewhere and it's getting dark'.

'I couldn't begin to think what she was going through,' Nicola recalled. 'I knew how protective she was with James. I never used to take him out because she wouldn't let anyone. It goes through my mind all the time, how we could have let him out of our sight. I saw him there by the door. It was a matter of seconds and he was gone'.

When the shops had closed, Mandy took Denise on another tour of the precinct. Denise remembers shop staff reassuring her. 'They all kept saying, "He'll turn up,' because nothing like that happens around here'.

Later Mandy took Denise out in her patrol car while Nicola and Vanessa went with other officers in a second police car and they spent a few minutes touring the immediate area. Again, there was no sign of James.

After about two hours of frenetic, fruitless searching, Mandy took Denise back to Marsh Lane Police Station, a typical red-brick modern police building on the corner of two busy roads, a matter of a couple of hundred yards from the Strand itself. Nicola joined her a few minutes later in a quiet little side office. Denise stared plaintively at her and said, 'Ralph will go mad. He always said not to let go of him in the Strand because you'll never get him back'.

Ralph Bulger finished work on his brother-in-law's fitted wardrobes late that Friday afternoon, and went to visit his mother Helen at her home in nearby Minstead Avenue. He had a chat with her and spent a few minutes playing on one of the children's Sega computers. He left to return to Eileen's house to meet his wife and son shortly before 6 p.m. Minutes after he left Helen's, the telephone rang. It was an officer from Marsh Lane Police Station, to break the news that James was missing.

'They said they were concerned because it was over two hours now since he had gone,' recalled Helen. 'My first thought was maybe someone who couldn't have kids had taken him. As time went on I was hoping that was the explanation. You start thinking about the funny people who are out there'.

The news caught up with Ralph when he returned to Eileen's. She was back from her trip to Birkenhead, and had also received a message from the police. Worried sick, she was busy telephoning other members of the family to break the news.

'I thought he might have wandered into a shop and sat down and fallen asleep,' said Eileen. 'That thought was keeping me going, thinking he was there all the time'.

Ralph said, 'Eileen told me James had gone missing at the Strand. I felt like puking up when I heard. It was just before 6 p.m. I went straight to Ray's house'.

Ray Matthews and his wife Delia were having their evening meal when Ralph arrived. 'Have you heard about our James? He's missing,' Ralph said.

Ray's first thought was that Ralph was talking about his elder brother. 'How can your James be missing?'

'Not my brother. The baby James,' Ralph said impatiently.

'What do you mean, he's gone missing?' 'He's been missing for a few hours down at the Strand'. An image of a blond-haired child waving excitedly from the back seat of a car flashed across Ray's mind. He dropped his knife and fork, grabbed his car keys and made for the front door, Ralph hard on his heels.

As they sped towards Bootle, Ray told Ralph, 'Don't-be worrying. They will have found him by now. He'll be in the police station drinking tea or playing with a toy, waiting for you to pick him up and go home'. He was trying to reassure himself as much as Ralph.

When they arrived and learned that James had still not been found, Ralph was impatient to see Denise and to get out and help in the search for his son. Instead "he had to go into an interview room, answer a series of questions and give detailed statements to the police. Then they drove him back to Kirkby where they looked around his flat and retrieved two unprocessed camera films of family gatherings which would include recent pictures of James. The films were dispatched by police motorcycle rider to Merseyside Police Headquarters for processing.

When they got back to Marsh Lane Police Station Ralph faced further questions. As he put it: 'All I wanted to do was to get out and look for James. I said to them, "Rather than sitting here talking we should be out looking." '

Denise, meanwhile, was also giving a statement to other officers. To the frantic couple, it all seemed a frustrating obstacle to their own natural instinct to get out and search for their son. However, everything they were going through was standard police procedure in a missing child case, and very necessary to allow the police to build up as full a picture as possible of the circumstances of the disappearance. At last, after well over two hours, Ralph was taken to the interview room where

Denise was sitting with Nicola. 'I can't remember what we said to each other. I just remember I was feeling sick,' said Ralph.

Jim Fitzsimmons was at his home in Bootle's neighbouring town of Crosby having his evening meal when his pager went off at about 7.07 p.m. that Friday evening. He had been promoted to the rank of Detective Inspector four days earlier and this was his first weekend on call providing cover for the whole of B Division of Merseyside Police. He rang the control room in response to his 'bleep' and was told that a two-year-old boy had gone missing from the Strand.

It was such a large and busy shopping centre that children regularly went missing there, but when DI Fitzsimmons heard that James had been missing for over three hours, it triggered immediate alarm bells. He drove the short distance to Marsh Lane Police Station where he was briefed by the uniformed supervision officer. All the stops had been pulled out. The force helicopter was up and searching, traffic patrols were touring the area with loudhailers, and police and members of James's family were searching the Strand. The Operational Support Division (OSD), which provides back-up manpower to divisions on major incidents, had already been mobilized.

Two further incidents had come to light during initial police inquiries. A suspected sex offender had been recognized in the Strand, and a child who had been separated from his parents in the area had said a man had tried to get him into a car. The incidents would prove to be unconnected, but were enough to satisfy DI Fitzsimmons that the circumstances of James's disappearance could be suspicious, and he took the decision to transfer the inquiry to CID responsibility. He called in all available detectives from the division's stations at Marsh Lane, Copy Lane, Crosby and Southport. Detectives had already gone to the sex offender's home but he was not to be found. About an hour later the man came in to Marsh Lane Police Station, having been told that officers had been at his house. Brief inquiries were enough to establish that he could not have been involved.

The local media were circulated with appeals for witnesses, and at 9.30 that night detectives traced a woman who had seen a young child crying on the bank of the Leeds-Liverpool Canal, which ran alongside the shopping precinct. A number of other children had been standing nearby. The divers of the regional police underwater search unit had already been alerted to begin a search at first light the next morning. DI Fitzsimmons now formed the grim conclusion that James had wandered out of the Strand down to the canal bank, and would probably be found in the canal.

The news of James's disappearance spread like wildfire through the Bulger and Matthews families, and as they got the news they made their way to Bootle to join the search for the missing child.

Early in the evening Ray Matthews drove Denise back to the Strand and as they peered through the outer glass doors a security man saw them and let them in. They went to the security office and then began another tour of the precinct with police officers and security staff, retracing Denise's steps from earlier that day. The precinct was eerily quiet now, in sharp contrast to the bustle of the afternoon. As they walked through the partially lit corridors, their footsteps echoing in the silence, Denise spotted her shopping bag, lying where she had dropped it hours before in her anxious initial hunt for her son.

One of the officers told Ray that it was unlikely James was in any of the shops because they were protected by infra-red alarms which would be triggered by the slightest movement inside. Nothing was being left to chance, however. All the keyholders were being called out, and a specialist search team from the OSD was making a careful check. It was a process that was to continue through the night.

'I remember thinking we didn't care how long it took,' said Ray. 'We still believed he was in one of those shops, either asleep or locked in a storeroom or something like that'.

They returned to the police station where Ray talked to a young police officer in the foyer for a few minutes while Denise was taken back inside. Then Ray, too, was invited to give a statement. Afterwards he had a cup of tea with Ralph, trying to keep him calm, and the two men headed back to the Strand. They looked around the front of the building and then explored every level of the multi-storey car park. Once again they trudged back to the police station to see if there was any news. It was a pattern that they would repeat endlessly over the next two days.

At one point in the evening Denise and Ralph were both invited back to the Strand security office to look at a image that had been found from one of the security cameras, showing a child running outside the butcher's shop. They were asked to confirm it was James. 'It was only a quick glance, but I knew it was him straight away,' remembered Ralph.

Denise confirmed this. 'It was definitely him. We could tell as soon as we saw him. I remember screaming, "That's him!" I was in a total panic'.

Several of the couple's brothers were arriving in the area by now, to begin a search which between them they would keep up around the clock for almost forty-eight hours. It was a bitterly cold night. A fine drizzle was forming.

Ralph's brother James, a former cab driver who used to work in the Bootle area, toured some of the seedier backstreet places he knew well from his taxi days. He searched until 1.30 a.m., returned home to Kirkby for his Uncle John and went straight back out to Bootle.

Nicola Bailey drove an exhausted and bewildered little girl back to her parents' home, collected fiancée Paul and returned to Bootle. They too would spend the night scouring the neighbourhood, occasionally returning to the sanctuary of Nicola's car to run the engine for a few minutes and warm themselves up.

Late that evening police persuaded Ralph and Denise that they should go home, and Ray drove them back to Kirkby. He left them at Eileen's with his wife Delia and sisters Sheila and Joan, and drove back to Marsh Lane. His brother Gary was there, and they decided to go back to Kirkby for some warm clothes and -torches. When he got back he found Ralph and Denise still sitting, drawn and shocked, in Eileen's lounge. They could not bear to stay away any longer, and returned to Bootle with Ray and Gary. By now it was 1 a.m.

Ray and some of the others spent an-hour or more searching along the canal, shining their torches into the bushes and the dark, impenetrable water. Later in the night they cast their search further afield, acting on snippets of information of possible sightings that had Come in to the police station.

Ray remembers their search of a derelict housing estate. 'It was a terrible place. It was like walking through a war zone. Litter, old broken furniture, glass and old toys were everywhere and the smell was vile. Most of the houses and flats were well shuttered with steel plates over all the doors and windows. There was no way into them, but some of the others had been entered. The steel plates had been pulled away at the bottom or had the corners bent upwards. I climbed in and made my way around while the others waited right outside in case of difficulties. You never knew who you might meet in those places, drug addicts, drunks, tramps, thieves'.

Paul and Nicola were checking out a building site. It was about 2 a.m. by now and the site was a sinister place in the pitch darkness. Paul made Nicola wait in the car with all the doors locked while he searched. It was treacherous going, and at one point he stumbled and fell, cutting his hand. Paul instinctively felt that if he found James here, the news would not be good. 'I didn't have a torch. I was searching using the flame from a cigarette lighter. In a way, I was a bit terrified I might find him'.

Ralph was having dark thoughts of his own by now. His brother Philip remembers going to the toilet at the police station with him, out of Denise's earshot, in the early hours. Ralph turned to him, haunted and lost, and said, 'I've just got a feeling I'm not going to see him alive again'.

Photographic technician Alan Williams was driving through Bootle on his way home from a long day's work when his thoughts drifted back to a day five years before. His son Michael had been three years old when he wandered off and got lost in T. J. Hughes's in the Strand Shopping Centre. It had been a nightmare incident, but Michael had turned up crying but safe, not far away. He was now eight and a half. Alan shook his head as he vividly remembered the sense of panic he had felt, and wondered what the parents of James Bulger must be going through. He glanced at the dashboard clock. Almost midnight. 'He could be anywhere,' Alan thought sadly.

Perhaps it was his own experience that made Alan act as he did that night, or perhaps it was just the natural dedication he and so many of his colleagues routinely displayed, for which the rest of us have cause to be grateful. Alan was a civilian employed by Merseyside Police, working in the photographic and technical support unit at the force's modern red-brick headquarters overlooking Liverpool's waterfront. That night he had been working late on another assignment, and had been asked to make copies of some photographs of James to help house-to-house inquiries and local media publicity. Later he had processed the two rolls of family film retrieved from Kirkby, found a good shot of James and ran off over a hundred copies.

He was not due to be on call through that night, but as he was booking off duty he considered for a moment and then went along to the force control room. He told the duty inspector, 'There's no one on duty from our department now, but I've got our mobile phone with me. I'll keep it switched on by the bed. If anything drastic happens during the night give me a ring on that'.

Alan had not been asleep for very long when something very drastic indeed happened. OSD officers, filling in time between searches of shops with their keyholders, were checking through the security videos of the Strand Shopping Centre when they came up with an extraordinary image. It showed James Bulger being led away by the hand by a boy, while a second boy walked just ahead of them. By the deepest of ironies, the picture was captioned to identify the camera location with the word 'Mothercare'.

DI Fitzsimmons, still at his desk in the early hours of Saturday morning, was called to the Strand security office by Inspector Peter Jones. 'They pointed out to me James leaving the Strand with two boys. It was then that we realized for the first time, that James had not wandered away but had been taken out'.

He contacted headquarters and the control room rang the mobile telephone number. Alan Williams, awakened by the trilling of the telephone, dressed rapidly and made his way immediately to join the others at the Strand. He asked for his colleague Colin Smith to be called out from home to meet him, took the-three-hour-long master videotape from the security office, and set off for the city centre and police headquarters.

A newly installed, £25,000 piece of high-tech equipment in the department's offices on the sixth floor of the building was the perfect tool for the task they faced. They had spent two years trying to get the Home Office recommended video enhancement gear, and by a remarkable coincidence it had been installed just three weeks previously. Alan and Colin had spent a lot of time familiarizing themselves with the equipment, but had only used it in practice once before on a relatively minor case.

Alan met up with Colin at the offices, quickly briefed him, and the two technicians went to work. The enhancement equipment was housed in a darkened room, air-conditioned to a constant cool temperature that protected both the complex electronics and the department's hundreds of stored video-tapes. The operator sat in front of a computer keyboard, with a screen in front of him which gave information about the video image and allowed him to select from an impressive array of enhancement functions. High to his right sat a colour monitor on which the video image being processed was displayed. Alongside the operator was a stack of boxes of various shapes and sizes that looked like a hi-fi buff's dream customized system. Among the boxes were video-players and enhancement equipment including a timebase corrector. To the right of this stack sat a laser printer which produced high-quality prints of the finished article.

There were immediate problems in analysing the tape. The general quality of the original was not good. A total of sixteen security cameras were deployed around the Strand, and all of them fed their images into the same recorder, one frame from each in strict rotation. The cycle took about fifteen seconds. Going through the fuzzy images and selecting the ones from the relevant cameras was slow and painstaking work that put a huge strain on the eyes. The two men took turns working at the machine in short bursts, while the other foraged for coffee to help ward off exhaustion. It took about six hours to go through twelve to fifteen minutes of information, working slowly backwards from the last sighting of James.

When they found an image worth working on, the digital image processing technique came into its own. The computer made a digital record of the image, reading the information that existed on it in pixels, tiny pinpoints of electronic light. The timebase corrector sharpened each chosen frame by clearing its field of the fogging effect of surrounding frames of the tape. The computer software then counted the number of pixels in each colour, and began the sophisticated process of sharpening and cleaning them up. The system only worked with the original raw data contained in the video image. The technology was capable of adding information which would have produced aesthetically better results but this would have rendered them useless to the police as a tool to identify suspects. The computer even encrypted an 'audit trail' showing every step taken in enhancing the image, which could not be altered and could be produced in court if necessary as evidence of how an enhancement was produced.

The two men toiled through the night. By morning they had produced the first series of usable images of the two suspects. They made copies for the media and for the house-to-house-police team and finally made their weary ways home. 'It was about 8 a.m. on Saturday when I got home,' Colin recalled. 'My wife wasn't up but my little daughter had just woken up. I went and sat with them and talked through what I had been doing. I couldn't believe the story that was unfolding'.

As Colin Smith was arriving home, DI Jim Fitzsimmons was returning to his desk. He had worked until 3 a.m. that morning. The discovery of the existence of the two boys had given the case a new significance and before finally going off duty he had briefed the night detective to ensure that a full major incident team from the Serious Crime Squad was available on Saturday morning to work with the Holmes computer. This system is the nerve centre around which modern police investigations of murders and similar major crimes now revolve. Its terminals were brought out to an incident room established at Marsh Lane, and plugged in ready to start sifting an anticipated flood of information from the public.

The enhanced photographs were waiting for DI Fitzsimmons on his desk. Detective Chief Inspector Geoff MacDonald was brought in to take charge of the investigation and a decision was taken to call a news conference for 11 a.m. that morning. Here the video photographs would be released to the media in a bid to secure the maximum possible publicity in the hunt for James and the two boys. Diane Halliwell, the civilian police press officer on call that weekend, was brought in to make the arrangements.

Denise, Ralph and their families were numb with tiredness and anxiety but keeping up their efforts to help in the search. Ralph's brother James recalled: 'Everyone was zapped. We were just on auto-pilot. Everyone looked rough physically and you could tell they were rough mentally as well. We feared the worst but we were scared to talk about it. Denise looked very old that morning. It was as though she had aged twenty years overnight'.

The family had been given a TV room on the CID landing at Marsh Lane in which to congregate. There were constant comings and goings by various members of the family throughout the weekend, as they asked for news of sightings or new areas to search. The detectives briefed Denise and Ralph first thing that Saturday morning about the sighting of James with the two boys. Denise recalled: 'A policeman came in and said they had found that two lads had taken him. He said they had probably taken him as a younger brother, and all they had to do was find him and take him back. When they said that I felt better. I thought two young lads couldn't harm a baby'.

At about 10 a.m. PC Mandy Waller arrived at the police station. With her kindly, sympathetic tone, Mandy had struck up a rapport with Denise and, as the officer who had been involved from the start, it was decided that she should continue to look after the family. Mandy said: 'It was just a case of keeping them up to date on what had happened as far as we could and providing tea and sandwiches. There was such a constant stream of family members that it seemed that everyone who turned up at the police station was a relative. It was a matter of working out who was who and what the connection was. Denise and Ralph hadn't slept at all. Ray had been out searching all night and looked really rough on the Saturday morning'.

Denise and Ralph were persuaded to appear at the news conference. It was a crowded briefing. All Denise can remember of it is a blur of lights and flashes from the cameras. She managed to say, 'I was buying meat at the butcher's. I turned round and he had gone. If anyone has got my baby, just bring him back'. Then she broke down and fled from the room in tears.

Then Ralph said, 'It could happen to anyone. She just turned away and the next minute he was gone. James is a bubbly kid who gets on with anyone. He will chat to people and we have taught him his name and address so if anyone asks him he will tell them'.

While the news conference went on at Marsh Lane, outside on the ground the police were continuing their search, widening the area in response to new sightings that were coming in. Over 100 officers were involved in the hunt for James. Police divers waded along the canal conducting a line search. Ray Matthews remembers one of them giving him an encouraging 'thumbs up' signal towards the end of their initial search late that afternoon. 'That was a big relief: said Ray. 'There had been a lot of reported sightings of him on the canal bank. We then thought we can't think the worst now. He's not in there. Someone's got hold of him'.

Late that afternoon, Mandy took Denise and some of the other members of the family upstairs to the bar area, for a break from the little TV room. The window commanded a view of the pavement outside the police station and, as Denise glanced out, she caught a glimpse of two little girls with a boy who, in his track suit bottoms and coat, looked very like James. She shouted to Mandy, who called out an alert on her personal radio. Within a minute a police patrol car, blue lights flashing, overhauled the little group. It turned out to be one more crushing disappointment. The toddler was actually a little girl.

Saturday night repeated the pattern of Friday. Police continued their full-scale search long after dark, the powerful searchlights of the police helicopter illuminating the ground as officers carried on line searches. At 10 p.m. the search was scaled down, though not abandoned, for the night. It was to resume in all its intensity early the next morning.

Most of the family had gone beyond exhaustion by now, but somehow drove themselves on to trudge around the area for a second bitter winter's night. They were still refusing to abandon hope, still inventing scenarios for James's disappearance that all had the common denominator of his eventual safe return. If sheer communal willpower could have brought James back safe and well, there is no doubt that by now he would have been tucked up in bed at home.

Ray said: 'We didn't feel tired, just bewildered by it all. We thought from the video pictures that the boys looked about fourteen. We thought they had taken James away somewhere for a prank, to cause a police search. They had dumped him somewhere and were lying in their beds thinking nothing of it, while James was out there wandering or huddled up in a corner. We even thought they might have sneaked James into one of their houses and their parents didn't know he was in the bedroom. Anything and everything was going through our minds'.

Sometime in the early hours of Sunday, Ray took Denise and Ralph back to Eileen's house. Denise said, 'I just sat up in the lounge with Ray's wife Delia. I was sitting in my Mum's chair waiting for it to go light. The police had said we would have to go home and get some rest because we

looked so bad. I was just waiting for daybreak. We kept phoning the
police station to see if they had heard anything. As soon as it went light
we went back down there'.

That Sunday morning the police called another news conference.
This time Denise could not face the ordeal, but she wrote out an appeal
for Ralph to read out. The television in the family's little room at Marsh
Lane was switched on in the corner, with the volume turned off. Ray
noticed that a religious programme was on. Suddenly James's photograph
flashed on to the screen, and a special prayer was said for him to be
found. Ray could read the words on sub-titles at the foot of the screen.
Life for the family had been a vacuum of constant, exhausting effort for
two days. For the first time Ray got an inkling of the extent to which the
thoughts of everyone in the country were with them.

Detective Superintendent Albert Kirby, head of the Merseyside
Police Serious Crime Squad, came in on the case that day, and took over
as Senior Investigating Officer (SIO) in charge of the inquiry. By now,
with massive police search resources and the considerable efforts of the
family still having drawn a blank, prospects were looking increasingly
bleak.

The press conference was scheduled for noon that day. During the
night a colleague of mine in the Press Association's London office had
picked up information from the police about the sighting of James with
the two boys at a reservoir. I had spent part of the morning looking
around the area expecting to find police divers searching a waterway. In
fact the reservoir turned out to be grassed over and enclosed. There was
no way that a child could have gained access to the underground water
source. At least, I thought, that was another potential source of danger
for the missing child ruled out. Now I sat with dozens of colleagues in the
overcrowded office at Marsh Lane used for the briefing.

DCI MacDonald eventually came in with Detective
Superintendent Kirby and Ralph Bulger. Mr Kirby listened as Mr
MacDonald read out an initial statement.

'It is now some forty-four hours since James went missing on Friday.
We have continued searching buildings, open land and the canal in the
area of the Strand. I would make an appeal for anyone living in the area
of Bootle and perhaps towards Walton to search their gardens, their back

sheds and anything of that nature as the child may have wandered off and found somewhere to sleep.

'We have had a sighting of James at round about 4.30 p.m. on Friday in the Breeze Hill area of Walton near a reservoir. This is a fully enclosed reservoir and no access can be made into the water area. A lady saw a small boy certainly answering his description with two other boys. She viewed the video pictures of the two boys and is quite confident that they are the two boys she saw and also, having seen the photographs of James, she is quite satisfied that that is James also. We are anxious to trace any more persons who may have knowledge of who these two boys are or who may have seen them in this particular area. I do have enlarged photographs of the two boys.

'We have been getting help from the public and we are anxious that anyone who has any information at all should come forward. We request vigilance from everyone to search the area for James'.

Ralph was then invited to make his statement. He looked gaunt and haggard as he sat slumped in his chair, reading from the note Denise had scribbled out for him.

'Me and my wife want to say to the lads who were seen with him, whoever they are, if they could come forward and get themselves eliminated or bring my son back, as long as he is safe nothing will happen to them ... just as long as he gets back. If they could drop him in to the nearest police station or somewhere safe or phone or something, or anyone who can give any information whatever, no matter how small it is, just get in contact'.

One of the reporters asked him if James had ever wandered off before. Ralph replied: 'He does wander but it's not something he does all the time'.

He was asked how Denise was. 'As well as can be expected,' he shrugged. 'We've never been through anything like this before. We are obviously het up about it–especially my wife'.

Finally Ralph was asked if he still had hope. His voice dropped almost to a whisper as he swallowed hard and replied, 'Yes, you've got to'.

DCI MacDonald then broadly reiterated Ralph's appeal. 'It may well be that they have taken this boy away and are now frightened to come forward. We are anxious merely for the boy to be returned'.

He then dealt with questions about the sighting at the reservoir, explaining: 'The witness asked the boys about the small child. They said they were in the area having just found the child. They then took him away and went off into Breeze Hill. She said they were round about twelve years of age. She is not totally positive but she is more confident that they are the boys than that they are not. She assumed that they must be together. It is a mile or just under away from the Strand. They left the reservoir area and went towards Breeze Hill, the main dual carriageway. It is a distinct possibility that they are frightened. We are also looking at the possibility of boys who have run away from home, either absconders or missing from their own homes, possibly squatting. Initially the woman found it unusual but then she was quite confident that they all seemed together because the boy seemed happy to go along with them'.

Then DCI MacDonald was asked if he feared the worst. His response was brief, but the look on his face spoke volumes. 'Sometimes, but you have just got to hope for the best,' he said.

He then took us through the security video in detail, dealt with a few more questions and called the conference to a close. We went off to file our stories, while the police got on with the search.

With that out of the way, Ralph, Ray and six more of their male relatives went to a new search area, close to the grassed-over reservoir. They parked the two cars they were using on the car park of the Mons Public House, and spread out to search the area, using A-Z street guides to coordinate their efforts. Police officers were doing a line search of school playing fields near a sports stadium in the area, and one of the detectives at the scene told them there had been a reported sighting nearby. 'We looked for him in parks and empty houses, garages, anywhere,' Ralph recalled. 'I don't remember what I was feeling. I was just looking for him and trying to find him. I was confused'.

Back at police headquarters, Denise sat in the TV room with Nicola and Mandy Waller. All Mandy could do was try to keep Denise and the other family members who were still regularly calling in reassured and fuelled with tea, sandwiches and platitudes.

Finally Denise could take the lack of activity no longer. 'I started to go off my head. I said I wanted to go out and start looking,' she recalled.

Mandy decided to take Denise and Nicola out in her own car, as much to give them a break and some fresh air as in the serious expectation of finding anything. She took a police radio with her and notified the radio room of their plans before they left the police station.

They set off at about 3 p.m., driving fairly aimlessly around the quiet Sunday streets, Denise staring vacantly out of the window. The expedition had lasted only about twenty minutes when Mandy's radio suddenly crackled to life. The radio room operator told her in a clipped, urgent tone, 'Come back to the station immediately ... and turn your radio off'.

Chapter Five

They thought at first that somebody had discarded a doll on the railway track. The bored teenagers were idling away a cold, dull Sunday afternoon, roaming about near their Walton homes, when they spotted it on the freight line from Edge Hill to Bootle. The boys, two brothers aged thirteen and fourteen, and their two fifteen-year-old friends, moved in for a closer look. Suddenly the awful reality dawned on one of the boys. 'It's not a doll. It's a baby!' he shouted.

The others could see it clearly now. It was a sight they will never be able to forget. Horrified, they turned and scrambled frantically off the embankment, sprinting all the way to Walton Lane Police Station, less than 100 yards away. They burst through the doors and up to the reception desk, breathlessly blurting out their story to the policeman behind the counter. Within seconds they were rushing back to the scene with uniformed officers to show them what they had found.

Police officers are used to unpleasant sights. Road accidents, sudden deaths and attending autopsies harden them against most things. Nothing in their experience could quite prepare these officers for the sight that confronted them that afternoon. James Bulger's tiny body was lying on the railway line in two pieces, cut in half by the impact of a freight train.

News of the discovery was transmitted to Marsh Lane Police Station at 3.15 that Sunday afternoon. The radio room made the call to PC Mandy Waller its first priority. The air would soon be alive with operational communications about the discovery. That was no way for James's mother to find out that her son was dead.

Mandy had no way of knowing for sure what had happened, but instinct and experience led her to the correct conclusion. She told Denise Bulger and Nicola Bailey, 'We've got to go back to the station'.

Denise instantly realized that something significant had happened. 'They've found him, haven't they?' she asked Mandy.

Mandy was noncommittal. 'I've just been told to go back,' she replied.

Denise was convinced they had found James. She convinced herself that when they got back to Marsh Lane, James would be sitting there waiting for her.

It was a short journey. Mandy parked in the enclosed car park behind the police station and the three women made their way to the rear entrance. They met Detective Superintendent Albert Kirby, Detective Chief Inspector Geoff MacDonald and Detective Inspector Jim Fitzsimmons in the doorway. Their faces were grim and taut. There were other police officers milling about everywhere. Denise shouted, 'Have you got him?' Nobody would answer. She turned to Mandy. 'What's happening?' Mandy's response was vague.

In the confusion, she managed to grab a moment with DCI MacDonald, out of Denise's earshot. He told her a body had been found and they were on their way to the scene to confirm that it was James.

The detectives left, and Mandy took Denise and Nicola upstairs, back to the TV room on the CID landing. Nothing was confirmed and Mandy knew she could not tell Denise until they were sure. It would have been too cruel.

A few members of the family were gathered in the room by now. Ralph's brother Phil, Denise's brother-in-law Denis Mather, her brother Paul, Nicola, and Denise's close friend Jeanette all kept her company during the anxious half-hour that followed.

Denise asked Mandy point-blank, 'They've found him, haven't they?'

Mandy said, 'I don't know'.

Denise asked her again.

'I honestly don't know'. These were uncomfortable moments for Mandy. She knew the strong possibility was that James was dead. Professionalism told her she could not tell Denise what was happening until the detectives confirmed what now seemed the almost inevitable outcome. Mandy had spent much of the previous forty-eight hours in Denise's company and they had developed a strong bond. She had realized as the time dragged on that things were looking less hopeful, but for Denise's sake she had allowed herself to go on hoping. Now she had to hide her own feelings, to spare Denise from despair until they knew beyond doubt.

DCI MacDonald drove as the three detectives made their way quickly to Walton. It was an area Jim Fitzsimmons knew very well. He had walked the beat there as a young bobby in the Anfield sub-division, soon after ending a brief flirtation with professional soccer as an apprentice with Liverpool FC. The detectives parked their car in the driveway of a transport depot in Cherry Lane, and made their way up the embankment and along the treacherous stone ballast to the crime scene.

When they arrived and saw the tiny, mutilated body, they had no doubt that it was that of James Bulger. It was equally clear that he had been deliberately and brutally killed.

Mr Kirby recalled: 'My reaction was one of disbelief. We went from a stage of not actually believing the gravity of what had happened into automatic pilot. You know what you have to do in a situation like this, and you set things in motion. In the odd quiet moments, waiting for people to arrive and perform their tasks, we were walking around up there and it was very hard to comprehend'.

The clues pointing to foul play were numerous. The most immediately striking was that the clothing had been removed from the lowest part of James's body. Blood-stained bricks were strewn about on the railway line around his body and it was clear that they had either been placed on top of his body or built up in a pile in front of it to conceal him from the driver of the train that had hit him. The scene was the site of an old, demolished former railway station. There were low brick walls at either side of the double, non-electrified track, the remains of the old station platform. The two halves of James's body layover the track at one side, yet there was blood splattered on the far wall, some 20 feet away. There were also drops of blood leading from there to where his body lay. The child had either staggered to where he lay after being injured, or had been carried there.

The process of preserving the crime scene for forensic examination began. British Transport Police officers had already thrown a cordon around the area to keep the public at bay. Officers from the police transport section were arriving with the lightweight, spring-loaded major incident tent, which was erected over the body. Detective Inspector Andy McDiarmid, in charge of the police scenes of crime unit, was called out from home, a call he had been grimly anticipating throughout the weekend. Home Office pathologist Dr Alan Williams and scientists from the forensic science laboratory at Chorley were also called out from home.

Meanwhile, DCI MacDonald left his two colleagues at the scene, returned to his car and drove back to Marsh Lane Police Station, on one of the hardest missions of his life. Recalled Mr Kirby: 'There was no question that it was James, and one of the first things we discussed was telling Denise and Ralph. Geoff immediately said that as he had been speaking to them and dealing with them right through, he would do it. He showed tremendous courage to volunteer to take that task on, and I know for a fact that it cost him a lot of heartache and upset'.

Nicola Bailey was staring at a frosted glass panel alongside the door of the TV room at Marsh Lane Police Station. She was convinced that at any moment a familiar little golden-headed shape was going to appear against it.

Half an hour had elapsed since she and Denise had returned to the police station with Mandy. Denise, too, was still expecting her son to be brought back to her. 'I honestly thought he would be all right. With him being with two young lads, that convinced me. I thought they had him in a shed somewhere and their parents didn't know. I imagined them taking out biscuits to feed him'.

Mandy Waller had stepped out of the room for a few moments when DCI MacDonald arrived back. He knocked on the TV room door and walked in. Everyone in the room looked at him. Denise and Nicola looked past him, down at toddler level. No James. Nicola looked at his face. The detective looked grey and suddenly exhausted.

Geoff MacDonald walked to where Denise was sitting, knelt down and held her hand. 'We've found him'. he began. Phil Bulger watched

Denise's face and saw a flicker of hope. '… but it's not good news, I'm afraid'.

Denise screamed. It was a terrible, anguished sound that reverberated through the very souls of all who heard it. She brushed DCI MacDonald aside and pitched forward on to the floor, moaning, 'Oh no, oh no'.

'I know there was a room full of people but I couldn't tell you now who they were,' recalled Denise. 'I remember him coming over to me, saying, "It's not good news, I'm afraid", but it's all a blur after that. I don't remember any more'.

Nicola threw her head in her hands. The others stood in shocked silence for a moment. Mandy walked in then and saw Denise crying on the floor. 'She seemed to go totally out, not unconscious but almost asleep. It was very odd,' Mandy remembered.

Geoff MacDonald, his own eyes filling with tears, was saying something about '… by the railway track'. He added the words 'I'm sorry'. Hands were reaching out to Denise, lifting her back into her chair. The detective walked out of the room. He knew there was nothing more he could say, not now.

He walked into another office, where some of the Murder Squad detectives had gathered. They didn't need to be told. They had all heard that scream. Detective Sergeant Phil Roberts saw DCI MacDonald pull a handkerchief from his pocket. 'There's very few things that move me, but this …' His voice trailed off.

DS Roberts recalled: 'I had been thinking, "I hope he has been kidnapped and he is alive". Then when we knew they had found a body, we hoped it would be some tragic accident. The bosses said there was no doubt about it, it was a murder. Everyone's hopes had been dashed. There was a terrible air of silence'.

Ralph Bulger was still out with Ray Matthews, searching relentlessly for James. They were near Walton Prison, checking a city farm site popular with children, when a police officer told them they should return to the police station. Ralph and Ray said they wanted to carry on searching, but the officer was insistent. He drove them in his patrol car back to the Mons Pub car park where Ray had left his car. The officer left them, but they then realized they had left two others from the car still searching, and decided they had better wait for them. A couple of minutes elapsed and a Volvo estate car pulled into the pub car park alongside them. Ralph's brother James climbed out. James had driven with Ralph's brother Gary directly from Marsh Lane, where they had just been given the news. James recalled: 'When I saw Geoff MacDonald he was a different man. All the police officers just seemed to look old, worn out. Everyone had been so hyped up wishing to get him alive, and then knowing the worst just sapped them all. You could see that they were visibly totally drained'.

Mandy Waller had broken the news to James and Gary and added, 'You tell Ralph when you get him. It is up to you how you tell him'. James accepted this. He knew it would be better coming from him than anyone else.

James motioned to Ray to wind down his window, leaned inside the car to him and put his arms around him for a moment. Then he walked to the passenger side, opened the door and embraced his brother. 'They've found James,' he said.

Ray said, 'Where is he?'

James shook his head. 'They've found him, but he's dead'. He looked into his younger brother's eyes and said quietly and firmly, 'You had better get back to the police station and see to Denise'.

Ralph nodded. James got in the car with them. 'I knew from the look on their faces, both of them, that it hadn't really registered when I told them,' he recalled. 'Ralph said nothing in the car'.

Ray has no recollection at all of his drive back to Marsh Lane Police Station. Ralph recalled: 'I remember James telling me. I had been hoping it was going to be all right. I was just cracking up. I felt angry'.

When they reached Marsh Lane, Ralph's silent rage exploded. He met Geoff MacDonald at the foot of the main police station stairs, just after being allowed through the front public foyer into the private part of the police station. 'Is it him?' Ralph asked the detective.

'Yes,' DCI MacDonald confirmed

Ralph pleaded. 'I want him now. I want to see him'.

'You can't see him now,' the detective said gently.

Ralph started kicking at the wall and shouting.

'Have you got them? What have they done to him? Has anybody had him?' Ralph was tortured by the possibility that his son might have been sexually interfered with.

His brother Phil managed to calm him down for a moment, but then Ralph went running to Geoff MacDonald's office, Phil close on his heels. The chief inspector was sitting at his desk by now.

Ralph smashed his hand down on the detective's desk and said through clenched teeth, 'Have you got them? Who are they? Give me five minutes with them. I want five minutes'.

Geoff MacDonald met Ralph's desperate, anguished gaze and vowed quietly, 'We will get them. Don't worry. We'll make sure we get them'. Philip Bulger saw the detective's own eyes fill with tears again as he spoke.

Phil took Ralph by the arm and led him out of the office to the toilets. Ralph's brothers watched over him as his outward rage slowly subsided. 'He was full of hate, and just said whoever it was, he wanted to kill them,' Phil recalled.

Ralph somehow got himself under control and went to Denise. She had refused the attentions of a doctor and was sitting in a daze in the TV room, crying. Ralph held her tightly and said, 'We will have to be strong'.

DI Andy McDiarmid arrived at the scene of the crime shortly before 4 p.m. to be briefed by Detective Superintendent Kirby. He then took charge of the scene and began organizing the scientific investigation.

'With a child of such young years, you are looking at the worst possible scenario,' he recalled. 'It was horrendous and very emotive. We knew we would have to get the maximum amount of evidence from the scene which meant we couldn't rush things. There are always conflicting interests in this situation. The SIO wants to get as much evidence as he can quickly so he can start his investigations. On the other hand you have the need to make sure you do a thorough job. It is a balancing act, and it is very difficult. From the outset we decided we were going to do this very thoroughly, no matter how long it took.

'Our major problem was that it was a very difficult scene. You had to walk 200 yards along railway ballast to get there. It was also quite apparent at that time that we were going to have problems with lighting,' he recalled. A Merseyside Fire Service team was called in to rig up emergency lighting to illuminate the scene. Members of the scene of crime team then video-taped the area and took photographs from all angles.

Mr Kirby took an early decision that there should be very limited, 'need to know' access to the photographic material and to detailed information about the nature of the attack on James. 'I decided from the outset that because it was so horrific it could affect the professional way the staff were working. I decided I would not tell them all the details of what we had seen on the railway line. I told them why and I assured them that it would not be allowed to affect the way they were working. It was purely because it was so heavy to handle. Without exception, the officers accepted that decision'.

Dr Williams and Home Office forensic scientists Graham Jackson and Phil Seamen were all at the scene by about 7 p.m. Dr Williams made his initial examination at the scene. One puzzling factor at that stage was some blue staining on James's eye, the side of his neck, his ear and the fingers of one of his hands The scientists took some blood swabs from the body at the scene, and it was agreed that the body should be removed to the mortuary before any further forensic samples were taken. Even the process of removing the body was meticulously photographed, to provide a record in the event of any piece of evidence becoming detached as it was being moved. Detective Sergeant Alan Carver went with Dr Williams to the mortuary at Liverpool's' Broadgreen Hospital where he was to conduct a full post-mortem examination, while DI McDiarmid stayed to supervise the investigation at the scene.

'I wanted to know from the scientists if they could give me there and then any facts based on the blood distribution about what had actually happened at the scene,' said DI McDiarmid 'They did an absolutely superb job. The scientists confirmed what we thought, that there had been some sort of assault that had taken place prior to James's death'.

Mr Kirby and DI Fitzsimmons made their way back to Marsh Lane, where they started setting up the complex procedures of the murder inquiry on which they were now embarked. 'It was a miserable, damp, freezing night,' said Mr Kirby. 'When we got back we were cold, upset, and generally in an awful state. But we switched into professional mode and got things up and running. There are a mass of things that have to be done in that situation. We had the major incident room to set up and get going, a management team to organize, and we already had a lot of people coming in with information. I was very lucky that I had worked with so many of the team on a lot of major inquiries before. I had a very good, experienced, balanced team to work with, which made life very secure. I knew everyone was pulling in one direction.

'I have dealt with far more complex cases, but none of us has ever dealt with anything as emotive. It wasn't just that which was difficult, but the intense attention we were getting from the media. No one in this force had witnessed anything quite like it before'.

Meanwhile a specialist search team from the OSD carried out an initial line search along the railway track. They discovered a tin of matt blue Humbrol modelling paint. They also found some new batteries. One of them was still inside the four-battery packaging, lying on top of the platform just above the point on the wall where the blood was splattered. The other three batteries were right in amongst the stone chippings of the railway ballast. One of them had blood-staining on it.

'They were obviously important,' said DI McDiarmid. 'We had a big dilemma about what to do. We could have tried for blood-matching or fingerprints. You have to make these decisions all the time. If you go for one type of evidence you ruin another type. If we went for fingerprints the fingerprint process would destroy the blood. Going for blood could wipe off the fingerprints. We decided to go for fingerprints and as it turned out we didn't get fingerprints off it. That is one of those risk decisions you have to take'.

The team also spotted that the polished top surface of the railway track itself was covered with a large number of footprints. They were difficult to see, even with the emergency lighting, but DI McDiarmid knew they had to be retrieved that night. There was every chance that they would disappear for good in the morning dew. The specialist photographer began painstakingly recording every footprint the team could find.

'The problem was that the young lads who had first found him had stood on the track. The initial police officers had been to the scene. The Fire Service had been there to put up lighting. You try to maintain a common approach path as far as possible but people were going to tread on the scene. All you can do is limit the damage they cause. I knew at the time that some of the footprints would be those of police officers and firemen, but in amongst them there could be an offender's footprint, so we had to record them all. It was a major job–a nightmare, in fact. In the end sixteen different types of footprints were retrieved that night, many of which we could eliminate right away'.

It was a long night's work for the team. They eventually wound up their initial examination of the scene at about 4 a.m. 'There is a danger in working too late because your attention span can be wrong and you can miss things after that length of time, but we had to get something quickly because this job had to be solved quickly. We were all aware of that,' said DI McDiarmid.

Helen Bulger had drifted into a few minutes of fitful sleep that Sunday afternoon at her Kirkby home. The telephone did not wake her. Her daughter Carol, thirty-two, took a call from Phil at the police station. Close to hysteria, Carol woke her mother, shouting, 'They've found him. He's dead'.

Helen recalled: 'I started shaking. I couldn't stop for nearly two weeks. It would go off and then it would start again. The doctor said it was my body's way of releasing the tension'.

Ralph came to visit her during that evening, hardly aware of what he was doing, lost in his shock and grief. Later still, she received a telephone call from a friend who said somebody had called the Pete Price phone-in programme on Radio City, Liverpool's independent radio station, suggesting that Denise had been negligent. 'That's why I rang. What they said was wrong. She was overprotective if anything. They were the most caring parents in the world. They were just in the wrong place at the wrong time'.

Denise's friend Jeanette drove her home to Eileen's house in Scoter Road. Phil, who was also in the car, recalled: 'Denise wasn't talking at all. She was just wound in on herself, really quiet, not saying anything'.

Back at home, Eileen too had received the news by telephone. 'I felt as though everything was drained from me,' she recalled. 'I had thought he might have wandered into a shop and sat down and fallen asleep. That thought was keeping me going, thinking he was there all the time. When I knew he was dead my mind seemed to go numb. I couldn't tell you what I felt like. It was a horrible feeling'.

Eileen retired to her bedroom, unable to cope. When Denise got home, she went upstairs too. The other women of the family followed. For hours they sat comforting Denise as best they were able. It was a time when the only thing they could really do to help was be there.

Ralph spent most of that evening in the kitchen, his brothers and Denise's all lending him what support they could in the terrible loneliness of loss. His rage was spent now. All he wanted was to hold his son.

Somebody had to shoulder the burden of making a formal identification of James's body. Ralph had forcibly volunteered himself for the task, but the detective team was anxious to spare him that further ordeal. Ralph was close to the edge now. Seeing the injuries for himself would simply have been too much. Ray and Denis had also offered themselves. In the end James's uncle and namesake, Ralph's big brother, said he would do it. He quietly told Mandy Waller that it had better be done that night. Come morning, nothing would stop Ralph from wanting to do it himself.

James Bulger felt some trepidation about what he had to do that night, but he was sure he could handle it. In his years driving taxis he had witnessed the results of some terrible road accidents. He was a tough man. He saw himself as the logical choice. 'If Ralph had done it, he would be lying there in bed for years remembering that horrible part. I didn't want that to be his memory of James,' he recalled.

At about 9 p.m. he was sitting at his Kirkby home with his wife Karen when the police telephoned and asked him if he was ready. Mandy Waller was in the patrol car that picked the couple up and drove them to Broadgreen Hospital a few minutes later.

Geoff MacDonald met them outside the mortuary. He warned James that it was important that he did not touch the body because there was still forensic work to be done. They had to wait about half an hour, and then James was asked if he was up to it. He nodded and went in.

Mandy stayed outside with Karen. 'Will he be able to cope?' Mandy asked her. Karen, staring apprehensively at the door her husband had just stepped through, said, 'I'm not sure'.

Nothing could quite have prepared James Bulger for what confronted him on that mortuary table. 'He was covered in blood and matted in blood. His blond hair was dyed red with his own blood,' James recalled, staring off into space, seeing again the image that haunts his every thoughtful moment. 'His eyes were open and his little mouth was open a little bit. You couldn't mistake him'.

He went on with the description, his voice dull and mechanical as he suppressed his emotions. When he had finished, he said, 'I felt anger. Real venom. If I could have got hold of the ones that did it ... I could hear James talking, shouting for his Dad while it was getting done. I could hear him saying, "I'll get my Dad on to you" while they were slapping him around and battering him. It was so unreal. It was him but part of me didn't want to believe it. Seeing is believing. It just struck me that what was there of him was so small. He was only a little kid anyway but he was even smaller. You tend to blank things out. Your mind works overtime'.

James looked down at his little nephew and confirmed quietly to the officers: 'That's our James'. He then asked one of the hospital staff, 'Can you fix his face in case his Mum and Dad want to see him?'

'Not really,' came the reply.

James told Geoff MacDonald what the detective already knew, that Denise and Ralph could not be allowed to see him. James recalled: 'I know he is their kid but he ... The sight will be with me till the day I die. For them to have seen it I think would have killed them'.

It took a cruel toll on James. He started drinking heavily and became, by his own admission, very aggressive, even to those close to him. 'I ate hardly anything for about three weeks, and my weight went down to 7 1/2 or 8 stone. I was full of anger and frustration at not being able to get hold of the fuckers that did it. I lived on ciggies and ale–that's all I'm living on now. I don't go out every night any more but when I do go out I can't even get drunk any more. If I sit here watching the television I see his little face on the screen. I hardly sleep. I eat one meal a day, when I can get it down. When I am sitting on my own it comes back, or in the dead of night when I am in bed asleep. It is in your dreams and it just wakes you up. I have nightmares where I see him getting killed and see what they are doing to him. I hear his voice. It becomes very real then'.

Following my early tip-off on events at Walton, I notified my London office and set off back to Liverpool mid-afternoon. During the forty-minute journey I got through on my car telephone to Detective Chief Superintendent Roger Corker, who confirmed formally: 'The body of a young boy toddler has been found on a railway embankment at Walton. It has not yet been formally identified'. I filed a newsflash which was rapidly transmitted by the Press Association.

The scene, near the corner of Cherry Lane and Walton Lane, had been sealed off by British Transport Police officers by the time I arrived. Other journalists began arriving within minutes. Press officer Diane Halliwell, later to be joined by Chief Inspector Paul Donnelly, met the press beyond the barrier and gave us what scant information was available. It is one of those strange situations that often arise in the early stages of a murder inquiry, when everyone knows that it is a murder and who the victim is, but police procedure forbids formal confirmation.

We waited for some hours, watching the comings and goings of the investigation team from the scene. Although the railway track was raised above the level of the road it was heavily screened with trees. We had no view of the murder site from the public pathway, though one or two enterprising photographers were able to find vantage points for long shots of the police tent. It was bitterly cold, and the crowds of young onlookers from the neighbourhood who gathered eventually got bored and drifted away. I remember idly speculating with colleagues at the time that the boys involved could have been among those local kids. It now seems possible that Robert Thompson was indeed standing there with the other curious spectators.

We sheltered in our cars through much of the evening, running the engines sporadically against the cold, climbing out when one of the press officers came to impart some snippet of news. It was confirmed that the death was suspicious and that a group of young boys had found the body, but there was very little else in the way of hard information. Eventually we were asked to go back to Walton Lane Police Station, where we were told it would be several hours before the post-mortem examination would be held. Finally we were persuaded to return to our bases, on the understanding that Chief Inspector Donnelly would notify me when there was any further statement, and I would circulate the information through the Press Association. It was late that evening when my telephone rang and Paul Donnelly told me: 'The body has been formally identified by an uncle as that of James Bulger. We are now treating the case as murder. Further details will be released at a press conference tomorrow'.

Detective Superintendent Albert Kirby and DI Jim Fitzsimmons worked late into that cold winter's night, briefing the inquiry team and laying their plans for the next day. At last they set off for home to snatch a few hours' sleep.

Jim Fitzsimmons recalled: 'I felt as though I knew James Bulger because I had been working on this since the Friday and everywhere you looked you saw his face looking back at you from the posters. At the scene it was as if I had been detached from myself, getting on with the job in hand.

'As I was leaving the police station to go home it hit me. I was extremely upset. I went home and my wife was aware of it. I was quite distraught for a couple of hours. Although I had never met him it was like a personal loss. There were an awful lot of people, members of the public, police, press and the like, who felt that way. This affected me on a personal level for those hours more than any other incident I have been involved with in seventeen years in the police.

'It is something we talked about in the aftermath. None of us volunteered for counselling because we were a very strong team, but some of us who are fortunate to have strong and supportive homes got our support there. We couldn't be breaking down left right and centre. We would have got nothing done. But that is not to say that in our private moments we weren't deeply affected'.

Detective Superintendent Albert Kirby held a management conference with his senior officers at 8 a.m. on Monday morning. They reviewed what was known of the case and discussed the strategy they would pursue during the murder investigation. Then Albert Kirby held a full-scale conference with the officers of the murder squad, to update them all on the course the investigation was to take. The inquiry team detectives who would go out in pairs to interview suspects and witnesses, and the officers from the Holmes team who would collate the information coming in and feed it into the computer system attended this conference.

Conducting a murder investigation in a modern police force is very different from the popular television fictional image of the senior detective dashing about interviewing every witness, seizing on a vital clue and moving in to make the arrest. In real life the senior investigating officer is the man at the top of a complex management structure. The buck stops with him, and he bears overall responsibility for the success or failure of the inquiry, but delegation of work to trusted and experienced officers further down the command chain is vital.

There was a steady flow of information from the public on the James Bulger case. The high media profile and the way the case had touched the public conscience ensured that everyone wanted to help. Processing such vast amounts of information, cross-checking and assessing it, sifting out the useful from the well-meaning but useless, is a slow and laborious job requiring thousands of man-hours. It is painstaking, very thorough work. Experienced senior officers prioritize the action required in sending the detective teams out to follow up on information. Every potentially useful lead is eventually followed up. Sometimes the results are swift. Often it can take days, even weeks, but it is a system that almost invariably gets results.

That Monday morning Detective Superintendent Kirby held his first news conference on the case. We gathered once again at Marsh Lane Police Station, to hear Mr Kirby confirm what some of us had already heard unofficially, that James had suffered 'absolutely horrific' injuries in addition to those inflicted by the train. He said there was no evidence of sexual assault, and that theft was not thought to be the motive. 'Two-year-olds have nothing to steal,' he said.

'I am inclined to think it is something that has taken place for some reason we cannot understand, where events have got out of hand. I believe James was probably alive until he arrived at the area where his body was found and was killed prior to the train striking him. What has taken place is horrific and has caused us a great deal of emotion'.

In an appeal to the boys pictured in the video to come forward, Mr Kirby said: 'My experience says no human being can contain the fact that they have been responsible for a child's death. They may be completely innocent. They may have stupidly led James away and what I don't know is whether, as a result, he has come into contact with someone else'.

He renewed his appeal for witnesses, and gave us an update on some of the sightings that had already come in.

While the news conference went on at Marsh Lane, detectives were already out bringing in youngsters who had been identified as possible suspects for questioning. Houses were being searched. 'We were dealing with juveniles all the time and the reliability of what they would tell us was a big problem,' recalled DI Fitzsimmons. 'The frustrating thing was that we had the people responsible for taking James from the Strand right there on video. We believed we would have the offenders within hours. The more we looked at a suspect and compared him with the video the more we thought it could have been him. It is only now, when we look at those responsible, that we realize how deceptive the video images were'.

Efforts to improve and enhance the video pictures were continuing. PC Billy Lightfoot at Marsh Lane spent long hours, day after day, going back over all the security camera footage frame by frame. As he found an image that might be relevant, he would identify it and send it to police headquarters. Ian Clague, manager of the photographic and technical support unit, had returned from leave that Monday morning and was now supervising efforts to enhance these images to produce identifiable shots of the suspects. Outside agencies were also offering to help, but were unable to produce results even close to those created on the unit's own new equipment. It began to rankle with Ian and his team, who were reading reports in newspapers crediting outside computer companies with images they had produced. 'It disappointed us because it was a vital time when we had just been funded with the new equipment and we weren't getting any credit for the work,' recalled Ian. 'We hardly left the machine during the first six days of the inquiry. We produced excellent results but morale in the office wasn't too high because of others claiming the credit'.

The only other agency who had significant success in enhancing the tapes proved to be the Ministry of Defence. DS Andy Rushton and DC Steve Montgomery took the security video to the top secret Joint Air Reconnaissance and Intelligence Centre at RAF Brampton. Experts in the air-conditioned, windowless unit worked for ten hours to enhance six images DS Rushton took them.

'The security in this place was incredible,' he recalled. 'We had to have a series of special passes and tags. It was so tight that even if we wanted to go to the toilet we had to be accompanied to get through all the checks'.

The scientists digitalized the images, sharpened them with a filter and enlarged them three times, before sharpening them once again. The contrast was then adjusted and the frames were printed. The results helped to sharpen the facial features of the boys, without altering them in any way as most of the outside agencies had done with their attempts. The experts were also able to calculate the height of the boys from the video at 3 feet 11 inches to 4 feet. 'They were very helpful people and brilliant at their job,' said DS Rushton. 'Everyone thought the boys must be taller than they were saying, but it worked out that they had hit their heights correctly'.

With the story attracting growing international attention, there had even been suggestions that the American space agency NASA could help enhance the tapes further, but DS Rushton was told by the Ministry of Defence team that there was nothing further that the Americans could have done. 'The chaps who helped us go to NASA two or three times a month, and there is a constant liaison and close relationship between them,' he said. 'They assured me there would be no way on this earth to get better pictures than they had'.

Down at the crime scene, DI McDiarmid and his team resumed their investigations early on the Monday morning. The OSD search team began a new daylight search of the railway track. James's anorak hood was recovered from a tree where it had been thrown, pinpointing the likely point at which James was first dragged on to the railway.

The bloodstained bricks had already gone to the forensic science laboratory at Chorley for examination, along with dozens of other scraps of potential evidence from the scene and from the examination of James's body. One mark on James's face, which had a very intricate pattern, was puzzling the detectives. 'It was almost as if he had been hit with a piece of carved wood, like a curved carving,' recalled DI McDiarmid. 'We were looking for something like that, and in fact anything that could be a weapon. The search team found metal bars, pokers, and even quite a number of knives from the area'.

One of the items recovered was an 'E' clip which was lying on the railway line. This was a clamp with a spring clip used to hold the concrete railway sleepers in place. The clip slots into a hole in the sleeper and is knocked in place with a hammer. The clip looked as if it could have caused part of the mystery face wound. British Rail provided the team with a similar 'E' clip and its assembly which was sent to Chorley to compare. Examination of the 'E' clip recovered at the scene was eventually to reveal minute traces of fair hair and blood.

As the detectives, uniformed officers and scientists worked behind the cordon, members of the public began to arrive and lay flowers and cuddly toys on the grass bank at the corner of Cherry Lane. What began as a small cluster of tokens was to grow into a huge tribute in the days ahead. The spectacle was widely covered by photographers and television cameras each day. For Robert Thompson, it was too much to resist. Later that week he took flowers and laid them with all the others near the scene of the tragedy in which only he and Jon Venables knew he had played such a central role.

While the police were using all their considerable resources in a massive effort to trace their son's killers, Denise and Ralph Bulger were lost in their grief at Eileen Matthews' home in Scoter Road, Kirkby. Denise spent all her time sitting in her bedroom at the house, most of it alone with her thoughts.

'A couple of times I went by the window, but there were people looking up at me,' Denise recalled. 'After that I couldn't go near the window. I was just sitting on the bed all the time. I didn't want to face anyone. I just wanted to be on my own'.

Ralph said, 'I was just moping around that week. We stayed in the house. My head was wrecked. We were just quiet. We didn't say much. I felt anger and grief'.

Helen Bulger came to the house that Monday morning to see Denise and pass on her sympathies. She still could not control the involuntary shaking that had gripped her the previous evening, and felt embarrassed about it during her visit.

Ralph and Denise hardly slept during those dark early days. One night Ralph arrived at his mother's in the early hours of the morning. Helen recalled: 'He brought me a little toy parrot. He said, "Last time James had this he was crying and he wiped his eyes on it". I just wanted to smell it all the time because you could smell James on it'.

DS Jim Green, who had taken the initial statement from Denise on the Friday night James vanished, was appointed family liaison officer along with Mandy Waller. One of his first tasks was going to tell the family on the Monday that James's body had been severed by the train. This information was known to the media and was likely to be published before long. He went to Eileen's home along with police press officer Wendy Johnson. Denise was persuaded to come down to the kitchen, where Jim and Wendy spoke to Denise and Ralph together. Wendy gave them some general advice about the press contact they were likely to encounter, and Jim explained about what had happened to James as gently as he could.

'Denise's head was down and it was impossible to know if she could even hear what you were saying,' Jim recalled.

'Ralph just developed an angry stare. I could have told them anything then. Denise didn't even lift her head. She just stared at the door'.

Mandy Waller also visited the family with Jim Green that day. 'It was a manner of introducing ourselves around so the family would know who we were,' she recalled. 'The first time was difficult. We didn't want to be there and they probably didn't want us there. Denise had retired up to the bedroom more or less from the first. I would go upstairs and talk to Denise while Jim talked to Ralph downstairs. We had various bits and pieces to do with the investigation that we had to fit in.

'Denise would talk about James quite a lot, not in the present tense as though he were still alive, which some people do. It was always in the past tense. She was very open. I was surprised at how much she did talk about him. She had questions about how the investigation was going each day, and whether or not we had got any further'.

During that week the beginnings of a massive flood of sympathetic mail and gifts of teddy bears and cuddly toys began pouring in to Marsh

Lane Police Station, addressed to Denise and Ralph. Thousands of concerned members of the public were to write to them. The prominent and the famous also offered their sympathy and support. Prime Minister John Major sent them a personal letter. There were letters from Church leaders including the Anglican Bishop and Roman Catholic Archbishop of Liverpool and Archbishop of Westminster Basil Hume. The mother of the late rock star Freddie Mercury wrote. Local politicians and the mayors of Sefton and Knowsley added their expressions of sympathy.

Officers at Marsh Lane carefully sifted through the mail. Jim Green recalled: 'We asked the family if they wanted to read any letters. There were sacks of them. They were all well meant but some were terribly depressing'.

Jim took some of the more appropriate letters out to Denise and Ralph in the days that followed. They were to prove a source of comfort. 'It shows that there are a lot more good people than bad,' Ralph said.

'I sat reading through a good few of them. They didn't mean anything to me at the time, but they mean a lot now,' said Denise.

One letter in particular summed up the kind of support, from all levels of British society, that the Bulgers were receiving. The neatly handwritten note read:

Dear Ralph and Denise,

I know you are inundated with messages and flowers, but I could not let James's journey to a better place go by without expressing my deepest, deepest sympathy. I am so shocked and upset that this could have happened, and cannot in any way comprehend the total suffering you must be going through.

Last night I went to see my little babies in their beds. I thought of James and the pain I would feel if I walked back into these bedrooms and could not see my girls in their beds and feel the suffering of knowing they would never come back. It made me cry and they were there. It was a small feeling of the agonies in your heart. You must be going over and over in your mind what happened, and if only...

But James is in a better place. This world we live in was not for James, and he was such a special person that God needed his soul. I know nothing can ever ease your suffering, you both have been through so much. If there is anything I can do at all to help you please let me know. I give you all my support and strength, for what it is worth.

With love, Sarah

The note had been sent from Buckingham Palace.

Tuesday began along a similar pattern to Monday, with Detective Superintendent Albert Kirby holding conferences for the senior officers and the entire police team.

As the various scientific and investigative aspects of the inquiry continued, another news conference was convened at Marsh Lane. James's uncle James Bulger was still badly shaken after identifying his nephew's body but found the reserves of strength to appear at that news conference. DS Jim Green picked him up from home and brought him to Marsh Lane, where the venue for briefings had been switched to the bar as the numbers of journalists and TV crews grew steadily. By now the media attention was massive. Television companies had their vans camped out permanently on the pavement outside the police station. The barrage of cameras, microphones and journalists became intimidating, as Mr Kirby recalled. 'It created tremendous pressure on us, but the press were very responsible. All the way through there was the feeling that they were pulling the same way as us. Every appeal we put out was sent out. There was never a feeling that we were fighting the press. When you went into those news conferences, they were trying to help you in the way they could'.

James Bulger was visibly shaking with emotion as he appealed for help in tracking down his nephew's killers that Tuesday morning. He cold the conference: 'He was only a baby and he was dragged away in broad daylight. I fear that they will do this again. If anybody knows anything, no matter how small, they should get in touch'.

Detective Superintendent Kirby revealed that a new security video had come to light, showing James being dragged along the street almost half a mile from the Strand on the way to Walton. The new footage came from a camera outside the premises of AMEC Building Ltd, on the corner of Hawthorn Road and Oxford Road. Mr Kirby said, 'The child appears to be in some distress. It looks as though he is either being dragged or they are on either side of him and swinging him'.

Mr Kirby also disclosed for the first time the existence of the tin of blue Humbrol paint and the Tandy batteries found at the scene. He told us that both items had been stolen from shops in the Strand, and confirmed that both had been 'in contact' with James's body.

He then made another startling revelation. 'Witnesses have told us that at about that time James had some injuries to his head,' said Mr Kirby. 'He was seen with bruising and grazing to his forehead which were caused after James left his mother's side but before he reached the embankment'.

This came at the end of a question-and-answer session, as the conference was being drawn to a close, almost as a throw-away line. Mr Kirby was asked how he felt about the fact that nobody had intervened in the light of these injuries. His voice dropping almost to a whisper, he replied, 'Horrified'. The conference was then drawn to a hasty conclusion.

That afternoon James Bulger's uncle had another duty to perform. He attended the formal opening of the inquest into James's death at the court of Merseyside County Coroner Roy Barter in Liverpool city centre. Mr Barter had spent an hour being briefed by Detective Superintendent Kirby. What he heard had a profound impact on him.

Mr Barter took brief evidence from James Bulger confirming that he had identified his nephew's body at Broadgreen Hospital late on the Sunday night. Mr Barter then told the inquest hearing: 'I have spent the last hour hearing the circumstances of the tragic death of this innocent child explained to me by Mr Kirby. All I will say is that this is the most dreadful and shocking murder case that I have had to open in the course of the last twenty-five years as coroner of this city'.

He said it took only a matter of seconds for a child to stray and become lost in a crowd, and that no mother loaded with weekend shopping could be expected to keep an eye on her child for every second. He added: 'The person or persons responsible for this must be brought to justice and this must be done as quickly as possible. The tragic facts of the case underline how important it is for mothers to safeguard their children when they are in crowded places like shopping centres'.

On the press benches we were scribbling furiously during the brief hearing. The coroner's reaction was one more strong angle on what had been a day of awful developments in the story. None of us could have guessed then that events were about to occur that would sweep all we had learned so far off the next morning's front pages.

Chapter Six

The first telephone call came through to the police incident room at about 4 p.m. that Tuesday. A man, who would not give his name, said he had seen his son in the Strand shopping precinct on the day James was abducted. He made reference to the batteries, but said he was not prepared to bring his son in to Marsh Lane Police Station because of the intense press interest outside.

Soon afterwards the man called again, giving further information, and said he would think about bringing his son in. A third telephone call followed. This time the caller said his son had denied being in the Strand. He said his mother was aware of it and his mother and grandmother had washed his coat. His grandmother still had the coat. He stressed that if the police went to arrest the boy they should not tell his wife and son that he was the informant. At last he volunteered his name as Mr Paul Green, of 8 Snowdrop Street, Kirkdale, Liverpool. He said his son's name was Jonathan.

DI Jim Fitzsimmons assessed the information. A tip-off from somebody as close as a boy's own father was in itself unusual. The intimation that the boy's coat had already been washed was worrying. Further vital forensic evidence could be in the process of being destroyed.

'We felt we needed to act immediately,' recalled Jim. 'When a suspect was brought in the house would be systematically searched by trained OSD search teams. We didn't have one available. Instead I took a small team of detectives, some of whom would wait at the address until a search team became available'.

It was shortly before 6 p.m. when Jim and his team of detectives pulled up near the Greens' terraced home in Snowdrop Street, in three discreet, unmarked police cars. It was a small residential street, one of a series of terraced side streets stretching down from Stanley Road towards Liverpool's docks. Night had fallen and the street was virtually deserted. None of the officers was in uniform.

The officers knocked at the door of the house, and it was answered by Jonathan's mother, Mrs Margaret Green. The detectives identified themselves to Mrs Green, entered the house and arrested Jonathan on suspicion. The boy, who was twelve years old and bore a strong resemblance to one of the boys in the blurred video images, burst into tears.

Jim Fitzsimmons put an arm around the boy to comfort him and they left the house, walking up the deserted street to one of the cars, parked some 20 yards away. Mrs Green went with the officers. They drove off without fuss, leaving the area as quietly as they had arrived.

DCs George Scott and Mark Dale were among officers who waited at the house with two other children, a male lodger and a friend of the Green family. They settled down to await the arrival of the OSD search team.

Soon afterwards there was a knock at the door. 'I thought it was the search team,' recalled DC Scott. 'I opened the door to be confronted by a blonde-haired female reporter, a sound recordist and a cameraman. She told me her name and said she was from GMTV and she wanted me to make a statement. I was shocked that they were there. It was only minutes since we had left the police station. I didn't understand how on earth they had gone to this address'.

George told the crew that he could not make any statement, and closed the door. He and Mark then kept an eye on the situation outside from behind the curtains of the house.

The television crew, its brilliant lights illuminating the street, quickly began to attract a crowd. George went outside again to speak to the reporter. 'She was persistently asking me to make a statement about whether people had been arrested and I refused to comment,' said George. 'I requested them quite firmly to move away from the house. I told them it was a free country but I was requesting them to move from the house. They then moved to the bottom of Snowdrop Street, about 75 yards away.

'Feelings were already high in the area. People came out to see what was happening. Everyone likes to take the bull by the horns in a situation like that, and they automatically thought the police had the right person and it was Jonathan Green. Soon there were about 150 people outside the address and we had to call for back-up. At no time did I feel I was under any threat from the people outside. There was no ill-feeling whatever towards the CID officers. My fear was for the other people who lived in the house who had nothing to do with the inquiry'.

By the time the OSD arrived in their police vans the street was packed with people. Other journalists and photographers had heard about the commotion and joined the initial television crew, and the crowds of curious and in some cases hostile onlookers were building up. The team conducted a systematic search of the house. They took away some clothing and other property for examination, and in view of the apparent danger from the crowd, the other occupants of the house were also removed in the police vehicles.

Jonathan and his mother were unaware of this commotion at the time. They were driven by the police initially to Stanley Road Police Station and then to St Anne Street, where Jonathan was to be held for questioning.

A team of detectives was sent out to collect Mr Green from an address in the Netherton area of Liverpool and bring him in to give a full statement. In his statement he repeated the claims he had made in his telephone calls. He said he had been going to a friend's house on the Friday and had seen Jonathan on the bus. His son, who was wearing a jacket like one of the boys wore on the video, had got off the bus at the Strand. When he got home that night Jonathan had been washing the jacket in the bath. Mr Green had asked his son about being in the Strand and the boy had denied it.

Mr Green was asked to be present while a police surgeon took what are known as 'intimate samples' from Jonathan. This entailed taking not just fingerprints but samples of blood and saliva which would be used for forensic tests as one of the methods of establishing if he could have been involved in the killing. When Mr Green saw his son he shouted at him, ordering him to 'tell the truth' to the officers, namely that he had killed James Bulger.

Jim Fitzsimmons confronted Mr Green in the medical room and warned him that in no circumstances should he speak to his son again about the murder. He was not allowed any further contact with Jonathan, because the officers did not want him influencing the boy in what he said.

DS Phil Roberts was given the job of questioning Jonathan. The boy was questioned with his solicitor present, and was not very cooperative, denying having anything to do with James's death. Almost from the start the detective realized that it was very unlikely that Jonathan was involved in the crime. 'I knew it wasn't him, but it was a case of proving that to the father. It was a case of ruling him out of the inquiry,' he recalled.

I received a telephone call at home from Chief Inspector Paul Donnelly in the police press office later that evening. His message was short and to the point. 'A person has been arrested in connection with the abduction and murder of James Bulger'.

I immediately telephoned a newsflash through to the Press Association, and heard it read back to me by a TV newsreader at the end of BBC TV's main 9 o'clock news as I was heading for the front door on the way to Liverpool in search of more information. The scene that confronted me outside Marsh Lane Police Station was one of chaos and confusion. Angry groups of men, women and youths, many of them clearly fuelled by drink, were milling about. It was a potentially explosive atmosphere. The police were wisely not saying which police station the boy had been taken to, and many had wrongly leapt to the conclusion that he would be taken to the headquarters of the murder inquiry.

Other journalists, the majority of them alerted by our newsflash, were also arriving at the scene. It is a very difficult situation for a journalist. You need to be there to find out what is going on. That is your job. Unfortunately your very presence in a situation like this only encourages the crowds to gather. There is always the risk that, to some extent at least, elements of that crowd will play to the cameras and create disorder for their benefit. As a reporter you can at least try to be relatively unobtrusive in such a situation, but for photographers and the broadcast media that is virtually impossible.

One very senior detective whom I have known for many years spotted me outside the police station that night and said to me, 'You ought to know better'. To this day I can't see how I or my colleagues could have responded differently that night. This had by now developed into a massive story of international proportions. It was by far the biggest murder case I had ever encountered. Based on the information given, that an arrest had been made in connection with the murder, we could hardly have been expected to sit quietly at home and wait for the next day's press conference. If any of us had, I suspect we might have been seeking another form of employment by morning.

Large numbers of uniformed police officers were being drafted in by now, and began moving on the crowds. Some people had to be restrained by police as tempers turned ugly. Similar problems were apparently being encountered in Snowdrop Street.

Superintendent Paul Burrell, the uniformed subdivisional commander at Marsh Lane, emerged from the police station and gave a quick, impromptu pavement briefing to the gathered reporters. 'During the course of today we have had a number of people who may be witnesses to help us with our inquiries,' he said. 'Those who would not come willingly we have arrested–about three so far. We have no evidence that any of them committed the murder. We are merely looking at their movements on the day of the event. I can promise you we are in no position to charge anyone with murder yet. These are young lads who will have been around the Strand shopping precinct at the time of the murder. We need information off them as witnesses at this stage. They are not like those in the video. We are still looking for them. We have not got the murderer in the cells at this stage, and this interest is premature'.

I duly filed this information to the Press Association, and then spoke to Detective Superintendent Roger Corker. His version of events was not quite so clear-cut. 'In relation to the James Bulger murder the person who has been detained at the present time is one of a number of people who have been detained in this inquiry so far. Merseyside Police will make a formal statement as and when someone is charged and it does not serve this inquiry for speculation to be made'.

The Bulgers were not immune to events in Snowdrop Street that night. They were receiving a series of telephone calls from friends and relatives telling them of the television news reports. Ray Matthews telephoned DCI Geoff MacDonald in a bid to find out what was really happening. Mr MacDonald assured him that the arrested boy had never been more than a 'possible' in the murder hunt. Mr MacDonald said journalists had found out about this particular arrest, but stressed: 'We are arresting anyone who fits the description, if they don't come willingly to help us'.

After hearing what they had of the television reports the family remained sceptical, and it was only when regional bulletins later in the night started carrying the later police statements that they were convinced that the police did not have the killers.

DS Jim Green went out to reassure the family. He recalled: 'The incident had caused them a lot of excitement and a lot of hopes were raised. They were reading more into it than was there'.

By now other journalists who had been to Snowdrop Street were arriving at Marsh Lane, bringing neighbours' graphic accounts of the arrest being made, the youth and his relatives allegedly being bundled into police vans with blankets over their heads, and mobs hanging on the vans and scuffling with officers as the convoy moved off. They were actually giving somewhat exaggerated accounts of the scene when the OSD team moved the rest of the family from the house for their own safety, but with the best will in the world and no way of clarifying the situation with the police that night, none of us could have known that at the time. Neighbours also gave some rather colourful accounts of the lifestyle of the Green family, who had moved to Snowdrop Street only recently and had clearly not made the best of impressions on some longer-term residents.

It was a late and difficult night for all of us. Police finally managed to restore calm to both Snowdrop Street and Marsh Lane, after making a handful of arrests of some of the more extreme members of the crowd. I eventually made it home, not satisfied that I had the full picture but resigned to getting things no clearer that night–by now it was well after 2 a.m. For DI Jim Fitzsimmons there was another hour's work before he finally set off for home at 3 a.m. 'By then we didn't trust the information' Paul Green had given us, but there were certain 'points that needed clarifying before Jonathan could be eliminated,' he recalled.

By the time he returned to his desk five hours later, the morning papers were dropping through letter-boxes around the country. Their headlines told of an apparent major breakthrough in the James Bulger

murder case. The Daily Mirror's splash headline that morning was
'Murdered Jamie: Cops Hold Boy, 12'. The Daily Mail led with 'Tragic
James: Youths Held' under the strapline 'Mob gathers at police station
after murder detectives swoop'. Liverpool's own morning newspaper, the
Daily Post, aided by its later edition times, was able to sound a note of
caution. Its headlines ran 'Three Held in James Probe' but the tag added
'Police swoop but "killer still on Loose." '

Jim Fitzsimmons told the other senior officers at the 8 a.m.
management meeting that Wednesday that they were now working to
eliminate Jonathan from the investigation rather than prove him
responsible. To that end a team of six detectives was assigned to check
his account against his father's with friends, neighbours and school staff,
who had to be tracked down at home because of the half-term holidays.

'We were able to establish that everything that Paul Green said
had happened on the Friday actually happened on the Thursday,' said DI
Fitzsimmons. 'We were able to convince Paul Green that the statement
he had given us was wrong. He then gave us a further statement agreeing
that he might have been mistaken'.

The results of forensic tests confirmed that there was nothing to
link Jonathan to the crime, and the boy was released on police bail later
that day. Detective Superintendent Kirby and DI Fitzsimmons
considered charging Mr Green with an offence of wasting police time.
'But we believed, and my report said, that these were the actions of a
man who really had been seeking to help,' recalled Jim.

In the light of the previous night's coverage an urgent review of
the handling of the media was conducted. Part of the problem had
stemmed from the fact that it had not been clear that the arrest of
Jonathan Green, while one of the more significant possible leads, had
been only one of a large number of arrests. It was decided that Inspector
Ray Simpson and his civilian colleague Diane Halliwell from the
headquarters press office would from then on be stationed full-time at
Marsh Lane, where they could maintain close links with the
investigation and keep the media updated.

'After the Tuesday night we decided we needed a strategy for
releasing information,' Ray Simpson recalled. 'We had to bear in mind
press deadlines. It is something detectives don't like doing but we need
to do it. We decided to have a press conference every day at 11 a.m. and

a written release with further factual information at 5 p.m. We opened up an office at Bootle on the Wednesday morning. All we had to start with was one telephone, though we got two extra lines put in that day. I don't think anyone could have foreseen the level of calls we were going to get. As soon as the press knew we were there the phones just erupted. The phone box in the public foyer at Marsh Lane took more money than it had ever done that week, just through journalists downstairs trying to ring through to us upstairs'.

Ray Matthews and another of James's uncles, Denis Mather, were invited to attend that morning's press conference, and were shown around the incident room and given a detailed explanation of the way the investigation was being conducted, to reassure them that everything possible was being done to trace James's killer.

The conference was opened that day by Chief Superintendent Dave Thompson, the commander of B Division of Merseyside Police, who made a direct appeal to the community. 'The primary aim of this investigation is to trace who abducted and murdered young James and all our efforts are directed to that end,' he said. 'I would like to appeal for calm from people and ask them to assist us to find who did this terrible thing'. He set the Snowdrop Street arrest in context for us by explaining that twenty youths between ten and sixteen had been interviewed at police stations on Merseyside and been eliminated from the investigation. He stressed: 'We don't regard yesterday's incident as a significant breakthrough in the inquiry. It is part of an ongoing inquiry'.

He then gave some detail about those arrested as a result of the disturbances, before saying: 'The distress caused to the family yesterday evening has had implications for the running of this inquiry. Today we have with us two of his uncles and they feel alone and isolated. They feel a sense of frustration and want to know more information, so today officers from the inquiry have shown them how we are conducting it.

'We had to divert police officers from the house-to-house inquiry to protect police stations and houses of people assisting us last night. It has probably put the inquiry back by at least twenty-four hours. We have only so many police officers we can use, and this kind of thing is taking our eye off the ball'.

He said the level of support from the public and the flow of information had been 'tremendous' and added, 'We need the public's support to catch the killers. We know there is a lot of frustration in the community and we appreciate that, and we are doing everything we can to achieve our main objective'.

It was then Albert Kirby's turn to bring us up to date on sightings and developments in the hunt. When he had finished, Denis Mather was invited to speak. 'I can only emphasize to the people of Bootle and the surrounding area to keep calm,' he said. 'We are just as enraged as they are. We don't want the wrong people to be brought in and charged with this. Last night we got some wrong information off the media. For the people of Bootle and the surrounding area I would ask them not to make a commotion, to keep it calm until these people are caught'.

He said the family had not been convinced that enough was being done by the police, but added, 'We have been shown around now and we know enough is being done. The information coming in is phenomenal'.

At noon, Ray Simpson stood in an office at Marsh Lane with Mrs Pauline Clare, the assistant chief constable in charge of crime investigation on Merseyside, Chief Superintendent Thompson and Detective Superintendent Kirby. Ray recalled: 'We watched the 12 o'clock news. It was well reported and accurate. The information we wanted was going out. Mr Thompson did well with his appeal for calm. Mr Kirby's requests for information had also gone well. This was what we wanted. I thought if we could keep it something like this we won't do too badly. This was the standard we had to maintain'.

That should have been that as far as the Jonathan Green incident was concerned. However, it was to become the focus of criticism in the days ahead that would put a dent in the morale of police officers who had been devoting every waking hour to their efforts to catch James's killers.

Prominent Liverpool solicitor Rex Makin fired the first shots. He gave interviews outside Marsh Lane Police Station that day critical of the police operation of the previous night. 'There is hysteria and I don't think there ought to be,' he said. 'I think the police have a job to do but whether they are doing it in a way that is calculated to restore peace and calm to the community is very doubtful. They are approaching it in a gauche way'. He went on to criticize the officers over the way in which

Jonathan had reportedly been arrested. At this stage he, like the rest of us, had no way of knowing that the actual circumstances of the arrest had not been as described by neighbours.

Mr Makin went on to represent the Green family, who were unable to return to their Snowdrop Street home because of the residue of ill-feeling towards them in the neighbourhood, and were accommodated by Liverpool City Council in various hotels for several weeks before eventually being rehoused.

By that Friday Mr Makin was demanding that the police should apologize to Jonathan. 'This boy's life has been ruined by the precipitate police action. He has never been in trouble of any kind at all,' said Mr Makin. 'The boy has never had any psychological trouble but he is now wetting the bed and waking up with nightmares. They have no home and don't know what to do or what is going to happen to them. Their plight is terrible'.

Jonathan and his family were then interviewed by newspapers. The boy claimed that he was so confused by what happened to him that by the time he was let out of the police station he had thought he had committed the murder.

His mother Margaret was quoted as saying, 'We are what they call a classic problem family. But that does not mean we are bad people'.

The police were sufficiently wounded by some of the criticism they faced from Mr Makin and the family to set the record straight by going public with the fact that Jonathan had been 'shopped' by his father. After that, media interest in the saga dwindled rapidly.

Mr Makin lost contact with the Green family after they were rehoused, but maintains his belief that they were unfairly handled. 'They were rather sad people,' he recalled. 'They were a problem family. Mr Green had his problems in the past and still has them. Jonathan was a problem child and no cherubic angel'.

But he said the conditions Jonathan was held in by police overnight put him in 'terror', though he did not criticize the police questioning process. He said he felt it was inconsistent for the police to bail Jonathan, rather than release him completely, once they had cleared him of involvement. 'It was only when I made a row that they voided the bail notice,' said Mr Makin. 'There was never any apology to Jonathan Green or his parents, which should have been forthcoming'.

Detective Superintendent Kirby remains deeply angered by the criticism heaped on his team by Mr Makin. 'My staff worked very hard to prove Jonathan innocent after he was accused of murder by his own father'. he said. 'It distracted us, and there was tremendous gratitude, especially from his grandmother, about the way they were treated'.

Most of the media coverage of the James Bulger investigation was positive and supportive from start to finish. What little criticism there was, notably a Sun story referring to the 'bungles' of Merseyside Police, stemmed from the Jonathan Green incident.

I did not consider that criticism valid at the time, and nothing in the extensive researches I have conducted for this book has altered that view. The police would have been failing in their duty if they had not acted promptly in the face of such apparently strong information. Once a television crew got wind of the arrest, given the huge media interest in the investigation, the events of that evening had a momentum which it would have been difficult to check. With the benefit of hindsight, perhaps we would have been better equipped to put that night's arrest into its proper context had we been advised earlier of the regular round of arrests of suspects that was going on. It was, however, a new situation for all of us. The media were not trying to be vindictive. The police were not trying to be obstructive. We were all doing our jobs, the best way we knew how. It was an unfortunate night, but one from which I believe useful lessons were learned on all sides.

DI Fitzsimmons said, 'I was criticized for my "heavy-handed" ways, but I knew that we had behaved beyond reproach. Considering the hours we had put in and the dedication we were showing, the criticism that came my way was very frustrating for myself and all the investigating team. We felt a sense of despair that Wednesday. It was now three days since we had found James's body, and we were five days into an inquiry where we had photographs of the suspects. We were really down. Then came the breakthrough ...'

Chapter Seven

It was 10.30 p.m. on Wednesday, five full days after James's abduction. The CID landing at Marsh Lane Police Station was quieter now, but far from deserted. DI Jim Fitzsimmons sat in his office researching the evidence that had come in. His spirits were low as he waded through the documents. The Jonathan Green episode had been the kind of distraction he and the team could have done without. The subsequent criticism that was already being aired left him seething with resentment.

There was a knock at his door and two uniformed officers came in, one of them from the station's front desk and the second from the OSD. 'Boss, we've had a woman call at the counter with some information,' the desk officer began. The woman had refused to make a formal statement, but the officer had made a note of what she had told him. She was a friend of the family of a ten-year-old boy called Jon Venables, from Norris Green, Liverpool. The boy had been 'sagging' school on the Friday of James's disappearance, with a ten-year-old friend called Robert Thompson. Jon had come home that night with blue paint on his jacket. The woman also thought she could recognize Jon from the way he was standing in one of the photographs from the video, which showed him from a rear view.

Jim read the officer's notes, asked him a few questions and thanked him. He discussed the development with two other detective inspectors, Ray Murray and Phil Jones, who were part of the team working on the Holmes computer. They agreed that the blue paint sounded promising, and Jim arranged for two detectives who were still on duty to go out and take a full statement from the woman, confirming what she had said. Meanwhile other officers were assigned to make initial inquiries into the backgrounds of the Venables and Thompson families. The information came back shortly after midnight. Everything seemed to stand up, although the boys were younger than everyone had been anticipating. They had to be classed as suspects. Background checks revealed that neither of the boys was known to the police, though the Thompson family was. Jim closed his eyes and muttered a silent prayer that they were not about to pursue another red herring, and started setting the wheels in motion.

DS Phil Roberts was relaxing with a pint in the Marsh Lane bar. He had conducted the questioning of Jonathan Green and was quietly relieved that it was out of the way. Jonathan was the second suspect he had quizzed and eliminated from the inquiry so far. It was tiring work, demanding total concentration over long periods, and he was relishing the breather. Then Phil was asked to attend a briefing with Jim Fitzsimmons, and realized that his temporary respite was over.

It was half past midnight when the officers gathered in the deserted police station canteen. Jim told them of the information they had received, and put Phil Roberts in charge of an operation early the next morning to arrest the two boys and bring them in for questioning. Phil would lead one team to arrest Robert Thompson, and DC Mark Dale would take the second, for Jon Venables.

Mark and his partner DC George Scott had been developing a promising lead of their own, after the children of a family they had spoken to that evening told them they thought they recognized the boys in the video pictures as two persistent school 'saggers' they knew who lived in the Walton area. The mention of paint made the Thompson-Venables lead stronger, so it was agreed that this action would take precedence for the moment.

During the night the overnight duty officer, DC Dick 'Shiner' Wright, made contact with the boys' headmistress at home, and got her to go into the school and check the correct home addresses for the two boys. In Jon's case this involved two separate addresses, his father's in Walton and his mother's in Norris Green. He then made contact with an 'on call' magistrate and had search warrants sworn out for all three addresses.

When Phil Roberts arrived at Walton Lane Police Station at 6.45 that Thursday morning, DC Wright was waiting for him with the

confirmed addresses and the warrants. He met the OSD team who were
to conduct the searches and briefed them that they were not to come in
at the time of the anticipated arrests but to wait for his direction. Mark
Dale, George Scott and the other detectives who were to take part in the
operation were also there, and Phil explained to all of them who the
suspects were and sorted out the details of who would go in each team
and to which police stations they were to take the suspects. It was a short
briefing. In a few minutes, the two parties of Murder Squad officers were
on their way.

The journey from Walton Lane Police Station to Robert
Thompson's home was a very short one. At 7.30 a.m. three unmarked
police cars pulled up in the little street. Even at that hour there were a
lot of parked cars on both sides, and the detectives had to park away
from the target house.

Detectives Larry Dalton and John Kent went down an alleyway to
cover the rear of the house, while Phil Roberts, Detectives Bob Jacobs,
'Shiner' Wright and John Forrest went up the steps to the front door.
Phil knocked at the door, and it was answered by Ann Thompson.

'I am Detective Sergeant Phil Roberts from the Serious Crime
Squad. Can I come in and see you?' he asked.

'What about?' she asked, her manner confident at first.

Phil told her they had come to make inquiries about the murder of
James Bulger. 'She started to panic then,' Phil recalled. They went down
the hallway and turned right into the front lounge. Robert was not in the
room. His little brother Simon was sitting in an armchair. He wore
spectacles and looked intelligent and a little apprehensive.

He could clearly sense right away that something was very wrong.
Ann's baby son was in his pram.

Ann brought Robert into the room, a tiny boy for his age with his
hair cropped close to his head. The boy sat down at one end of the sofa,
leaning on its arm. He was wearing his trousers and socks, but no shoes.
Phil crouched down to the boy so they were face to face with each other.
The pram was right behind the burly detective's back, and easing himself
into the gap was a struggle for him. One thought immediately ran
through Phil's mind: 'For crying out loud, could a small boy like this
have done it?'

Phil cautioned the boy, simplifying the formal words used with adults so that he would understand what he was being told. 'Robert, I have reason to believe that you are responsible, or involved in some way, in the death of James

Bulger. You don't have to say anything to me. If you do say something I might have to give it in evidence against you.'

Right away Robert responded, 'I didn't kill him'. He started to cry, but it was not a normal cry. Phil could see no actual tears. His panic seemed genuine enough, but the crying looked like a pretence.

Ann too began crying. Soon she was on the verge of hysteria, and Phil and the others tried to calm her down.

'I'm not saying he has done the murder at this point. I only suspect he has,' Phil told her gently.

They found a neighbour who knew the family to come in and look after Simon and the baby. Then Bob Jacobs and John Forrest took Robert and his mother out to one of the police cars and drove them back to Walton Lane Police Station.

At the house, Phil set the other officers to work making a preliminary search for obvious things like shoes and clothing, while they waited for the expert OSD team to conduct their more thorough search. Simon was getting upset by now, and Phil reassured the child that nothing was going to happen to him. 'That is what his worry was,' Phil recalled. 'He was a very astute boy. I thought 'to myself, he is young and intelligent, but it is going to be thrown away. He will end up like a lot of the children round here'.

When he was satisfied that everything was under control at the house, Phil left. He decided to walk back to the police station. Soon after he arrived he received a telephone call from an anxious Jim Fitzsimmons. Jim wanted Phil's initial opinion on whether they were on to something.

'I can't comment, Jim. I'll tell you after we've started interviewing him,' Phil replied.

Phil recalled: 'I never commit myself even in my own mind till I interview them. That is the way I deal with things now. I used to go straight in and think "guilty" or "not guilty". Not any more. I was a uniformed bobby for ten years and I've had fourteen in the CID. It's down to experience really'.

Mark Dale's team made their first call to Jon Venables's father's house in Walton. Mark was accompanied by partner George Scott, DS Mike Gunney, and Detectives Dave Tanner, Ray Gorbett and Carl Shelton. As with the team assigned to Robert, they made the short journey in three unmarked police cars. The OSD search team who were eventually to search all three addresses followed them to the area, but held back as they had been told.

It was 7.50 a.m. when Mark Dale knocked at Neil Venables's door. Neil answered, and the officers explained why they were there. Not surprisingly, he was shocked at their visit. The detectives emphasized to him that they were there to establish if Jon was involved rather then saying they definitely suspected him. 'There was no point in frightening the guy,' George Scott recalled. 'We knew it was going to be a horrendous experience for the parents'.

It was half-term, and Jon's thirteen-year-old brother and nine-year-old sister were still in bed. Neil told the officers that Jon was at his mother's house. Mike Gunney and Carl Shelton remained with him at the house while the OSD team moved in. With Snowdrop Street fresh in everyone's minds, they were warned to move in as quietly and surreptitiously as possible. They wore standard-issue blue overalls to conduct the search.

Mark Dale and George Scott drove off towards Susan Venables's address in Norris Green, Dave Tanner and Ray Gorbett following them in a second car. They arrived at 8.10 a.m. Dave knocked at the front door, and Susan answered it. The officers introduced themselves and said they had come to see Jon about the James Bulger case. She led them into the hallway and called out to Jon, who appeared in a few seconds and came downstairs still wearing his green pajamas. They all went into the front lounge of the house.

Mark told Mrs Venables: 'We have had information that Jon had been seen in the area of Walton and we want to speak to Jon and see what the situation is'.

Susan responded: 'I knew you would be here. I told him you wanted to see him for sagging school on Friday'.

Her manner startled the detectives. It was almost as if it was a joke to her that they were interviewing Jon. It was evident at once that she did not believe in her wildest dreams that he could actually be involved.

Mark verified with her that it was Jon she was referring to, and she turned to her son and said, 'There you are, sagging, I told you they would be here'. She then told the officers, 'He came home on Friday, coat full of paint'. Looking at her son again, she added, 'Paint, sagging, I told you they would be here'.

George Scott asked her for the coat she was referring to, and she and Jon went to a row of coat-hooks on a board under the stairs and began rooting through a pile of coats. Jon found it eventually, and threw it in the doorway leading into the living room. George picked it up. It was mustard-coloured and had blue paint on its arm. The paint mark was to prove to be where a child's hand had grabbed hold of it.

Mark Dale cautioned Jon and told him he was being arrested on suspicion of the abduction and murder of James Bulger. Jon instantaneously burst into tears. 'I don't want to go to prison, Mum. I didn't kill the baby,' he said.

Susan, still convinced beyond doubt that her son was not actually involved in the crime, said, 'Don't be silly, Jon. They won't send you to prison. They are just doing their job'.

'It's that Robert Thompson,' Jon sobbed. 'He always gets me into trouble'. Jon later asked, 'Are you going to speak to Robert Thompson?'

'Do you think we should?' asked Mark.

'Yes,' said Jon.

Dave Tanner recalled: 'Jon was frightened. I am not small by any stretch of the imagination, and I was looking down at a ten-year-old frightened little boy who didn't look as though he could hurt a fly. I have children of my own and your heart goes out when you see a child like that'.

They told Jon to get dressed and Dave Tanner and Ray Gorbett led him out to their car, leaving the two younger detectives at the house with Susan to await the arrival of the OSD search team when they had finished searching her husband's house.

The unmarked Serious Crime Squad cars routinely carry search kits including bags and labels for collecting evidence. The coat and some other items were bagged by the two officers while they waited for the van bringing the team who would conduct a more thorough search.

Susan made the detectives coffee, and showed them the other clothing Jon had been wearing. She told them she had already washed his grey school trousers because they had also had paint on them. Jon had been covered in dirt when she found him that Friday evening. Mark Dale recovered the trousers from a pile of clothing waiting to be ironed.

'I sat on the settee and we had a chat with her,' recalled George. 'It was a clean, respectable house, and not untidy, especially considering there were three children who lived there'.

Meanwhile Jon was still crying as he sat on his own in the back of the police car on the way to Lower Lane Police Station. Dave Tanner turned round from the front passenger seat and engaged him in small-talk to try to lift his mood. He asked him what he would like for breakfast.

'Rice Crispies,' was Jon's reply.

As the car came to a halt at a set of red traffic lights, Jon wanted to know: 'Is someone with Robert Thompson now? Which police station will he be going to?'

By the time they reached Lower Lane, Jon had stopped crying. Dave and Ray led him into the police station and presented him before the custody officer. They were expected. The police station was shut down as a custody centre for all other prisoners for the duration of Jon's stay.

Dave Tanner telephoned Jim Fitzsimmons to tell him they had brought Jon in. Jim asked him the question he had asked Phil Roberts: 'What do you think?'

If anything, Dave's response was even less encouraging than Phil's. 'Gut reaction ... I can't believe it,' he said.

Dave recalled: 'I do not normally come to a decision that easily but before me was a picture of a wide-eyed ten-year-old boy in pajamas. Even now it seems incredible'.

There were no Rice Crispies at the police station. Dave fetched the boy a cup of tea and some toast, and he sipped and nibbled nervously while he waited for his parents to arrive.

It was 10.15 a.m. when Mark Dale and George Scott arrived with Susan Venables. They found Jon sitting in the custody suite with the two other detectives and the custody sergeant, who then took Jon's details down for the custody record. He was told to turn out his pockets and asked whether he understood his rights. They were read to him again, and his mother was asked if anyone else should be notified, if she wanted a solicitor and if she wished to consult a copy of the codes of practice on arrests. Solicitor Laurence Lee was contacted to represent them.

Dave Tanner interviewed Susan at length to get information on the family's background and took a statement from her. It was a process that was to take several hours, during which the detective struck up a rapport with her that was to prove vital later in the inquiry.

Mark Dale and George Scott headed back to Bootle to debrief with Albert Kirby and other senior officers on the events of the morning. George Scott was in confident mood when they arrived. He told Chief Superintendent Dave Thompson, the divisional commander, 'It's them. It is definitely Venables. We've got the paint. It's looking good'.

The families of both boys agreed to them supplying 'intimate samples'. A woman police surgeon took these, first from Jon and later from Robert.

While she was with Jon, he asked her, 'Can you get fingerprints off skin? Can you get skin under your nails if you drag a person?' A policewoman who was present recorded the remarks, and they were relayed back to Marsh Lane, where they further reinforced the growing conviction among the detectives that this time they were on the right track.

When the doctor later took samples from Robert, taking nail clippings proved particularly difficult, as his nails were bitten right down. He was nervous of the syringe used to extract the blood sample. He claimed that it had hurt his arm. When he was interviewed later he would play on the pain in his arm in a bid to deflect attention when questions got awkward.

The developments looked promising, but there was still a long way to go before anyone would feel confident that they had detained the true culprits. This posed a particular dilemma for DS Kirby. He had been invited to go to London that evening to appear on BBC television's

Crimewatch UK programme. He had used Crimewatch before and knew what a useful tool it could be in bringing in information from the public. This was something unique for the programme. They had never before featured a crime in detail so soon after it had been committed. It was a monthly show, so if the Thompson-Venables lead fell through, it would be four weeks before they could take advantage of it again, if they had not caught the killers by then.

Merseyside Chief Constable Jim Sharples, who along with Assistant Chief Constable (Crime) Pauline Clare and Police Authority Chairman George Bundred had been regular and supportive visitors to the Murder Squad during the investigation, was at Marsh Lane once again that day, and Albert Kirby canvassed his advice.

Mr Sharples asked him, 'Are you happy that these boys have done it?'

Mr Kirby replied, 'No'.

The Chief Constable advised him to go ahead with the broadcast.

That day PC Billy 'Lightfoot, still straining his eyes through endless flickering images from the security video cameras, came across a profile shot of the two boys that looked the clearest so far. It was sent to Ian Clague and his technical team at headquarters. They started working on it shortly before midday. By 1.18 p.m. they had produced a startlingly clear image. It showed up what appeared to be a blue patch on the elbow of the dark jacket worn by the short-haired boy. DS Andy Rushton, who was watching as the team worked on the enhancements, telephoned Jim Fitzsimmons, who by then was able to confirm they had recovered a dark jacket from Robert Thompson's house with a blue patch on the elbow. A cheer went up in the room.

'There was a warm glow that all the work we had done on these images had paid off,' recalled Jim. 'To know that what we had done would form part of the evidence to charge them was really satisfying'.

DS Rushton was to take that image to Marsh Lane. Along with the improved facial shot from the Ministry of Defence they were to be taken down to London by DS Kirby and DS Rushton to be used on the Crimewatch appeal.

Albert Kirby flew to London late that afternoon after a police traffic car rushed him up the motorway to Manchester airport to catch the shuttle. It was to be a close-run thing. Researcher Helen Phelps, the

Denise and James, on holiday.

James with his grandmother, Eileen Matthews.

The original frame taken and printed by the
enhancement equipment from the security video.

The computer 'zooms in' on the critical area of
the frame to produce an enlargement.

The contrast is enhanced by the computer.

An 'image processing median filter' is applied by the computer. This 'rounds off' the square edges of the pixels–the tiny individual squares of which the picture is composed, which become more obvious to the naked eye with enlargement.

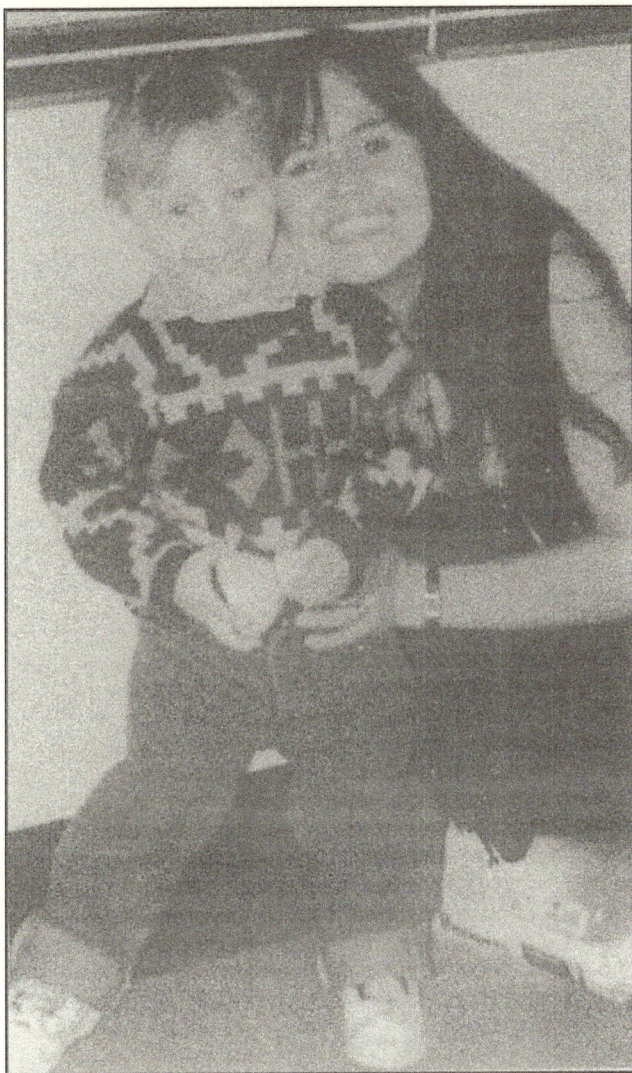

James with Nicola Bailey

James and Antonia, with Sheila Matthew's
boyfriend.

Detective
Superintendent
Albert Kirby.

Detective Inspector
Jim Fitzsimmons.

Interview team: Detective Constable Bob Jacobs
(left) and Detective Sergeant Phil Roberts.

Ralph Bulger (right) and Ray Matthews (left) bear James's casket out of the church. Denise follows, head bowed, eyes hidden by the wide brim of her hat. (The Press Association)

A policeman wipes away a tear outside the church where the funeral service was taking place. (The Press Association)

Detective Sergeant
Jim Green.

PC Mandy
Waller.

former policewoman and on-screen presenter who had prepared the item, met them with a car at Heathrow and took them to BBC Television Centre. Presenters Sue Cook and Nick Ross and the programme's producer met them at the studio and explained what the format was to be.

'We were to be the first item on,' recalled Mr Kirby. They had never before put something on their programme in such a short period from the actual incident. The way they pulled the stops out to accommodate us was a tremendous credit to them. The heat in the studio was intense and I was feeling exhausted by then. I said, "I am going to have to freshen up and have a shower." '

It was a decision that almost caused the poor manager apoplexy, as they were about ten minutes from transmission time of the live, networked programme. She need not have worried. Mr Kirby arrived, refreshed and relaxed-looking, just in time for the rolling of the tide credits.

Back in Liverpool, the police had given us the new enhancements under embargo, so they did not appear on other television news programmes in advance of the Crimewatch broadcast. I went into Merseyside Police headquarters in Canning Place that night to watch the scenes in the two rooms where teams of officers manned a bank of telephones ready to take calls from the public. I did not have sight of a television screen to see the programme go out, but I had no doubt about the moment when the hotline telephone number was first transmitted. Every telephone in the room started to ring simultaneously. It was a remarkable moment.

A great deal of useful witness information came in as a result of those calls. 'Crucial witnesses came forward who we might not have traced had it not been for the impact of that broadcast,' said Mr Kirby.

The response also served to underline the difficulties in recognizing the boys from the video shots. A total of only thirty-six of the several hundred calls suggested possible names for them. Of those only one suggested Robert Thompson, and that caller was very unsure. Nobody at all came up with the name of Jon Venables.

Mr Kirby spoke to the Murder Squad by telephone after the programme and was briefed on progress with the interviews with the two boys. The picture was looking stronger all the time.

'I didn't want to be away from it any longer, and I decided if I had to go two nights without sleep, so be it,' he recalled. Assistant Chief Constable Clare sanctioned the force helicopter to be sent to London to collect Mr Kirby. He travelled from the BBC to a helicopter pad at Hayes in Middlesex, where the helicopter touched down to collect him.

The first part of the flight home passed uneventfully, and the helicopter touched down to refuel, a midget in an army of giants among the Jumbo jets at an increasingly windy Birmingham Airport. A surreal encounter was to follow in which the driver of the tanker that came to refuel them disputed the rating of the pilot's credit card and would not fuel the helicopter. Things were eventually resolved and a second tanker topped up the helicopter which took off again into the teeth of a ferocious headwind. 'It was like being in a corkscrew as we tried to fly over the wind,' recalled Albert Kirby with a wan smile" 'I was really tired and we were getting knocked about all over the place by the weather. I thought if I was going to die at least I wouldn't know much about it! It was about 4 a.m. when we eventually reached RAF Woodvale near Southport. It was a great relief when we landed'.

Mandy Waller sat in Eileen Matthews' house in Scoter Road, Kirby, watching the Crimewatch broadcast go out with the family. Later Jim Green, who had been manning headquarters' telephones on another Merseyside murder inquiry over which a separate appeal had been made on Crimewatch that night, went out to join her after the programme. 'There was a bit of concern at the house,' recalled Jim. 'They couldn't comprehend that nobody knew who they were from the video picture. It was getting very frustrating for them'.

Ralph recalled Jim taking a telephone call at the house not long after his arrival. He then gave them the news that two more boys had been detained for questioning.

'I was going to go down to the police station but Jim wouldn't let us go,' Ralph remembered. 'I was very angry. I felt like going down and beating the crap out of them, really. Jim said it would cause a big commotion if we went down there. I was punching the walls in the kitchen. My head was chocker. We stayed up through the night, and Mandy and Jim stayed until the early hours with us'.

Jim recalled: 'I tried to remind them of Snowdrop Street and tell them not to expect any more, although by then the inquiry team were getting more confident. As time went on and we got to Friday the family began to realize the two boys had been in custody quite a long time. They kept asking, "Is it them?" I was telling them, "Wait and see. Things are going well." '

Albert Kirby arrived home at 4.30 that Friday morning, went to bed and took more than an hour to get to sleep. He was completely drained, but his mind remained active, running over and over the events of the last twenty-four hours. Almost before he fell asleep, his wife Sue was shaking him awake with a cup of tea. Jim Fitzsimmons had arrived at the house. As the Detective Superintendent forced himself properly awake, Jim sat on the end of his bed and brought him up to date on events while he had been away.

When he arrived at Marsh Lane that morning, DS Kirby held a briefing for the detectives interviewing the two boys. Phil Roberts had worked with him a lot and thought very highly of him. 'As far as I am concerned no other boss could have dealt with this case better,' recalled Phil. 'He was the right man for the job. What he says goes and you respect that, and he is usually right'. But Phil got a shock when he saw Mr Kirby that morning. 'He has such a small frame, and he looked so tired,' he remembered. 'It was the first time I had ever seen him like that. I thought, "He is killing himself here." '

Shattered as he was, Albert Kirby was to face the biggest barrage of media attention yet that morning. The handling of the press conferences had now fallen into a more workable routine, with press officer Inspector Simpson discussing what should be released with Mr Kirby each morning and arranging the late afternoon updates. Since Thursday morning Ray Simpson had arranged for the news conferences to be held away from Marsh Lane itself, where the swarms of journalists were putting added pressure on the murder team. The Salvation Army had donated the use of its Citadel hall, near the corner of Stanley Road and a mere two minutes' walk from the police station. Jim Green was attending each press conference and immediately telephoning the family to tell them what had been released, so that they were not learning of developments first by hearing radio or television news reports.

That morning there must have been a hundred of us in that hall. With the new photographs and the Crimewatch appeal, there was a sense of expectation in the air. The atmosphere grew tense as we waited for the conference to start, when rumours began to filter through that there had indeed been a major development. Before walking round to the hall, Mr Kirby and Ray had carefully planned their strategy. Ray knew well enough that if they began by announcing the arrests the conference would immediately dissolve in chaos as everyone dashed for their telephones to transmit the news. There were still further appeals for information and updates to be made.

It worked just as they had hoped. Mr Kirby made his appeals and gave his update on the response to his broadcast, and fielded a few questions from the media. Then he read a statement: 'Following the abduction of James Bulger from the New Strand Shopping Precinct in Bootle on Friday, 12 February 1993, and the subsequent finding of his body on the railway line in Walton on Sunday, 14 February 1993, two boys aged ten years from the Walton area have been arrested and are currently being interviewed by Merseyside Police at police stations on Merseyside.

'It is stressed that the boys are currently being interviewed in relation to these matters. At this stage it is not known if charges will follow as this will depend upon the results of these interviews and other inquiries'.

He had hardly finished speaking when the first mobile phones began to bleep and reporters made a dash for the door. The final press conference of the James Bulger murder hunt dissolved in pandemonium.

The arrests of Robert Thompson and Jon Venables had brought a new rush of work for scene of crime officer DI Andy McDiarmid. Trains were once more using the line where James's body had been found, but searches in the general area continued. A psychologist who was an expert in offender profiling techniques had been taken around the various locations involved in the crime, and had given the police what proved to be very accurate insights into the natures of the boys they were seeking. Now there was the clothing recovered from the homes of the two boys to examine. The OSD had not found Jon's school shoes at his mother's home, but had gone back to his father's house late on the

Thursday afternoon and found them, a pair of black brogues. They were stained with blood and paint.

One baffling factor was that the paint they had found on James's body appeared to be of a different consistency to that on the shoes. The answer, when scientists conducted tests, proved deceptively simple. It turned out that the matt modelling paint consisted of a pigment and a vehicle fluid which carried it. Every schoolboy who has ever put together a construction kit knows what those little tins of paint are like. The pigment sinks to the bottom of the tin, and has to be stirred in with the vehicle fluid before paint is applied. During the interviews the boys made reference to throwing the paint at James. When they had taken the lid off the paint and thrown it at him, a lot of what had hit him was the vehicle liquid, which was why it had a different consistency.

Another part of Andy's job was to check out information given during the interviews, by relating it to physical evidence at the scene of the crime. Once they knew the paint had been thrown they went back to the railway track and tried to find traces of paint to indicate the point where this had happened. 'Finding a grey-blue paint on railway ballast was like looking for a needle in a haystack,' recalled Andy. 'It seemed impossible, and Alan Carver and I were just about to come down off the track for the last time when we looked down and there at our feet on the ballast were some drops of greyish paint. It was right on the edge of the railway bridge at Cherry Lane. On the walls of the bridge you could also see some speckles of paint. We were able to show this was where the paint was thrown. Most of it had gone on James but some splashes had hit the wall and some had spilled on the ground. We could dig the ballast out and there was quite a lot of paint there underneath. This was a useful bit of evidence to prove that what they were saying was true'.

In the weeks and months that followed, the results of a series of state-of-the-art scientific tests Andy had set in motion would provide a lot more corroborative evidence. Blood matches and DNA testing techniques would help to fill in the details of what had happened on that bleak, lonely railway track.

The huge investigative resources of the police and the Home Office forensic science laboratory could provide some of the picture, but the only ones with all the answers were Robert Thompson and Jon Venables, and they weren't telling. Technology can only achieve so much. In the end, as so often in murder cases, it all came down to human beings, sitting in a room, asking questions.

Chapter Eight

The little boy looked frightened. He looked tiny next to the burly figure of DS Phil Roberts sitting alongside him at the table in the interview room at Walton Lane Police Station. Robert's mother Ann sat at his left-hand side, a portly, unkempt woman who appeared almost as scared as her son. A solicitor, Jason Lee, sat at the end of the table next to her, while DC Bob Jacobs sat at the other end, to Phil's right. In front of them all on the table was a tape-machine which would record every word said in that room, in accordance with the Police and Criminal Evidence Act. It was a small room, grey and formal, with the only natural light coming from one high window above the solicitor's head. The back of Robert Thompson's chair was touching the wall behind him. The door to the room would have caught Phil's chair if anyone had been brave or foolhardy enough to open it in the middle of the most important sequence of interviews he had conducted in his career.

It was three minutes before six o'clock on the evening of Thursday, 18 February, when Phil began his questioning, recording the precise time on the tape-machine and stating who was present for the legal record. Robert had already been cautioned that he was under arrest on suspicion of the murder of James Bulger. Now, to ensure the legal proprieties were carried out, Phil had to caution the boy again for abduction.

'I am also arresting you, right, for abducting James Bulger, OK?'

'What does abducting ... ?'

'On suspicion of abduction, meaning taking away from,' said Phil.

Robert looked even more frightened after that. 'But I never took him away,' he insisted plaintively. It was a line he stuck to doggedly during this first short interview session.

Phil knew that his first job was to try to put Robert at his ease. It would not be easy, but if anyone could bring it off, it was Phil Roberts. He had been on a special course to learn the techniques of interviewing distressed children involved in child abuse and had successfully investigated a number of such cases. But there was more to it than that. The forty-two-year-old rugby-playing Welshman may have been a farmer's son from the Valleys, but he was a born detective, a Serious Crime Squad man with the kind of instincts and experience you can't teach on a course.

The first thing was to establish eye contact. Phil sat hunched forward, crouching in his chair to keep his head on a level with Robert's It was an uncomfortable posture for such a big man, but one he would maintain throughout the interviews, to help make Robert feel secure. An occasional touch on the knee helped reassure the boy. It was warm in the room, and Phil was in shirt-sleeves. He spoke softly and slowly, making his sentences short, his questions simple.

Phil began with establishing if Robert knew the difference between telling the truth and telling lies. He kept the tone light, trying to gain the boy's confidence. At one point Phil actually had him laughing as he broke the ice.

'What football team do you support? 'Phil asked him.

'Everton'.

'Everton. Right, if I said Everton won 10-nil last Saturday what would you say that was?'

'A lie'.

'OK, and if I said there was five in this room, what would you say that was?'

'True'.

After ten minutes, the detective sensed that Robert was relaxed. The time had come to move on to the facts of the case.

Now Robert's legs began to move, swinging listlessly back and forth under his chair. It was a small body language clue that Phil learned to spot whenever be believed Robert was not telling the truth. Robert readily admitted to 'sagging school' that Friday and going to the Strand with Jon Venables and he had claimed he had seen 'little James' holding his mother's hand in the precinct. He confirmed he had beard about the

James Bulger case, revealing that he had taken flowers to the scene on Wednesday.

The boy then confirmed that he knew the difference between right and wrong, and was asked: 'We're talking to you about things and you said you've seen James on that day, haven't you, and you know that James was killed, don't you?'

'Not on that day, I never knew'.

The detective then asked: 'Now is it right or is it wrong that James should have been killed?'

'Wrong'.

'It's wrong, isn't it?'

'Yeah'.

Phil already sensed that Robert was lying with his account of the events. He was claiming that he and Jon had spent half an hour in the library. He could describe James and Denise, whom he had only seen for a few seconds, yet be could not describe the librarian beyond saying she had dark hair. Asked about this Robert's natural cunning came to the surface as he said: 'There's a board there that you can't see the lady'.

Some forty-three minutes had passed and the first of the forty-live-minute interview cassettes was about to run out. Phil was only too conscious of the need to keep the interviews short. This was, after all, a boy of ten. He decided to take a break. Already, Phil's antennae were starting to twitch.

Exactly five minutes after the start of Robert Thompson's first interview, detectives at Lower Lane Police Station began questioning Jon Venables. DC Mark Dale, the arresting officer, led the questioning, backed up by DC George Scott. The interview room, on the ground floor in the cell complex, was more spacious than its Walton Lane counterpart. Jon sat at a table placed under the room's one frosted glass window. The wall-mounted microphone was close to his face. He was positioned there because of concern that a child's small voice might be lost to the recording equipment. Jon felt cold at times, and a heater was placed behind him, to be turned on whenever he asked. The heating of interview rooms is a perennial problem for detectives. They almost always seem to be either too hot or too cold.

Mark Dale sat at the other end of the table from Jon, his notes and paperwork resting on the tabletop alongside the tape-recording machine.

The others in the room had space to sit spanned out in a semi-circle from the table. Jon's mother sat next to him, with lawyer Laurence Lee next to her and George Scott between him and Mark.

The detectives were aware that Jon had never been in a police station before, and would be frightened, regardless of whether he had been involved in James's death. Everything was kept deliberately low-key as they began their patient questioning process. 'The last thing we wanted to do was frighten or alienate this child,' George Scott recalled.

Mark Dale began by explaining to Jon what the tape-machine was and how it worked. He was told to speak up if he felt cold or hot, and Mr Lee was invited to monitor closely what went on.

The interview that followed was little more than a general chat. Jon was asked to talk about himself. They talked about football, and his likes and dislikes, until Jon, like Robert, began to feel more at ease. He confirmed that Robert Thompson was his 'mate'.

'I don't go near him at school sometimes, 'cos he causes trouble at school,' he said. When he was playing out with Robert he came in 'dead late', he said. 'He just wants me to stay out late and say we can do good things and I say to him what is there to do in the dark?'

Asked Mark: 'And what does he say?'

'He says just come on the railway with me and that ... you know, by the police station'. Jon claimed that Robert slept on the railway and lit fires, by the bridge near the police station, but he insisted that he had never been on the railway with Robert. He said Robert was not a good friend because he got him into trouble and added: 'He's much of a girl. He sucks dummies ... and sucks his thumb'.

He then described some of the mischief they got up to when they 'sagged' school, climbing into back gardens and getting people to chase them. 'We rob bouncy balls and throw them at the windows, and one day this fat man came running out getting his mop and throwing it at us'.

'You have a riot, don't you?' asked Mark.

'Yeah'.

He said that on the Friday of James's death Robert had tried to get him to go 'pinching'. 'He just steals. He just goes "I'll have that and that" and just stuffs it in his coat'. Robert would then give him things outside.

Jon claimed that when he played truant it was always with Robert. 'We leave at playtimes. We just open the gate every minute and then when it's wide open we hide behind the wall and when nobody's looking we run'.

Nothing more significant was asked by the detectives, or volunteered by Jon. The name of the game, in this softly-softly interview approach, was to build a rapport and give Jon the confidence to talk openly. The interview ended after forty-five minutes.

DI Jim Fitzsimmons is not a man given to inactivity. Mentally and physically agile, he was selected by legendary soccer boss Bill Shankly as an apprentice for Liverpool FC, choosing a police career ahead of a football career in the lower divisions only after 'Shanks' retired and his successor Bob Paisley decided to let him go. He carried on playing football for the police, while rising to the rank of detective sergeant. An experienced field detective, he was still only thirty-two when he was offered the chance of a university scholarship. His three-year combined honours course in management, policy studies, computers and Spanish saw him spending eight weeks each summer studying the language at colleges in Spain. In January 1992, he returned to the force with a good honours degree, and now, at thirty-six, had just become one of the youngest officers to have risen through the ranks to CID inspector. He was married with children aged twelve, ten and six, and somehow found time to manage a children's soccer team.

Jim had been working the same back-breakingly exhausting hours as the rest of the Murder Squad ream. Now he was getting a crash course in the particular pressures of management. When Robert Thompson and Jon Venables were arrested, Jim's every instinct was to drop everything, head for one of the two police stations and start the questioning. That would have been wrong, and Jim knew it. He delegated the task instead to top-class CID men whose professionalism he knew he could depend on. Now, sitting in his office at Marsh Lane Police Station, he had done his part for the moment. All he could do was wait for the telephone to ring. It was very hard work.

The interviewing officers were to call him after every session and report what they had been told. Jim sat, waiting for their calls, to discuss what had been said at each session.

Those first three-quarter-hour interview sessions seemed to take an eternity. At last the telephone rang, twice within a few minutes. Jim listened, asked questions, thanked the detectives and put the telephone down. Robert Thompson's interview sounded promising. Jim sighed, crossed his fingers, and waited.

Mark Dale and George Scott started the second interview with Jon Venables at exactly 7 p.m. the same day. George had got Jon a can of Coke and a Mars bar from a machine in the police canteen. Jon sat sipping the Coke during the interview.

George recalled: 'We questioned Jon about where he had been on the Friday James Bulger was abducted. He led us on a wild goose chase. He told us he went everywhere, all over Walton and even as far as Scotland Road, but he never went to the Strand'.

Asked about the paint on his coat, he claimed that Robert had thrown it over him.

Jon claimed he had wanted to go to school that day because his mother had given him a letter giving him permission to bring gerbils home for the half term holiday. He said Robert had made him 'sag', and had told him: 'You had better come with me or I'm getting these lads on to you'.

Jon said it was 'a bit' exciting being with Robert, and Mark asked him: 'Do you do things with him that you wouldn't normally do with your other friends?'

'Yeah,' said Jon. 'I wouldn't do anything with me other friends'.

'Why?'

'Because they're good'.

Jon agreed that Robert led him 'along the path a little bit'. 'And then you get under your own steam and you're up and running?' asked Mark.

'Yeah'.

The interview was concluded at 7.43 p.m. Again there was nothing significant to report to Jim Fitzsimmons. As soon as the interview ended, Jon hungrily demolished the Mars bar in a few quick chomps. As he was obviously still hungry, and the station canteen was closed, they asked him what he fancied from the fish and chip shop. Jon chose his favourite Chinese special fried rice, a beaming smile on his face as he ordered.

George and Mark went with his mother to a Chinese 'chippie' in nearby Longmoor Lane to get his food.

Robert Thompson was given a break until 8.12 p.m., when Phil Roberts and Bob Jacobs resumed their questioning at Walton Lane. Although the sessions were short, it was a break the adults valued as much as the child.

'The concentration you have to have is unbelievable, though they aren't very long interviews,' explained Phil. 'I'm thinking should I say this or that and how am I going to broach it. I am looking closely at Robert's reactions and asking myself if I am doing it the right way. You have to be very self-critical. Bob Jacobs and I had never interviewed together before but he was coming in at just the right times. It worked very well between us. When I felt as though I was going to dry up he would ask a question. We just gelled'.

Phil had given up smoking less than three weeks before, and was wearing nicotine patches under his shin to help with the withdrawal symptoms. But now he was in serious need of a cigarette.

'I was totally focused while I was interviewing him. The thought of what happened to James Bulger never entered my mind at all. I was there to do the job. You can interview someone and the horrific side of it doesn't enter your mind because you are there for one purpose—to find out what the hell went on'.

Robert told the detectives his hobby was 'skipping school'. They put it to him that boys wearing clothes similar to his and Jon's had been seen with James on the security video, and Robert said: 'I never touched him'.

The officers asked him again about the video and Robert said: 'Yeah, but that may not have been me and Jon that killed him. But I know it wasn't me that killed him, or Jon'.

He admitted stealing from shops in the precinct but insisted again: 'I never took the baby'. Asked what did happen, Robert repeated: 'No, but I never touched him'. Phil said: 'Well, we're going to find out what happened to him'. Robert started to cry then and insisted: 'I never touched him'.

Then Robert admitted that James had been walking round the Strand on his own and added: 'He (Jon) grabbed the baby's hand and just walked round the Strand and then he let him go loose. When we were by the church he let him go'.

Phil's heart jumped. 'You don't lose concentration but you lose the focus for a moment,' he recalled. 'I thought, "Oh, my God. I might have the boy responsible for taking him." ' I still wasn't confident that he had murdered him but the fear he had escorted him out of the Strand was a big step. He blamed everything on Jon.

Robert said James had been asking for his mother, actually mimicking the toddler's voice as he called for his Mum.

Later Robert insisted: 'I told him to take him back'. He started to cry again and added: 'I'm getting all the blame'.

The officers asked him to calm himself and made sure he was all right. Robert said again: 'Yeah, well I'm going to get all the blame'.

'Well, if you tell me the...' began Phil.

'For murdering him, but we left him by the church'.

'Did you? We only want the truth from you, son. Nothing else'. 'We did, we left him by the church'. Robert's crying was not winning the detectives over to his side. 'When he admitted things he would cry at the same time, but there were no actual tears,' recalled Phil. 'It was part of his act. I really thought he was evil, looking at him. He was astute and very streetwise. He wasn't educationally intelligent but he was shrewd'.

Later Robert spoke again of James 'running around' in the Strand. 'Jon said, "Come here" and then he grabbed his hand and walked out the Strand by the ... think it's Marks and Spencer's shop'.

At the end of the interview Robert asked: 'Will I be able to go home tonight?'

'We don't know yet, we don't know yet. OK?' was the gentle response.

Phil concluded that interview at 8.55 p.m. and went straight to a telephone. Jim Fitzsimmons answered at once, and Phil said, 'It looks good.

At the end of their conversation Phil peeled off the nicotine patches and headed for the cigarette machine. 'That's £64 up the Swanny,' he thought with a grim smile.

Jon Venables tucked into his special fried rice with enthusiasm at Lower Lane Police Station. When his meal was over, Mark Dale and

George Scott held a third brief interview with him. It was getting late by now, so they kept it deliberately short. The session began at 9.40 p.m.

Jon was asked again about being at the Strand. This time he eventually admitted it, but he denied taking any children. He also admitted to some petty pilfering from shops and general mischief.

'As he was telling us about these escapades he seemed to be pleased with himself,' George recalled. 'There was glee on his face. He seemed on a high about it.

The officers were careful not to register disapproval over what be was telling them. If they bad given a negative response to this, there was no chance that he would admit to anything more serious. His mother Susan, however, had a sharp word with her son about his conduct. Jon was wary after that, anxious not to upset her.

The interview ended at 10.01 p.m. and Jon was bedded down for the night in the unlocked juvenile detention room. Susan stayed with him on the specially arranged mattresses in the room. As the whole police station had been shut down as a reception center for other prisoners and the adult cells were empty, nothing but their own thoughts and fears was to disturb their night.

At Walton Lane, Robert Thompson also went through one last interview, from 9.35 until 9.59 that night. Robert admitted that they all left the Strand together but insisted it was Jon who had actually taken James. 'You'll get his face up on the video,' he added.

Earlier, Robert had denied that it was Jon and he who were seen by a witness on the enclosed reservoir site at Breeze Hill. He actually suggested, 'Well, you know she might be lying, mighn't she?' By the time this interview concluded, Robert had admitted that it was them. He said they had taken James to Breeze Hill and left him there on top of the hill after playing with him.

He said James was not crying when they had left him on the hill. 'He was crying ... and then he was quiet 'cos we said that we'd get his mother soon'.

At one point Ann Thompson said to Robert: 'Do you want to sort all this out tonight?'

'Yeah,' said Robert.

Tell the truth,' said his mother.

'I am,' he replied.

After the interview, Robert was settled down for the night. Phil Roberts and Bob Jacobs headed for Marsh Lane Police Station. All the detectives from the two interview teams and their back-up teams went to Marsh Lane, for a general debriefing on the day's events.

They went to DCI Geoff MacDonald's office. 'I've never seen as many bosses in my life as were in that office,' Phil remembered with a grin. 'I was mentally whacked. I was trying to repeat what Robert had said. The bosses were full of questions. They were excited. We had a general chat about it. There were questions people wanted asked, but you have to take things so slowly with children. Interviewing a man who is used to having questions popped at him is different. You have to take things much slower with a child and explain things to him. I said, "It is like a jigsaw, Robert. I have got one piece up here where James goes missing and at the bottom James is found dead. I have to find out what happened in between." '

Jim Fitzsimmons was breathing more easily by now. Progress on the interviews was slow, which was to be expected, but it was moving in the right direction. Forensic experts were working on analysing Robert and Jon's clothes and shoes. Paint traces on one of the coats matched paint found at the scene, and there were splashes of blood on shoes. The video enhancement team had confirmed a blue patch on Robert's sleeve. DS Kirby's appearance on Crimewatch had brought more information from the public. 'At that time progress was encouraging. We certainly needed to clear up a couple of important issues, but the picture as a whole was starting to look very positive,' recalled Jim. For the police, if not for Robert, the jigsaw was coming together.

Friday morning began on a sombre note for the interview teams. Albert Kirby, back with his feet gratefully on the ground after his helicopter trip north, had reviewed the progress made so far with the interviews. He decided it was time they were told more about the details of the attack on James. He called the detectives together at Marsh Lane Police Station for a special briefing. They listened quietly, absorbing the details, trying to stay detached and unemotional. In a few hours they would again have to face the boys who had done this, and try to be their friends. It was a supreme test of their professionalism.

It was also decided that the Serious Crime Squad's 'downstream monitoring' equipment should be brought into play. This grand-sounding device is actually just a recording-machine similar to those standard in all police interview rooms under PACE, but with the addition of a special outlet plug into which a cable connected to a loudspeaker is plugged. The loudspeaker can then be placed in another nearby room, enabling the back-up detectives to monitor the interviews word for word. It can be used only with the consent of the suspect, his legal representative and in this case his parents.

Only one such machine was available, and the detectives decided to use it on the Jon Venables interviews at Lower Lane. Mark Dale, George Scott, and back-up team members DS Michelle Bennett and DC Dave Tanner took the machine with them when they returned to the station. It was carried in a silver metal box like a photographer's equipment case. They simply disconnected and removed the existing tape-recorder from the interview room, hooked up the new machine in its place, and ran the cable out under the door to a nearby room where Michelle and Dave were to listen in on the loudspeaker.

If it was proving a difficult time for the interviewing detectives, the back-up teams were finding the experience no less harrowing. Michelle Bennett was the mother of three young children herself. She was a personable, well-liked officer with a penchant for outrageous practical jokes that could lift the tension of the most critical investigations. There were no jokes this week.

Dave Tanner, a forty-five-year-old detective who relished working on major murder hunts, had returned to duty on the Monday after watching his father succumb to cancer on 2 February. His father, also called Jon, was sixty-five and had been diagnosed as suffering from the disease at Christmas. 'There was nothing they could do for him so I brought him home and he died in my home on 2 February,' Dave recalled. 'I gave him his morphine, and I was with my dad when he died. I had all the funeral arrangements to make and the business matters to sort out. The funeral went from my home. There was just no time in between. I had no time to grieve, no time to get over it. But on the Monday I thought I was ready to come back to work'.

Dave had spent five years with the Serious Crime Squad before his current posting to the CID in St Helens. It was the happiest and most rewarding period of his twenty-six years in the police. His supervising officer at St Helens was well aware of this and when he was asked that Monday to provide officers to help the Murder Squad, he thought, without knowing too much about the James Bulger case, that it might be just what Dave needed. Dave's wife Diane was furious about what she felt was an unfeeling decision, and the officer who took it apologized to Dave later when he realized the full ramifications of the case. Dave had no recriminations, however. 'If I had said at the time that I wasn't ready for it I know he wouldn't have sent me,' he said. 'I had no second thoughts about going on the inquiry and when he apologized to me I was ensconced in it'.

Dave had been keen to take part in the interviews, but his initial role was to support George and Mark from outside the interview room. Dave was a huge man, but his experience with people and his gentle manner more than compensated for his bulk when it came to communication. He put his skills to work in forming a bond with Jon's parents, and with Susan in particular, that was to prove crucial in establishing a major breakthrough in the interviews.

Jon and Susan were awakened at 8.15 that morning when their solicitor, Mr Lee, arrived at the police station. At 8.20 the station superintendent reviewed Jon's detention and authorized his continued detention, with Susan and Mr Lee present. Jon's father Neil was brought to the police station at 9 a.m.

No objections were raised to the downstream monitoring equipment being used, and when Mark Dale and George Scott started questioning Jon once again at 11.06 a.m., Dave and Michelle were listening intently to the loudspeaker in a nearby room.

'Monitoring is a wonderful system because when two of you are interviewing it is very easy to be side-tracked and lose the vein of the questioning. Your partner will pick up on it and bring it up later, but to sit back and listen in you can pick up so much more than actually being in there and taking part in it,' said Dave.

Mark and George began by reviewing with Jon the ground they had covered the previous evening, and his admissions about going to the Strand and shoplifting. 'It was a new day, and we were trying to get him back into the flow of things,' George recalled.

Jon talked about going to various shops with Robert, including Tandy, from where police knew the batteries found at the murder scene had been stolen, and Toymaster, from where the modelling paint had been taken. He spoke about annoying an elderly woman in the Strand, and claimed that they had left the Strand and walked to County Road in Walton alone. Robert, he claimed, had thrown the paint over his coat. The interview concluded at 11.50 a.m.

Phil Roberts and Bob Jacobs began their fourth interview with Robert Thompson at 11.35 that Friday morning. Phil had the feeling that Robert was ready to tell him more. Armed with more detailed knowledge about the use of the paint that was found on James, Phil steered the questioning in that direction. Robert then admitted for the first time being in possession of a small tin of enamel paint. He said it was Jon who had taken James, and that they had taken him up by the railway. He was asked about blood on his clothing and said it was his own blood when Jon's mother hit him. He claimed that Jon threw paint in James's face and also threw the hood of his anorak on the line.

'He threw it in his eye,' said Robert.

'Why was that?'

'I don't know and I ran away from him then, from Jon'.

'What did baby James do?'

'He sat on the floor'.

'Was he crying?'

'Yeah. I was crying myself'.

'Why?'

"Cos he threw it in his face. He could have blinded him'.

He said that after they threw the paint in James's face they ran off but Jon might have hit him slyly. Crying now, Robert insisted, 'We never killed him'. He said James had been crying because he wanted his mum. Robert added that Jon had stolen the paint from Toymaster.

This information came out during two interview sessions. The initial one lasted until 12.15 p.m. but with the tape running out Phil wanted to keep the momentum of the interview going. He resumed after a gap of just six minutes, at 12.21 Phil let the interview run for seven minutes, and then called a halt at 12.28, more than satisfied with their progress that morning. 'It was important that the interview progressed slowly so that everyone understood what was being said,' Phil recalled. They left interview room, Robert to have his lunch and Phil to light another cigarette. He could not smoke in the interview room, but between sessions he was now chain-smoking at the rate of forty a day.

Jon Venables was still denying virtually everything. Mark Dale and George Scott began their fifth interview with him at 12.23 p.m., gently increasing the thrust of their questioning. Jon admitted being in the Strand,' but refused to accept that he had ever crossed to the far side of Stanley Road. Mark told him bluntly that his fingerprint had been recovered from the window of a building society on that side of the road, alongside a McDonald's restaurant.

They began asking him more questions, and putting to him some of the admissions that Robert had made. Mark told him Robert said he had taken James by the hand. Jon had a tantrum now, looking really upset, insisting that Robert was lying. 'I never killed him. We took him and left him by the canal, that's all,' he said, sobbing.

Susan comforted her son. 'I believe you, Jon, I believe you,' she said.

Outside in the monitoring room, Michelle and Dave exchanged a meaningful glance. It confirmed an impression that had been developing between them all morning.

'It was obvious to us by listening. Whether it is something you pick up after twenty-six years, or whether it would be obvious to anyone, I don't know,' Dave Tanner recalled. 'Jon wanted to talk and was getting very agitated. It was as if he had some horrific things to tell and they were causing him a lot of concern. But you had this stabilizing effect of his mum saying, "It doesn't matter. I know you wouldn't do anything of the sort". Mark and George were doing very well with him under very difficult circumstances. Our impression was that while Susan was in that frame of mind Jon wouldn't start talking in a month of Sundays. Michelle and I simultaneously came to the same conclusion. Susan was the stumbling-block to him talking. Neil had got an inkling by now that his son was involved, but Susan was still exactly as she had been on the Thursday morning, with no inkling at all'.

The problem had not been lost on Mark and George. 'Jon would be telling us a story and then he would break down crying and would go to his mum,' George recalled. 'When the questions got too hard or we would ask him if he was telling the truth, or he didn't like answering questions, he would turn to his mum. She didn't realize it, and she certainly wasn't doing it intentionally, but she was continually giving reassurance to her son'.

The interview broke off at 12.56 p.m., and while Jon went back to his detention room Dave Tanner and Michelle Bennett took Susan Venables for refreshments. 'Throughout the inquiry she would eat and drink, whereas Neil wouldn't,' recalled Dave. 'To say he was destroyed is the best way of describing him. We took Susan to an upstairs office, got her something to eat and told her what we thought. We explained that her constant reassurance was hindering the interview. She was doing what any mum would do, consoling him when he was upset and distressed and crying. I asked her if she and Neil would speak to Jon and tell him that whatever he had to say, whatever it might be, it did not matter and they still loved him.

'Susan and I ... and Neil for that matter ... got on very well together. I am fairly certain that during that conversation the truth suddenly started to dawn on her. She agreed to cooperate with us. Neil was a bit reluctant at first but she bolstered him up. It was a case of persuading them to listen to what Jon had to say, be supportive, but step back from their natural instincts and let him talk'.

The juvenile detention room where Jon was having his lunch was changed beyond recognition. The bare room with a bench most prisoners encountered was largely covered by full, thick mattresses and bedding. Jon's favourite toys and comics littered the room. Dave Tanner walked down to the custody suite with Susan and Neil, but hesitated in order to allow them to go in alone through the open, unlocked door.

Susan paused, turned to the detective and said, 'Dave, can you come in?'

Jon Venables was sitting on the bench when his parents and the big, kindly-spoken detective entered the room. Susan sat alongside Jon, and Neil sat on the other side. Susan held her son in a tight embrace, Neil resting a slightly hesitant arm around him.

'I love you, Jon,' she said. 'I want you to tell the truth, whatever it might be'. Jon Venables began to cry, and just blurted out, 'I did kill him'.

Dave Tanner had heard him cry before and lose his temper, and had not been convinced about his authenticity, but this time the child was absolutely sobbing.

The boy looked across the room at the detective and asked, 'What about his mum? Will you tell her I'm sorry?'

Susan continued cuddling her son, telling him she loved him. No matter what he had done, she wanted him to tell the truth. She did not cry. Jon's father said very little. He was ashen, a look of indescribable agony on his face.

Dave Tanner let slip a quiet sigh. The outcome had been about what he had been expecting. 'I had formed the impression in the interviews that Jon wanted to talk. Once Susan removed the stumbling-block she was creating with that act of the embrace, he came off the starting-blocks and rushed it all out. It was almost as if he was thinking, "If I say it quickly they mightn't realize I've said it". Once they get over the hill and admit it, it is always a tremendous weight lifted off their shoulders'.

Dave was leaving the room when Mark Dale arrived and started to come in. Jon said to the two officers, 'Can I tell you about Robert trying to get another lad away?' He was referring to the second attempted abduction.

Everyone left the detention room and went into the custody suite, where the supervising officer gave Dave Tanner the boy's custody record. The detective endorsed it and wrote into it everything that had happened, including the remarks Jon had made. Susan, Neil and Jon all read and signed the entry. When solicitor Laurence Lee returned from his lunch-break he also read and signed the document.

While these procedures were going on, Jon had a quiet word with his father. Neil went to Dave Tanner and said, 'Do you know what he's done? Because he's just told me'. He was looking even more shocked.

Dave Tanner knew from Albert Kirby's briefing that morning that the details of the attack were going to be deeply unpleasant. He told Neil firmly, 'It is time to stand up and be counted. If he's going to be truthful now in interview there are things his mother shouldn't hear'.

Neil Venables reluctantly agreed to take his wife's place in the interview room. Susan did not wish to go back in. Dave Tanner and Michelle Bennett took her out for a drive in an unmarked, rented car, to get some fresh air and a break right away from the area. The officers sat in front with Susan in the back. At one point Michelle, who was driving, glanced in her rear-view mirror and could not believe what she was seeing. Susan Venables, who had just learned that her son killed James Bulger, was busy adjusting her make-up. Robert Thompson was questioned twice more that afternoon, the gap between the sessions only that required to change the tapes in the recording-machine. The first session ran from 2.14 to 2.57, and the second from 2.59 until 3.11.

Robert was becoming more objectionable in his attitude. His manner was contradictory and sarcastic. He was streetwise and seemed to have an answer for everything the detectives said to him. More often than not, the answer was cheeky.

He totally denied murdering James. At one point he asked: 'Why would I take flowers over to the baby ... if I killed him?' He claimed at first that he did not see Jon attack James. Ann said to him: 'It will all be over in a few minutes if you just tell them the truth'. Then Robert volunteered: 'Jon threw a brick in his face.' Then he said Jon threw another brick and hit him in the stomach, and hit him with a fish plate, a metal bar with holes used to join tracks together on the railway. This blow, claimed Robert, had knocked James out. He was lying on the railway track. His eyes had been open but he was not breathing. Robert said he had put his ear to James's stomach and he was not breathing. They had left the scene and had not discussed it together since.

Ann Thompson listened, numb with horror, the second mother that day who had to come to terms with the unthinkable.

While Robert was busily blaming everything on Jon, his best friend sat in another police station a few miles away, blaming everything on Robert.

Jon's only interview of the afternoon began at 3.57 and lasted until 4.30. His father Neil was in the room, which was about all that could be said of his contribution. He looked a broken man, sitting hunched forward in his chair with his eyes closed and his fingers in his ears. George Scott feared that Mr Venables was having a nervous breakdown in front of him. Both parents were examined by a police surgeon before the day was out.

During his account Jon started looking anxiously at his father for reassurance, but quickly realized that the man might as well not have been in the room. 'I can understand why he blocked it all out, but he wasn't doing his son any favours by doing it,' George recalled. At certain moments of extreme emotion Jon actually got up and went to Mark Dale, putting his arms around him for reassurance rather than his own father.

In another extraordinary moment Jon stood up, clenching his fists in an astonishing display of sheer frustration and rage. For a moment the officers were convinced he was about to punch his father.

Jon's interviews from then on became an increasingly dark descent into horror. He confirmed for the tape, 'I killed James'. That afternoon he spoke of their attempt to abduct Diane Power's toddler son. He said it was Robert Thompson's idea, and the plan was that he would go into the road and get knocked over. Jon said he had told Robert: 'It's a very bad thing to do, isn't it?'

He said they found James outside the butcher's shop. He said it was his own idea to take him but it was Robert's idea to kill him. They took him to the canal, where Robert planned to throw him in. James would not kneel down to look at his reflection in the water as they wanted, so Robert picked him up and threw him on the ground. This was how James had first injured his head. He said James just kept saying, 'I want my mummy'.

Jon admitted going up to the reservoir and to the railway, and told how he took James's anorak hood off and threw it in the trees.

'I can't tell you anything else,' he said then. Mark Dale asked him why, and Jon said: "Cos that's the worst bit'.

'Now let me tell you I know that's the worst bit but you know what you did and you know that if you try hard you'll be able to tell us. What you need is to have a little rest, think about it and just tell us what happened'.

'We took him on the railway track and started throwing bricks at him,' Jon said, in a subdued tone.

He claimed Robert threw bricks at James and hit him with an iron bar. Jon had thrown small stones, but Robert had thrown housebricks, he said.

Mark Dale, reassuring, keeping his composure against frightening odds, asked Jon what he thought about what they had done to James.

Jon, tearful, said, 'It was terrible. I was thinking about it all the time'.

Robert and Jon met briefly for the first time since their arrest, later that Friday evening. Detectives from the two interview teams drove the boys in unmarked cars to South Sefton Magistrates' Court in Bootle, where a private application was made before a panel of three magistrates for them to be detained for a further thirty-six hours. Robert went to court in Phil Roberts's unmarked police Rover 416, and Jon in an equally anonymous but high powered police VW Golf GTI. The fast cars were to elude any attempted pursuit by the media or the public, but as it turned out all was quiet as they arrived at Bootle shortly before 7 p.m. and drove straight into the secure area of the building.

Albert Kirby gave evidence to the magistrates about the progress being made in the inquiry, and after hearing from defence lawyers who raised no objections, the bench granted the application. The boys had been kept separate from each other in court. Jon had expressly said that he did not want to have to meet Robert again. He had been told they would have to be in a room together but they would not have to speak.

Jon was taken back to his car in the enclosed underground area beneath the court first, and was sitting in the back seat of the Golf between his father and Mark Dale when Robert was brought downstairs and walked past the car towards the Rover parked behind it. George Scott, who was driving, saw Robert's face. There was a big, beaming smile from Thompson, and then he walked past and was behind us,' he recalled.

Phil Roberts, alongside Robert, could see into the car and caught Jon Venables's expression. 'Venables smiled in a sort of coy way and shrugged and looked at Robert. I thought "Oh God". It was a look that said, "We've got secrets here." '

That night Ann Thompson finally broke down. 'She didn't want anything to do with Robert by then,' Phil recalled. 'Whenever we asked a pertinent question of Robert she was always crying, which was hard. I had to tell her afterwards how difficult that was making things. I think she knew that he had done it before I knew for sure. She had really gone and had broken down by the Saturday. She was scared of being attacked. She didn't come in to the interviews after that'.

Saturday morning came, and Albert Kirby met his interview teams again, disclosing to them further details about James's death. Then it was back to Walton Lane and Lower Lane for the officers, and another day of questioning.

Phil Roberts and Bob Jacobs started the ball rolling with a session with Robert from 11.46 a.m. to 12.38 p.m. A social worker had now taken over Ann Thompson's role in the interviews.

Robert still maintained his line that he had nothing to do with the attack on James. The boy was shrewd enough to realize there would be forensic evidence against him, though. During this interview he volunteered: 'I never touched James. I just lifted him around my chest and put him back because I didn't want to get full of blood'.

He denied taking any of James's clothes. He said Jon bad thrown paint in the child's face 'because he felt like it'. He said Jon had thrown bricks in his face and stomach and hit him with a metal bar, and claimed that afterwards Jon had a smirk on his face. He cried when reminded that Jon was telling a different story and said: 'Well, you can go and ask our teacher who's the worst out of me and Jon, and she'll tell you Jon'.

At 12.33 p.m. Mark Dale and George Scott started their seventh interview with Jon Venables. Once again, they began by recapping on the admissions he had made the day before.

Jon went on to deliver the most graphic and terrible account of the attack they carried out. He described James screaming and falling down under their ruthless assault, but getting back up again. He claimed Robert had told the helpless child, 'Stay down, you stupid divvie'.

Mark asked Jon why Robert had said this. 'He wanted him dead, probably,' Jon responded.

'Why?'

'I don't know. I didn't want to, really. Robert was probably doing it for fun because he was laughing his head off'.

'That was as full an admission as we were ever going to get of what happened on that railway line,' George recalled. 'It was utterly horrific to think that this child of ten sitting before me in the interview room could carry out the acts that he did to another human being'.

Robert Thompson was 'interviewed again at 1.55 p.m. During that interview he was formally arrested for the attempted abduction of Diane Power's son.

Everything was still Jon's doing, according to Robert Phil kept going until the tape was nearly' full, at 2.35 p.m. He halted the interview for a short break, reloaded the tape-machine again and resumed four minutes later. He pressed on, but Robert was still not about to admit to any involvement in the attacks on James. 'He never actually told me the truth in the end, far from it,' recalled Phil. 'He said some things in the interview that never rang true. He had lied from the minute we started to interview him'.

He called a halt to the interview at 3.09 p.m. It was to be his last formal interview session with the boy. '

Phil took his team out for some Kentucky Fried Chicken, and they commandeered an empty office at the police station where they sat chewing on chicken legs and reviewing their three days' work.

Jon Venables's eighth and final interview at Lower Lane began at 2.23 p.m. and lasted for just twenty-nine minutes. The object was to try to get more details from Jon about exactly what happened. Jon said he knelt down by James who grabbed his coat and said: 'Don't hurt-me'. Jon replied: 'All right'. He said James was scared of Robert and added: 'He wasn't scared of me because I never hit him as much'.

He told Mark and George it had been Robert's idea to put bricks over James so nobody would see him. Robert had kicked him. Jon admitted stamping on him. Robert had kicked him in the face lots of times'.

The officers had heard enough. After concluding the interview they took Jon out in an unmarked Fiat car specially rigged with microphones and recording equipment. They left the police station at 3.35 p.m. During this 'mobile interview' Jon was driven to the Strand and from the back seat of the car described every step of the journey, clearing up any gaps in the account of the exact route they had taken as they walked James to the spot where they killed him.

'He was pleased to be going for a ride in a police car, going out with me and Mark, who he regarded as his friends,' George recalled. 'It was the child in him coming back into it. Somewhere on the route he saw a poster which had two separate photos from the video. He asked why Robert's photo was in colour and his was only black and white'.

They got back to the police station at 4.36 p.m. Jon sat playing with some computer games his parents had brought in for him. He told George how to do a 'cheat' on Sonic the Hedgehog to get to the final level. He was sitting on a stool with Susan and Neil, and started drawing simple pictures on some paper given to him by a policewoman. George said to him that he thought Diane Power's son was the luckiest boy alive the day James was killed.

Jon looked up at George and said, 'Yes'. There was a big, beaming smile on his face. It was a moment that will haunt George Scott and Michelle Bennett, who was also watching, for ever.

Phil Roberts's Rover was similarly rigged up with recording equipment, and Robert was taken out by the detectives and asked to retrace the route as Jon had done. They set off at 5.53 that night, with Phil driving and Bob Jacobs and a woman social worker in the back with Robert. Dominic Lloyd, who had now taken over as Robert's solicitor, sat in the front passenger seat.

'Even now Robert was lying. Some of the route he showed us was true, but it didn't tally with what Jon said. Robert was being shrewd. He was trying to recall what he had told us on the tape and relate it to what was on the journey'. said Phil.

Liverpool FC had played at home that afternoon, their fans observing a minute's silence for James Bulger while a banner was unfurled on the Kop with the message 'RIP James'. Some of the match traffic was still about, and the car got caught up in it at one stage. 'We were on tenterhooks wondering if people would put two and two together and realize who was in the car, but nobody noticed. We were silent in the car,' Phil recalled.

Later they drove to Cherry Lane and the scene where all the flowers were. There were still a lot of people standing there looking at the display and adding their own floral tributes. A note of panic crept into Robert's voice for just a moment as he asked, 'You aren't taking me up there?'

'No, we aren't,' Phil told him.

Phil was tense, waiting to make a quick getaway if someone in the crowd spotted their little passenger. 'If they only knew who we've got in this car,' he thought, grimly aware of their vulnerability. But it was just another car to the mourners, and nobody noticed anything unusual. They did not linger at the scene, and drove back to the police station. 'We didn't take very long. I had a feeling he was lying so I wanted it over and done with,' recalled Phil. 'I knew we weren't going to get what we wanted out of him'. They were back at Walton Lane at 6.15 p.m.

Throughout the interviews the teams had been reporting dutifully back to DI Jim Fitzsimmons at Marsh Lane. By now he had fairly frank admissions from Jon Venables, although he still sought to transfer most of the blame to Robert. Robert, on the other hand, had conceded being there but still had not admitted to his own involvement in the attack.

Jim Fitzsimmons was continuing to monitor the interviews and the evidence that was still coming in steadily from outside. 'The law is that when you have sufficient evidence you must charge,' he recalled. 'Mr Kirby, as the investigating officer, decided at that stage that we had sufficient evidence to charge them with murder'. Jim picked up the telephone, called the two police stations and notified the interview teams that he was on his way.

Driving his own car, Jim went first to Lower Lane Police Station, where at 6.15 p.m. he formally charged Jon Venables with the abduction and murder of James Bulger and the attempted abduction of another boy. Susan and Neil Venables were holding each other and crying as their son was charged, and Jon also began to weep. Laurence Lee watched quietly as Jim explained the charges in simplified terms to Jon after completing the formalities.

Jim then made the short journey along the East Lancashire Road to Walton Lane Police Station, where he put the same charges to Robert Thompson at 6.40 p.m.

Phil Roberts had seen a few people charged with serious offences in his time, but this, even to him, seemed unbelievable. 'His head was just about peering over the top of the charge desk,' Phil recalled. 'I felt good that we had got him. I also felt that we had prevented a lot of other tragedies. In my view the boys wanted tragedies. Putting James on the railway line was supposed to make everyone think an accident had happened. I think, had the first child been killed, James Bulger would not have been killed. They would have been happy with that'. He shook his head at the thought. 'Unbelievable, but that was their buzz. They wanted a tragedy and to make it look like an accident. I think they thought James's death would be taken as an accident. At ten years of age I suppose they didn't have the intelligence to realize otherwise'.

Robert Thompson seemed completely unconcerned when Jim Fitzsimmons read the charges out to him. He replied, simply, 'It was Jon that done that'.

Phil recalled: 'When he was charged he had no problem at all with it. I suppose he knew that if he was found guilty he would have a better life than he would outside. I thought to myself, "This boy has caused so much misery and evil". I didn't look for the three sixes on the back of his head, but at that moment I thought he was the devil'.

Denise and Ralph Bulger had been aware of the arrests of the two boys since the Thursday night. DS Jim Green, the family liaison officer, and PC Mandy Waller had been keeping them advised of developments. By late on the Friday they were beginning to realize that these boys had been in custody a long time. Jim kept telling them, 'Wait and see. Things are going well'.

James's uncle Ray Matthews told Jim, 'You know something you aren't telling us'.

Jim recalled: 'Ray bad made up his own mind. We spent most of Saturday in the police station waiting for authority to tell them. When I heard that a story that they were about to be charged had been broken in the Liverpool Echo I spoke to Ray Matthews. His reaction was relief.

When the final decision was taken later that afternoon, Detective Superintendent Albert Kirby went to visit Denise and Ralph with DCI Geoff MacDonald and Jim Green. 'We felt it only right that the senior officer was the man who came to give them the news face to face. I'm sure they appreciated that,' said Jim.

'They didn't really show a great deal of emotion when they were told. It was a very thoughtful time for them. There was still a lot of hate there,' said Jim.

The news was relayed to press officer Inspector Ray Simpson within seconds of Robert being charged. Ray's telephone had not stopped since the Echo ran its front page splash that lunchtime saying the boys were about to be charged. When they ran the story no definitive decision had been taken, though by then it was obvious to all of us covering the case that with the thirty-six hours' detention set to run out early on the Sunday morning, something had to happen soon. They would have missed the story completely until the Monday evening's edition if they had not taken a chance, and fortunately it went well for them. There may have been a few sweaty palms around the editorial floor when more than two hours elapsed after the original off-the-record estimate we were all getting of the boys being charged by 4.30 p.m., but that's the newspaper business.

Ray Simpson rang me as we had arranged to confirm that the boys had been charged, and I sent the information by computer to the Press Association's London office, from which the first news of the charges was flashed across Britain and the world, within about three minutes of their being brought.

A battery of television camera crews from several countries had been laying siege to Marsh Lane Police Station throughout the afternoon. Each time Ray had walked down the police station steps every camera light was turned on. It became a running joke between them, and Ray finally spared their batteries by slipping off his jacket and promising them that until they saw him with the jacket back on, they could rest assured that he had nothing to tell them.

After finishing his call to me, Ray slipped his jacket on and walked down the stairs into the full glare of the camera lights. He moved outside the station foyer and read the official statement confirming that the boys had been charged from the police station steps. 'Albert Kirby had read and approved the statement earlier, and I had told him I thought that as senior investigating officer he should read it out. He said he was happy if I did it. They say everyone has their fifteen minutes of fame, and I suppose that was my minute and a half'.

Sean Sexton, the Bulger family's lawyer, was waiting just behind Ray, to read a statement he had prepared on behalf of Denise and Ralph Bulger. Jim Green had brought him into the station earlier that afternoon and introduced him to Ray.

Sean's statement read: 'The family are of course relieved at the progress that has been made but are still trying to come to terms with the situation. They would like to thank the police and the public for their support. They do not wish, however, to make any further statement at this time and would ask the media to respect their privacy'.

Later that evening Phil Roberts managed to coax Ann to go into Robert's room and speak to him. Like Jon, Robert was finding his detention room had all the comforts of home. He sat playing with his cards and reading his comics. He seemed happy-go-lucky, as if the charges were no problem. It took some persuading for Ann to go in to him. She wanted nothing to do with the boy, and even when she was in the room she could hardly find a word for him.

Phil, a widower with two teenaged daughters, accepted the thanks of his superiors for his efforts without any sense of euphoria. Traditionally, when the suspects are in a murder case there is a celebration amongst the murder team. This time, nobody felt much like celebrating. The mood among the police officers was like the mood everywhere on Merseyside that weekend, sombre and thoughtful. A few people bought drinks for Phil in the bar at Marsh Lane that night, and Chief Superintendent Ray Walker made sure he was given a lift home.

Phil remembers sitting watching the television at home when his daughter Shán answered a telephone call from his mother. 'He's just been staring at the TV. I don't think he's watched anything,' she said.

Phil recalled: 'Shán was very attentive, much more so than usual, because I was so quiet. The girls wanted to know everything, but there was no way I could tell them. For about a month every time I went to bed or I was on my own I always thought about it. I was going over the interviews and asking myself, "Did I say the right things?, Did I remember to say this or ask that?" '

Most weekends, when the job allowed, Phil headed for his home village of Penybontfawr, near Lake Vyrnwy in Montgomeryshire, staying on the family farm his brother had taken over from his father or with his mother in a neighbouring village. It was a tiny rural retreat, with a Welsh name that meant 'End of the big bridge', and Phil loved it there. He planned to retire to the area when he finished in the police. He played rugby in the second row for Welshpool. They called him 'the old man' or 'granddad' these days, but at forty-two he was still second-team player of the year. It was his outlet and his escape from the pressures of life in the police force. A week after Robert and Jon were charged he was back down there, playing an away match for Welshpool seconds. The team stopped for a few drinks on the way back, and when he got back to Welshpool home, he went out with his rugby pals and completed the job, getting seriously smashed.

Dave Tanner vividly remembered Michelle Bennett breaking down and crying under the emotional strain on the Friday night of the interviews as they drove back to Marsh Lane Police Station. It was her birthday. Dave bought her a bottle of wine to try to lift her mood, but all Michelle wanted to do was get home to her kids.

Dave Tanner had a nineteen-year-old daughter at Liverpool University and twins aged seventeen studying for their A levels. When he got in that night his wife Diane was sitting in the lounge and his seventeen-year-old daughter was on the telephone. Dave walked right up to his daughter, wrapped his arms around her and gave her a bear hug that made her gasp.

'Detectives with a lot of service tend to try and hide things and we all did, but it was still obvious,' recalled Dave. There was no euphoria, no sense of "We've got them!" The atmosphere was dead. My wife and kids are the only ones who see me in my true light. I don't show my feelings at work but I will in the confines of my home. I could talk to Diane, but on a job like this I would never in my wildest dreams tell her the horrific things done to this child. You bottle it up. On the Sunday I rang my partner at St Helens CID and he and his wife came to our house. We are very close. The two of us went for a walk and ended up at a pub and I told him. He had a daughter James's age and I said I was glad he hadn't gone on it because I know it would have affected him. My mate listened. He was my release. If you took it all home with you on every job you would go under. You have to be able to bat things off, but it was difficult this time'.

George Scott's wife Elizabeth, a teacher and pregnant with their first daughter at the time, gave him the support he needed so badly. His sister-in-law, also a detective, was very supportive, too. 'It has affected every single one of us. It is something I will never forget and that has upset me and continues to upset me,' said George. 'I have got a picture in my mind of that kid on that railway embankment before he was struck for the first time, and it will haunt me for the rest of my life. There is no doubt about that. I am convinced that they both killed him. Who actually caused the fatal blow may never be known, but there was obviously mayhem on the railway line. What I can't understand is what on earth triggered two ten-year-old boys to do this. It would be nice to know, to get to the bottom of it fully so it can be prevented from happening again. How, in such a short lifetime, can they get to the stage of doing what they have done?'

Chapter Nine

The questions that haunt George Scott are those that trouble us all. We know, to our collective horror and continued astonishment, who killed James Bulger and how. Understanding why is much more difficult.

Lawyers and psychiatrists spent the months between the arrest and trial of Robert Thompson and Jon Venables trying to understand. Much of what passed between them, we on the outside will never know. Their dealings with the boys remain shrouded under the protective cloaks of law and professional ethics. Robert and Jon will undoubtedly have been examined and interviewed at length. Detailed confidential reports will have been drawn up. Yet even the access these professionals will have had to the two boys will not necessarily have answered the questions surrounding them to any satisfactory degree. Experts I have spoken to say it could take months, even years, before the layers of secrecy and disturbance are peeled back sufficiently to get to the core of their motivation. It is more than possible that we will never really know.

George Scott has had the advantage over most of us in trying to fathom this terrible crime. George spent three days sitting in a room with one of these ten-year-old killers, helping in a careful and painstaking questioning process. Yet even he, a skilled and experienced interrogator, was left frustrated, wanting to know more.

We, the public at large, have no opportunity to speak to these boys. If you or I could break through the protective walls of the state and sit in a room with them to ask them questions, we would probably be little the wiser at the end of it all either. These frightening little children have secrets inside them that they may not be prepared to admit even to themselves.

What we can try to do is analyse the facts of that terrible day and seek the guidance of experts in the field at least to make some intelligent guesses. It is extremely unusual to find children of quite such tender years capable of killing another human being. Yet much of their behaviour conforms to patterns familiar to those who have studied such crimes in older children and in adults.

12 February was the last day before the half-term holidays. The day a school breaks up is the most popular day of term for playing truant. Children often have a short span of awareness of the consequences of their actions. If you 'sag' school and you don't have to go back to face the music for a whole week, the risk seems worth taking. Maybe, the logic of the child runs, it will all be forgotten by then anyway.

That Friday morning a little girl who was in the same class as Robert and Jon spotted the two boys near an off-licence as she was on her way to school. The boys were running off down an entry, away from the direction of the school itself. She reported what she had seen to the class teacher and then the head teacher, who in turn notified the educational welfare office and telephoned Mrs Venables, getting no reply.

Recalled Mr Venables: 'Jon had gone off to school all happy that morning because he was taking gerbils home for half term. I went to the school and saw a little girl coming out with the gerbils and I said to her: "Where is he?" A dinner lady came running up to me and said "He's not here. He's gone missing." '

At 3.15 that afternoon Mr Venables was to arrive at the school to meet his son at the gates.

How the boys spent their morning is unclear, but the video security cameras at the Strand picked up their presence in the precinct for the first time at 12.23 p.m. that lunchtime. It was around this time that they encountered Mrs Diane Power, a twenty-seven-year-old mother out shopping with her lively little son and daughter. Diane had bought a pair of track suit bottoms in a sportswear shop as a Valentine's Day gift for her husband. After visiting another couple of shops and stopping to let the children play on a toy giraffe ride outside a newsagent's store, the trio made their way into T. J. Hughes's. Robert and Jon were already in the department store when the family went in.

Diane was standing by a display of sweatshirts and saw her two children gravitating towards the two boys. One of the boys was kneeling down and as she approached she heard him call out to his friend. 'Shall we take one of these?' At the time, Diane suspected that they were considering stealing a purse. With hindsight, she wondered if they were actually talking about one of her children.

When Diane approached, Robert and Jon froze and shut up. 'My two were looking at the boy looking at the purses,' recalled Diane. 'When he realized I was there he stopped. He wouldn't look at me and kept his side to me. I had thought they were just ordinary boys, but I wasn't happy about them'.

Diane took her children to join a queue at the till to pay for her purchase, but her son was fascinated with the boys and kept wandering over to them. 'I left the till three times to bring him back,' Diane recalled. 'I couldn't keep hold of him. I had to ask people to keep my place in the queue.

'When I was paying, he disappeared. I asked my little girl where he was, and she said, "He's gone out with the boys". I went to the purse counter and looked up the aisles of the shop, but I couldn't see him. I started to panic then. I kept thinking, "Where are you? Pop out of the aisle!" Then I went to the door and outside the shop. I had tight hold of my girl and I couldn't see my son.

'Then I just caught a glimpse of him, dashing round some benches. He was running very quickly. If I hadn't looked in his direction at exactly that moment, I wouldn't have seen him. As I came round the benches I saw one of the lads run and stop and then run and stop. He was enticing him to follow him. He dived behind a big post and was hugging it. He had his hand out beckoning to him. I thought, "What is going on?" I screamed to my son. I shouted and shouted and he still wasn't coming. He was in a trance. He was more interested in the boys than in me. It was fun to him. They were running and stopping and he was catching up. It was a big game..."

'Then, as I was shouting, the boy stopped beckoning and said, "Go back to your mum". That threw me. I didn't know what to do. The boy had been surprised to see me. He was a pleasant-looking lad. He was smiling all the time.

'He headed back to me and I told him off. I shook him and said, "What are you doing?"' The boys were already disappearing, cutting through another store to make a quick getaway. Bewildered and relieved, Diane did not know what to make of the incident. 'I thought they were having a joke, getting him lost in the passageway,' she recalled. She considered reporting the incident, or going after the boys, but she thought they were probably with their parents and the whole thing could end up in a row. Her little boy was still very restless and Diane was badly shaken, and she eventually decided to take her children home.

Like many others who saw the boys at various stages that day, the awful words 'if only' have tormented Diane ever since. She wishes desperately that she had notified the police or the store security staff, but she could have had no idea at the time of the evil in those boys' hearts. 'I thought the boys had gone home. I didn't know they were staying all day,' she said. 'On the day I honestly did my best. If the kid hadn't said, "Go back to your mum", I think I would have done more, but he definitely did say that. They didn't even run off'.

The boys' claim that they planned to lure the toddler into the road to be hit by a car is bad enough. There may have been still more dreadful wickedness in their plans.

'They were after my boy,' Diane recalled with a shudder. I don't know if they had been following me around. I was under a lot of pressure that day, keeping an eye on the kids without the pram with me. I know exactly how Denise felt that day looking for James. When I saw the video of him with them later I felt like picking him up and putting him to my heart and saying, "Don't go". I wish I could have done something more. They were really clever kids, really crafty. They knew exactly what they were doing. I still can't believe it. My son loves playing with older boys. I thought he was just playing with them, but I had left my child in a death-trap.

'For the first three weeks afterwards the children slept with me every night. I had to have them close to me. My husband and I would lose our tempers with them really quickly if they tried to move away. The two children are very close. It was my daughter who alerted me that something was wrong. Her dad picked her up afterwards and said, "Do you know what you did? You saved your brother's life". I think they will look out for each other for the rest of their lives now.

'Who could hurt such a young child? It is hard to believe of children that young. I thank God my son survived. I don't want to say I was lucky because I don't know if it was luck or a miracle or what. I wish they had never got James and that it had never happened. I am relieved it wasn't my son but I can still feel, very deeply, what his family have been going through. It is just fate that it wasn't us'.

There is clear evidence in this incident alone of premeditation and pre-planning. But there is much more. Police traced an office worker who had his lunch in the Strand each day, and saw two boys looking at the window of T. J. Hughes's on a day towards the end of January. He described them as excited and very lively and saw one of them tapping on the glass to a toddler inside the shop. He beckoned the child towards them, and he made a movement towards the door but then returned to his mother, and the two boys ran off. The man described the boys as very similar to Robert and Jon, and went on to successfully pick out Jon from an identification parade.

Let us not forget the incident when Robert and another boy took Robert's younger brother to the Strand and abandoned him, clearly upset, alongside the canal. Could there have been more to that incident?

Another factor is Jon's agitated, difficult behaviour in class on his last day at school, the day before the killing, the worst behaviour his teacher could ever recall from him. Was this evidence of a child excited at the prospect of carrying out a wicked plan?

David Glasgow is a lecturer in forensic clinical psychology at Liverpool University, who also practises at Ashworth Special Hospital at Maghull, near Liverpool. Ashworth is one of Britain's four special hospitals, providing accommodation and treatment amidst conditions of maximum security for some of the country's most dangerous killers and psychopaths. Moors murderer Ian Brady is Ashworth's most notorious inmate. Mr Glasgow's specialist area is young offenders, and particularly young sex offenders. We spoke, before the trial, in June.

He is convinced that the factors we have discussed point to what he would expect to find in such a case, a pattern leading up to the commission of their final, awful crime. 'Hardly ever do you get what is just described as a motiveless crime. The behaviour is planned,' be said.

'What is interesting about the case is that they were acting together, which often in my view reduces the abnormality of the individuals involved. When one person alone does something like this that person has to be very weird. Some of the "worst documented killers have an isolation and sense of apartness that goes way back to their childhood. " '

'When you get children acting together, particularly pre-adolescent and adolescent, they often do quit serious things, including killing people, that to an adult would be horrifying. The elderly are often the victims of these children. Often their psychopathology as individuals isn't so great.

'It sounds to me as if there was likely to be if not a plan then a rehearsal of it. When you are talking to one person who has done something horrible, as a psychologist you ask, "When did you first know it was going to happen and when did you think it might happen?" These are questions that never get asked by the forensic process, but are the most interesting ones.

'There would have to have been rehearsal. They may have done other things. Abuse and torture of animals would be likely. You often get that in the most sadistic murders. It is a relatively common occurrence. Children who go on to kill someone are often horrible to animals'.

So it seems possible that Robert Thompson and Jon Venables discussed and plotted their crime together over days, weeks or even months. We now know from witnesses and the security videos that the boys spent the next several hours of that Friday afternoon hanging around the Strand, presumably waiting for the next opportunity to strike. They stole tins of Humbrol modelling paint from the Toymaster store, and a packet of batteries from Tandy. Was their use in some way in the attack on their victim part of the original plan? Perhaps we will never know, but it appears likely.

The security footage shows Robert running up and tapping an eighty-three-year-old woman on the shoulder at 3.16 p.m. She remembered telling both boys off for messing around near an information desk distributing leaflets about tranquillizers. They continued to mess about and she told them off again and said they should be in school. She chased them away from the stand and one of them shouted something at her, but she was hard of hearing and could not tell what he said.

Eunice Gray, sixty-three, was looking in the window of T. J. Hughes's alongside the butcher's shop at about 3.30 p.m. when she heard the sound of a crack. She saw that two boys standing by the side window had dropped a small tin of paint, which was forming a pool with splashes. The boys were talking to each other, and she nearly stopped and spoke to them because she was concerned that someone might have stepped in the paint, but then went into the butcher's shop and did not see them again.

Another shopper, Janet Meyer, thirty-five, also saw the boys drop the paint, and then went into the butcher's shop. She queued at the cooked meat counter behind Nicola Bailey, and also saw Denise. She heard Denise say, 'I can't find him outside', and then saw her go to the door of the shop and come back inside, where she told an assistant, 'The little boy's gone missing from outside'.

The frames of the security video tell us' precisely the sequence of events that followed. It was 3.39 when James was pictured leaving the butcher's shop and looking towards the boys. At 3.40 Denise is pictured outside the shop, beginning her frantic search. At 3.41 James is on the top floor of the precinct with the two boys and they are crossing Mons Square. By now Denise is heading towards the security office to report him missing. At 3.42., three minutes after leaving the butcher's shop, James and the boys are passing the Mothercare store, turning left towards the precinct exit. At 3.43 Robert Thompson and Jon Venables are turning out of the precinct, by the door of Marks and Spencer's. Four minutes and ten seconds were all they needed to lure him away, cross the precinct and get out into Stanley Road. Witnesses confirm the impression the video footage gives that James, a trusting child who loved the company of his older cousins, was actually skipping. In that time Denise had made her own initial quick search and reported his disappearance to the security office. It is difficult to see what more she could have done. But Robert and Jon had laid their plans well.

It did not take long for James to start registering that something was wrong. He did not like to be away from his mother for long. His Uncle Ray Matthews remembered giving Denise, Ralph and James, a lift to a dental hospital in Liverpool on one occasion. He went back to the car for cigarettes, taking James with him for the walk. 'Halfway to the car he started asking for mum and dad. Suddenly he got really hysterical, and he knew me very well. What was going through his mind when he was being led away?'

A woman saw two youths holding a child between them in Stanley Road, near Marks and Spencer's. The child was crying and holding his head down. She could not see his face. She heard one of the youths say to him, 'Are you all right? You were told not to run'. She was about to enter the post office when she saw the boys by the steel railings leading to the canal. She heard one of the youths say, 'Do you want to go this way?'

Another woman walking along Stanley Road across the canal bridge saw a child on the canal bank, extremely distressed. There were three or four other children standing near him and she assumed they were all together and did not intervene. We know from the police interviews with the boys that some attempt was apparently made to get James into the canal itself, and he was thrown to the ground, injuring his head.

After coming back up from the canal to the pavement, the boys took James across busy Stanley Road and up Park Street, turning right into Litherland Road, and left into Langdale Street. They went into the car park of Viz Williams architects offices, climbed a wall into the grounds of Merton Towers, and another wall into Merton Road. They then crossed Hawthorn Road into Oxford Road by a roundabout, and were picked up by another security camera.

Mark Pimlett, twenty-five, was driving along Merton Road towards this roundabout, and his car was stationary in a queue waiting to get on to the roundabout. His eye was drawn to three teenaged girls in short skins walking towards the roundabout. As his car reached the 'Give way' sign for the roundabout he glanced to his left and saw Jon and Robert with James. 'They were stood either side of him and both older lads were holding one of the younger lad's arms,' he told police. 'They were both using their arms to hold his arms and they were dragging him in an effort to make him move. The child in turn was leaning back as if he didn't want to go with them. I would say I watched them pull the lad until the point where I had to move off. I could see the little lad crying because his face was red and puffed up. At this stage I thought it was an older brother taking him home and they pulled him like this as I moved off. I started around the roundabout and I looked into my interior mirror to make sure there were no cars coming upon my nearside. I was on the roundabout…when I saw in my mirror the lad in the black clothing kick the little boy in the ribs under his right arm. He kicked him with his left foot. It wasn't a real full-blooded kick but a persuasion kick. Both lads kept hold of the little boy who continued to lean against the direction the older boys were going. This had an immediate effect on me as I said to myself, "You are going to be a real scally." '

They carried on dragging James up Oxford Road to the top, where they turned right into Southport Road, crossing a pedestrian crossing to the far side by Hillside School. Then they walked towards the city of Liverpool to the junction with Breeze Hill, crossed the road and then turned left along Breeze Hill. A woman passing on a bus with her eleven-year-old daughter spotted' them in Breeze Hill. 'Each had hold of the baby by one hand and they were swinging him up in the air,' she told police. 'Although the two boys were about nine years old they were swinging the baby quite high. I didn't see whether the baby fell to the floor because of the traffic but when I next looked both of them were swinging him again. I thought the two boys were brothers taking the baby out. I did think they were playing rough with him because I said to my daughter, "What kind of parents have they got to let him play out with kids like them? They are going to hurt him. They'll be in trouble when they get home." '

Robert and Jon then reached, the raised, grassed-over reservoir site in Breeze Hill with James. It is thought that it was about 4.20 p.m. by now, the time security staff at the Strand first notified the police of James's disappearance. They were already almost a mile away from the shopping centre. The boys led James up the steps on to the top of the reservoir and led him around the field. A woman saw Jon Venables with James from the front window of her home in nearby Stuart Road. He was holding him by the shoulders, near the neck, and the woman saw him shake James very briskly, possibly to quiet him down.

An elderly woman walking her dog, on the reservoir, as she regularly did, saw James with both boys. The child was sobbing and the woman asked the older boys what was going on. One of them said they had just found the toddler at the bottom of the embankment. The woman could see two bumps on James's forehead and told the boys that he should get some attention for his injuries. They assured her that they were going to take him to a police station. They led James back down the reservoir steps into Breeze Hill, and turned right just beyond the reservoir site into Stuart Road. They followed Stuart Road until it came out in County Road.

County Road is a busy main route leading out of the city of Liverpool through Walton, lined with shops along most of its length. Astonishingly at this stage Robert and Jon took their bewildered little captive into at least two shops. First, just after 5 p.m. they went into a DIY shop and asked the owner where the nearest sweet shop was because they wanted to buy sweets for their brother. The shop owner noticed that James seemed 'slightly distressed'. Then they went into a pet shop where they paused to watch a 'weather coach' fish lying at the bottom of its tank.

Perhaps the idea of these diversions was to calm James down, with so many people about. Whatever the plan, it appears that James's shock and distress had made him more subdued by now. The boys took him across County Road and turned right into a side street called Hampden Street, walked its full length, turned left into Dunbar Street and then right almost immediately into Church Road West. As they wove their way through these Walton back streets, so familiar to Robert in particular, they met two older boys. One of them, a twelve-year-old, knew Robert.

'The little boy looked sad and seemed to have been crying. He had a little bump, with little red dots and lines on it,' recalled the twelve-year-old.

'What happened to the lad?' he asked Robert.

'He fell over at the top,' Robert replied.

'Where?'

'At the top'. The boy thought Robert must mean back up by County Road. Robert had then volunteered, 'Look at his hair, as well'.

The boy looked and could see more 'red dots and lines' under James's hair. 'Who is he?' the boy asked.

'His brother,' Robert replied, gesturing towards Jon.

'Where are you taking him?'

'Home'.

The boy considered his options. Finally he warned Robert, 'If you don't take him home now, I'll batter you'.

Robert and Jon walked on, James still in tow. They turned right next, into City Road, crossed to its far side by the railway bridge and turned left into a back entry running parallel with the line, which took them towards Walton Lane. They took the hood of James's anorak and threw it into a tree on the corner of City Road.

In the entry they met a forty-two-year-old local man who knew the Thompson family. He was walking down the entry towards Walton Lane carrying shopping from a nearby supermarket when he came upon the boys. One of the boys was standing on the wall. James was standing near the other boys, crying, 'He wasn't screaming, more of a moan or a sob,' recalled the witness.

The boy standing on the ground looked straight at him and said, 'I'm fed up having my little brother. He's always the same'. As they passed, this boy looked up at the boy on the wall and said, 'I'm not bringing him again'.

A fourteen-year-old girl was walking with her father along Walton Lane near the railway bridge. It is another very busy main road, and at this point is a matter of yards from Walton Lane Police Station. The girl saw Robert and Jon pushing James out into the road. To her it appeared as if James was laughing. Whether that was in fact the reaction he was displaying is a matter for speculation. When one of the boys spotted her approaching with her father they stopped, picked James up and scrambled up the embankment and squeezed through a gap in the fence on to the railway.

This little girl was the last to see them. From this moment on, Robert and Jon had the privacy afforded by the quiet, rarely used railway track to carry out their crime.

It is difficult to imagine the emotional state James was in by this time. The sheer exertion of a forced 2-mile walk through a warren of back streets must have been torture for his tiny legs. Add to that the terror and distress of being lost, away from his mother and encountering for the first time in his life two older children who turned out to be anything but friendly and protective. How he must have longed for one familiar face, for someone, anyone, to end his living nightmare and take him back to the warmth and security of his family.

Robert Thompson and Jon Venables were not only aware of his distress. Through their low animal cunning, they were actually making excuses for it to the adults and the older children they met along the way. Forming a plan was one thing. They had been pitiless in its execution in the face of the reality of an innocent child who was seriously distressed for a prolonged time before they finally killed him.

Jonathan Hill, Professor of Child and Adolescent Psychiatry at Liverpool University, finds this area of the boys' behaviour particularly hard to come to terms with. I told him of the boys' backgrounds, and he found plenty, particularly in Robert's case, to explain quite major behaviour problems. Robert's 'sly, manipulative' nature is a very common description of a child who is trying to get some control of his circumstances, in the face of a home life where, however the child behaves, the parents' mood and behaviour are difficult to predict.

'A child may sometimes be aggressive and may sometimes get control by means that might be called manipulative, and probably feels his aggressive impulses are not controllable and there is no one around to take control for him. That is all fairly common,' said Professor Hill. 'But there is still a gap in our understanding here. What is it that leads a ten-year-old child to systematically set out in a sustained way to commit this crime? What might it be that would lead a ten-year-old to sustain the intention to kill another child, over many hours, and to carry it out in the face of clear distress from the victim? If we break it down into intent, initiation, failure to stop in the face of distress and whatever other components there are in terms of sadistic or sexual components, it is hard enough to understand how they might form the intent to do that. It is possible that the original intent was different. One is bound to think, was the boys' state of mind and were their actions part of something you could have seen if you had interviewed them a week before? Was there something regular or habitual about the way one of them felt and acted and saw the world or was there something more particular about that day or the previous few days that made a difference? In older people, in young adults, for instance, you would think about an episode of psychiatric illness, but that is very unlikely to be the case in a ten-year-old'.

There may well be secrets in Robert and Jon's past, suffering that they have faced, which we cannot know. But, as Professor Hill points out, many thousands of children today go through the traumas of broken homes, poor parenting and even outright abuse, without turning into fully fledged killers. Many children have aggressive and destructive fantasies, and though it is likely that in Robert and Jon's cases these fantasies may be more sadistic than most, it is difficult to perceive how they could have taken all the steps involved in converting fantasy to terrible reality. Professor Hill said: 'I would say, and quite a lot of my Colleagues would say, there is in most people a very destructive, cruel and sadistic element. Usually it is held in balance by other impulses and concerns, and stays at the level of thoughts and fantasies, and is dealt with by not becoming action.

'I suspect that what has been going on in their minds in terms of fantasy is not necessarily substantially different from what might go on in the minds of lots of other children, but that it could be linked to action and carried out without something breaking through to stop the sequence, that is what it is very hard to understand.

'Most people can perceive the space between the strange things that go on in their minds and acting on them. Nothing I can think of in general would be enough to bridge that gap. I could imagine that it would be a little less puzzling if, for instance, one of them had been the victim of extreme cruelty, be it physical or sexual or a combination of the two. But even that kind of account leaves one saying there is still a significant minority of children who do experience quite severe cruelty but at the age of ten don't behave in this way. If I met one of these lads I would try to understand whether their normal equipment had somehow got disrupted or suspended, or whether' there was something habitually sadistic or cruel about the thoughts or actions of at least one of them'.

Science can only go so far in revealing exactly what happened to James on that railway line. Forensic examination provided no evidence of sexual interference. But the removal of his lower clothing may well point to the secret heart of this crime. It was not adequately explained by the boys when the police questioned them.

David Glasgow said a sexual motivation would make this case much easier to understand. The extraordinary findings of his own

Liverpool University research project into child sex abuse were that more sexual abuse of children was committed by adolescents aged twelve to seventeen than any other five-year age group throughout life. The next greatest group was pre-adolescents aged seven to eleven. These two groups together accounted for 30 per cent of all such assaults on children. That same research showed that when children under seventeen committed these offences there would be no positive medical evidence of the assault. 'The absence of evidence is not evidence of absence,' said Mr Glasgow. 'It is not unknown for young children to be sexually exploitative at all'.

He added: 'If there was not sexual motivation in this case you would have to come up with a much more complicated alternative involving issues of power, control and sadism. At Ashworth Hospital 25 per cent of offenders are sexual. Professionals working in sexual offending have led the way in seeing the ways thoughts, precognitions and fantasies turn into behaviour.

'Getting back to the rehearsal phase, which I am convinced was there and had probably been developing for some time, I think that would give the clues to the function it served for the two of them. Their fantasized or playing version would often reflect what they wanted out of it. If you talk to sex offenders they may often give you an account of what they think in their head is going to happen. Often the differences between that and what actually happened is quite revealing. Of course they lie and minimize their own wrongdoing. Indecent assaulters or indecent exposers, for example, have a fantasy of reciprocation. "This child would see me and then come up and start stroking my penis", the fantasy would go. It is a fantasy of a kind of sexual activity that is their goal but of course never happens'.

Mr Glasgow explained that the prelude to a sexually motivated crime would consist of three domains, with huge overlaps. The first, cognitive rehearsal, would be having the thought: 'Wouldn't it be great if there was a brand-new car there with keys in and I just drove off in it?' The second area, sexual fantasy, would involve masturbating and thinking up a story to go along with it, the function of which was to assist masturbation. Then there would be the planning phase. Often a small incident can lead to an overlap, which starts to convert into behaviour.

As an example, a sex offender masturbating and fantasizing about children in a playground might one day think: 'I could go a different way home past a recreation ground'. He might think about that and masturbate about that part of the story for a long time. Then it might develop into an action of rehearsal. He would walk past the recreation ground, but then walk on. By then it has become a piece of pre-offence behaviour, part of the chain.

David Glasgow said: 'I would suspect a sexual motivation in this case. Their motivations and cognitive rehearsals might not be identical, but their interactive part would be, raking each other along by energetic communication. It is really quite common to get two people feeding off each other like this.

'You get cases with one person acting solo, and you get a delinquency peer group acting together. There are a number of sexual cases where about five lads sexually assault two younger children.

'Then there are the little dyads that float around together. They are often isolated as a dyad, not part of a peer group'. Experts agree that the absolute classic example of that was the Moors murderers. One said, 'They were quite different in their needs but together they formed the potential for actions which possibly they may never have acted out alone. I don't know. You get the sense of something special about their interactions and relationship.

'The evidence is that these two boys would have had serious problems even if they had not met. I would like to know how important the rehearsal phase was in this crime, how exclusive it was, and what other sorts of things the boys did together'.

Mr Glasgow said that often with killers, the ultimate death of the victim is not the prime target of the offence. 'The process of abuse, humiliation or sex abuse may be what they want to do for various reasons. The difficulty is that they get trapped into escalation. Partly they get carried away. Having done what they wanted their options get narrower and narrower. Once the victim is covered in blood and cut and marked and screaming for Mummy they may think, "Now what do I do?" Their actions may have led them to face a decision. "Do we walk off and leave him or try and make it look like an accident?"

'The alternative is the rehearsal one. "Let's get a dog and put it on the railway track and see what happens". Maybe they did something like that. The entire pattern was rehearsed and the whole thing was what it was about - killing and making it look like an accident'.

Professor Anne Burgess, of the University of Pennsylvania in Philadelphia, is one of the pre-eminent psychiatric experts in the area of children who turn killers. She, too, felt that a sexual motive would be likely in a case like this. 'The fact that the victim's lower clothing was removed would be a sign of that,' she said. 'They probably would not admit to any sexual interference. That would be the secret part that they wouldn't admit but it would be a very important motivation. The murder sometimes occurs to silence the victim.

'Clearly these boys are very young. A ten-year-old committing such a crime is very unusual. Some of the things one would look for in their backgrounds would be a history of previous signs of serious aggression, injury to animals or fire-setting, and whether there is a history of abuse in their lives. Very often children may repeat acts that have either been committed on them or that they have seen or had some access to. In the study I have done of juveniles, more often than not it is a situation of one egging the other on. You do have that dynamic very often'.

I suggested to her the theory expounded by some of the detectives that the boys simply wanted to create 'tragedies' for which they thought they would not ultimately be blamed. 'That doesn't seem very logical: said Professor Burgess. 'My hunch is that there is another motive that they are keeping very secret and won't talk about. When they are in the legal arena it is very difficult to get them to reveal these secrets. I doubt if they will be able to do anything until the legal aspect is completed. The only way to get them to talk is to put them in therapy and get a relationship going where they feel safe enough to talk about things.

'One of these boys certainly had the masterplan. It isn't difficult for young people to get someone to go along with them and be an accomplice. There is probably one of these boys who is primary in this. Even though they are very young it fits the pattern of the juveniles I have covered where they tend to operate with two people rather than singly. Probably because they are so young, it isn't something they could do on their own'.

When James was dead and they had covered his broken little body with bricks and left it on the railway track for a train to run over, Robert

Thompson and Jon Venables went to the video shop near Robert's home. The boys ran a message for the shop staff and were paid £1 for collecting £3 on an overdue video from a nearby house.

It was there that Susan Venables found the two boys later that evening.

Recalled Mrs Venables: 'I went out at about half past five looking all round the area again and decided to go down to where Robert Thompson lived, looking around there. I went to the police station to report that he had gone missing again with this same boy and I wasn't happy about it at all. I told them I would go out and have another look around. I even went up to the railway because I knew Robert had a den up there and was on the railway nearly all the time. I wasn't actually on the railway track because there is a fence but I went up the side. There is like a little paint factory. It was very dark and I shouted down, shouted his name. That's the thing that upsets me because obviously where I was standing poor little James must have been not far'. She sobbed at the memory of the moment, make-up running down her face.

'I look around and spotted them going into the video shop,' she added. 'Me and my other son stood back a minute just in case they saw us and then I went in the video shop and grabbed hold of the two of them. Their clothes were absolutely filthy and Jon's beige coat was splashed with paint. She grabbed hold of Jon, and Robert was to claim that she also hit him, which Mrs Venables denies. The angry mother dragged Jon back to the police station and asked the officer behind the desk to give him a good telling off.

When Robert got home he told his mother Ann that Jon's mother had hit him. She took Robert to Walton Lane Police Station and complained about Mrs Venables assaulting her son.

It was one of the most extraordinary ironies of this strangest and most terrible of cases. The two boys who were to become the most wanted individuals in Britain over the next few days were both dragged into the same police station by their mothers within hours of committing their crime just a few yards away.

They kept their secret well enough over the next few days, Jon avidly studying the newspaper reports, Robert actually going back to the scene to add his flowers to the huge mound of floral tributes. Some parts of their secret may remain just that, and become lost, ultimately, even from themselves as they grow up. Professor Hill said: 'We rightly try and understand how people whether children or adults, behave in relation to their experiences, but we are always left with that element which is that everyone differs in ways that we cannot understand in relation to circumstances. New-born infants differ enormously and that is almost certainly a difference of constitution or make-up. Sometimes we have to stop at the point where we say we can go so far in our attempts to understand, but that's it'.

Chapter Ten

It was 6.45 on a bleak Monday morning in late February when the first of the two blue police vans arrived on the tarmac driveway leading to the double-airlock security gates of South Sefton Magistrates' Court. It was a modern, brick and glass monolith of a building occupying a large site on the corner of Stanley Road and Merton Road, Bootle, a matter of a few hundred yards away from the Strand Shopping Centre. The outer gates slid back with a low metallic whirr, and the first van drove inside. The outer gate closed, and only then could the inner gate be opened. It was an efficient outer security system similar to that employed in most of Britain's prisons and secure institutions, designed to prevent escape by the most hardened and determined criminals. Today, as the perimeter security faced its sternest test since the court complex had opened two years earlier, the problem was not to be one of keeping the suspects in, but keeping the public out.

Robert Thompson and Jon Venables had made an early start to their final morning in the custody of Merseyside Police. Since being charged on the Saturday evening with the abduction and murder of James Bulger and the attempted abduction of another boy they had been left in peace to play with their toys and read their comics, in their comfortably appointed rooms at Walton Lane and Lower Lane Police Station. The law permitted no further questioning.

They were still bleary-eyed and yawning when they were driven off to Bootle that Monday through the light early morning traffic. When they arrived, the only onlookers were a couple of discreetly placed uniformed police officers there to keep a watchful eye on any potential crowd build-up.

You didn't need to look beyond the masses of flowers that had by now accumulated, in Cherry Lane, Walton, and in the Strand to appreciate the pitch at which emotions were running in the city. You could sense the air of depression and disbelief everywhere, and particularly in the affected communities of Bootle, Walton and Kirkby.

Police were grimly aware of the likelihood of a darker side of that emotion manifesting itself as the boys made their court appearance. Memories of Snowdrop Street were fresh in people's minds. On the Sunday, Bootle-based Police Superintendent Paul-Burrell had appealed for calm. 'The last ten days have been stressful for the whole of Merseyside, in particular the family and friends of James Bulger, the police who had to investigate the crime, and the local communities of Kirkby, Walton, and Bootle,' he said. 'As we move towards a court appearance I would ask the communities, the community leaders and the clergy, with whom we work so closely, to continue to show and encourage the level of compassion and dignity which typifies them. We ask all of Merseyside to remain calm'.

Sean Sexton consulted with Denise and Ralph Bulger and issued a statement backing Mr Burrell's appeal. 'Having spoken with Ralph and Denise Bulger today they fully endorse the appeal made by the police. The last thing the family would want is for there to be any public disturbance'.

Security was understandably extremely tight. Juvenile courts, or youth courts as they are now known, are not open to the general public like adult courts, which removed one problem for the police. Journalists, on the other hand, have a right to attend and report youth court proceedings. I was one of a small group of reporters who were to be allowed in to cover the court hearing on a pooled basis, supplying copy to anyone who wanted it. Inspector Ray Simpson had made the arrangement after consultations with court officials.

'Superintendent Burrell went through with me the steps he would take to get the boys in and out of court,' recalled Ray. 'We knew we could fill the court with media and nobody else, but strictly speaking it wasn't a police matter. Once we got the boys into a court situation and they appeared before the court, technically they went out of police custody. We went to the court and asked them how they were proposing to deal with the media and if we could be of any assistance. They said they didn't know how they would deal with that amount of journalists and asked us to help them. We decided we couldn't leave it to run on its own, and that we had to manage how many members of the press would get in. Once we had all the media needs covered with as small a party as possible that is what we worked to. I assured Paul Burrell we would take the press in, look after them and take them out again'.

The six of us who were to be allowed inside the security net faced as early a start as the two boys that morning. The Bootle Times, the Liverpool Echo, the Daily Post, Liverpool-based Mercury Press Agency and the Press Association were the five nominated organizations. In addition, an artist from ITN was to be allowed in to draw an illustration of the scene inside the court, again on the understanding that it would be made available to all. When I drove past the court building, soon after 7.30 a.m., one or two eager photographers and cameramen were already in position, but there was no sign of spectators yet. We met Inspector Simpson and civilian press officer Diane Halliwell at Marsh Lane Police Station before 8 a.m., and drank coffee in the canteen while we waited for the moment when we would be allowed into court.

When we walked down Stanley Road to the court building, just after 9 a.m., the media, international as well as local and national, were beginning to gather in force. Among them was my colleague Stephen Guy, who was to keep an eye on events outside the court while I was covering the hearing itself. By now a handful of members of the general public had also started to gather outside. At this stage the mood seemed calm and peaceful.

Since their early morning journey, the two boys had been waiting with their representatives in a special juvenile detention room beneath the court complex. After passing through the airlock the police vans had driven directly into a tunnel under the building where the boys had been transferred inside behind closed doors, safely out of the view of even the most powerful telephoto lenses.

Several adult courts were also sitting that day, so it was not possible totally to shut off the court complex from the public. However, the youth court was behind frosted glass screens and double doors at one end of the wide main corridor on the first floor off which the adult courts were situated. Dozens of uniformed policemen and women were gathered behind those double doors, to ensure that nobody could force their way in. Reinforcements who had been held in reserve were also arriving on the streets outside, as the handful of onlookers expanded.

By the time the boys were due to appeal in court at 10 a.m. over 300 people were standing in the street. The mood was quiet and grim.

It was about seven minutes after the appointed time when our little group of reporters was allowed inside the court. To our surprise, it was already in session. Three magistrates were sitting for the hearing, at their long, raised wooden bench looking down, on the well of the court. It was a light, airy, magnolia-walled courtroom illuminated by fluorescent lights under a suspended ceiling. Everything was designed to avoid, children being intimidated by their surroundings as far as possible. We were ushered to seats with their backs to the rear wall of the court. Ahead of us were two long desks, running virtually the width of the room. At the rear desk sat Detective Superintendent Kirby, DCI MacDonald and DI Fitzsimmons. Sean Sexton also sat in one of the seats. 'I am simply trying to keep the family informed of what is happening,' he was to explain afterwards. 'They didn't specifically ask me to be here'.

On the front row sat defence solicitors Dominic Lloyd, for Thompson, and Laurence Lee, for Venables. Further along sat a woman lawyer representing Liverpool City Council's social services department and 'lawyer Robert Watts, who was prosecuting on behalf of the Crown Prosecution Service.

We did not have long to wait for the two little boys at the centre of all this attention to arrive. A door in the side wall of the court to our left opened and Robert and Jon were brought into the room, Robert accompanied by a social worker, Jon by his father.

Seeing them at last was as disturbing as it was incredible. Walking into the room were two little boys I would have walked past in the street without a second glance. They looked tiny, and very, very young. It was instantly apparent why so many people had hesitated to come forward in response to the video images. The perspective of the cameras made them appear much taller than they actually were. I found it hard to believe that they were even ten years old.

Robert, his mousey hair cropped close to his head, wore a dark blue track suit with red, elasticated cuffs. He could barely be seen over the tops of the desks as he was led to his seat. Jon was slightly taller, with hair just touching the collar of the red polo shirt he was wearing under a white crew-necked pullover. Grey corduroy trousers completed his outfit. If they were nervous, they did not show it. There was nothing in their demeanour that indicated any apprehension as they sat meekly alongside their lawyers during the six-minute hearing. Nor, come to that, was there defiance or nonchalance. If anything, they appeared faintly bewildered by what was happening around them.

Clerk of the court Peter Horan, facing the boys from behind a desk below the magistrates' bench, addressed them in turn. 'Robert, are you Robert Thompson?'

'Yes,' said Robert.

'And how old are you, Robert?'

'Ten'.

There it was. Confirmation of the unbelievable. Mr Horan turned his attention to Jon, who also confirmed his name. He just nodded when Mr Horan asked if he, too, was ten years old.

Then it was Mr Watts's turn to speak. 'My application this morning is that both these boys be remanded to the care of the local authority until Wednesday, 3 March,' he began. The first of the grounds he cited was that the boys should be in care for their own protection. The scenes that were to develop outside the court building were to lend powerful weight to that particular argument.

He briefly outlined the facts of James's disappearance and the discovery of his body, and told the court: 'Robert and Jon were arrested and have been interviewed separately at different police stations. The prosecution say both boys have admitted being involved in the abduction of James and to being present. They have each blamed each other for the predominant number of blows struck on James'.

Robert sat with his chin resting on his hand, elbows on the desk, as Mr Watts spoke. Jon stretched and yawned at one point. It did not look like insolence as much as the natural action of a child who had got up earlier than usual that morning, and who did not really appreciate the full gravity of his situation.

The two defence lawyers stood up in turn to offer no objections to the application. Mr Lee asked the prosecution if they might be able to fix a provisional date for their committal to the Crown Court. As he was speaking, Robert shot a glance down the desk towards Jon, who looked back at him for a moment. It was the only apparent contact between them.

Bench chairman Mr Jim Dixon then formally remanded the two-boys to the care of the local authority until 3 March. He issued an order that the two boys' names and anything leading to their identity could not be published. This was something of a 'belt and braces' procedure, as the law covering youth court reporting would in any event have prohibited such reporting. At that point, we were asked to leave the court while the social services lawyer made representations to the bench.

We were later to be told in a statement issued by Liverpool City Council that Health Secretary Viginia Bottomley had given approval for Robert and Jon to be placed in secure facilities outside Liverpool. The statement added: 'The families of both boys are known to Liverpool Social Services Department although not as a result of any concern surrounding the two charged. The Directors of Social Services and Education are working together to ensure a full response to the wider family and community consequences of the situation'. Robert and Jon's families were being secretly rehoused for their own protection and the other children were being placed in care, it was to emerge later.

We were taken by Ray and Diane to a room in the court complex where we were able to file our copy before going outside to brief the rest of the waiting journalists. When the remaining matters had been dealt with inside court, Robert and Jon were taken back down to the juvenile detention room to await transfer for the first time to the secure facilities that were to become their new homes over the coming months. Throughout the hearing, the actual charges of attempted abduction, abduction and murder were never formally read out to the boys.

Outside in the rain, skinheads rubbed shoulders with mothers pushing prams as the crowd waited impatiently for a glimpse of the killers. There were children among them too, 'sagging' school for the morning to be there. It was a charged atmosphere, which reached fever-pitch when two windowless blue police vans drove up Merton Road and turned into the court complex, passing through the gate airlocks. A line of police motorcycles gathered on the court car park, ready to provide an escort for the vans.

Then the gates were opened again and the vans moved out. People surged forward, urged back by a thin line of police officers. Some in the crowd screamed, 'Hang the bastards!' A balding, bearded man broke through the police line and ran into the side of one of the vans shouting,

'Die!' A police sergeant got an arm round his neck as a constable put him in an arm-lock, and he was forced to the side of the road and arrested.

A half-brick crashed into the side of one of the vans, and an egg smashed over the second. Another man tried to attack the convoy and was dragged off to a police van shouting, 'We've got fuckin' kids too, you know!' Two of the skinheads were then arrested. Minutes earlier one of them had been telling reporters, 'I'm here to see justice done'.

A lot of people stood and watched as the vans moved off. Some took the side of the six people eventually arrested during the brief scuffles. A chant of 'Let them go' went up. Others just stood there for a while, and then slowly began to drift away.

The brave individuals who apparently wanted to try to kill two ten-year-old boys that morning will be disappointed to hear that their actions had no effect whatever on Robert Thompson or Jon Venables. They were still sitting quietly in the detention area with officials while police ran their decoy operation and waited for the crowds to disperse.

The crowds were smaller and much more subdued the following week when the boys returned for their next appearance, and quickly dwindled to nothing as the weekly remand visits to Bootle became something of a ritual for all concerned.

That disturbance was a shameful incident. However awful the crime, behaviour that suggests the mob lynching of two ten-year-old boys is beyond the bounds of the acceptable in any civilized society. Only a small section of that crowd actually took part in the violence. To the cameras it unfortunately looked like a virtual riot. Some of those who stood and watched, adding to the impression of a rampaging mob simply by their quiet presence in the background, have no doubt felt ashamed about it since. Others would probably do the same again tomorrow in similar circumstances. Scenes like these are sadly by no means unique to the James Bulger case. Child killers, rapists and notorious murderers often encounter similar receptions from their local communities when they are brought to court. This is not a Merseyside phenomenon. If this case had happened in the East End of London, in Birmingham or in Glasgow, there would have been similar scenes. We all feel terrible anger and frustration in the face of such crimes, perhaps in this case more than almost any other. There are some among us who seem to have a compulsion to vent emotion by such public displays as this.

The crowd's actions made the lead item on TV news bulletins, and front page headlines in the national press the next day. The tone of all the reports I saw was rightly critical of the behaviour. They developed, however, into an unfounded attack on Liverpool as a whole. There was a particularly nasty piece in one of the nationals which implied that the city was 'getting off' on the city-in-mourning theme. It was one of several deeply unkind pieces that appeared in the national press in the wake of James's tragic death. The Liverpool Echo, its sister morning paper the Daily Post, and local politicians and Churchmen did their best to fight against the tide of criticism.

If newspapers feel so strongly that they have a case to make, about Liverpool or any other place, I would defend to the hilt their right to make it. It just seems sad that in this case it was done with such crass, insensitive timing. 'Self Pity City', a particularly scathing piece, appeared on the day before James's funeral.

Chapter Eleven

They buried James Bulger on the coldest day of the winter. It was a Monday, the first morning of March, and an icy north wind whistled through the streets of Kirkby under a bleak grey sky. Some had expected the street outside the church to be crammed with thousands of mourners. They had missed the mood of the town. The streets were almost unnaturally quiet. On a morning fit to freeze the tears on your cheeks, the people were saying their farewells quietly and in private, behind closed curtains in the familiar, reassuring surroundings of their own homes.

Denise and Ralph Bulger faced a double ordeal that morning. They had lost their beloved son and faced the natural grief of any parent who loses a child. That terrible burden of pain was made even more acute by the knowledge that James had not been taken by some childhood illness or accident but by a deliberate, calculated act of evil. If all this was not enough for this bewildered young couple there was an added cross to bear. Their names had become famous around the world and the thoughts of every parent were with them that morning. But their unsought celebrity carried with it a responsibility. Hundreds of journalists and photographers would be watching them. Live television coverage meant that millions more would share the funeral service. Since James's death the couple had kept themselves hidden away in their flat, surrounded by the support and love of their family. They had been insulated from the mass of attention that surrounded them, but now they had to face the world. Somehow they had to summon the composure and dignity to get through that awful day under the spotlight. It was a test of courage.

Often in murder cases there is a delay of several months before a funeral can be held. Defence lawyers frequently require their own experts to conduct independent autopsies in an attempt to uncover evidence not disclosed by the Home Office pathologist's initial post-mortem examination which might be helpful to their clients. In this case, thankfully for the Bulgers, that did not prove necessary. Lawyers for both the accused boys quickly indicated after the initial court hearing that they did not require independent autopsies, and coroner Roy Barter was able to sign the papers authorizing the release of James's body for burial on Tuesday, 23 February.

That same afternoon Sean Sexton released a statement announcing that the funeral would take place on Monday, 1 March, at Sacred Heart Church in Northwood, Kirkby. James was to be buried 4 miles away at Liverpool's Kirkdale Cemetery. The Bulgers requested family flowers only at the funeral and asked that anyone wishing to mark their respect should make donations through the funeral director to Liverpool's Alder Hey Children's Hospital.

Funeral director Graham Clegg had carried out the funeral for James's grandfather, and was not surprised when he received a telephone call from the family asking him to make the arrangements. It was to be the biggest ceremony his company had ever arranged, and Graham decided at the outset that there would be no bill for their services.

He had met Ralph and some of James's uncles at Kirkdale Cemetery and helped him pick out a suitable plot, right on the main driveway, in the shade of a tree. 'It was opposite the site of an old chapel. Ralph decided that was the place he wanted. In the circumstances he coped very well'.

The casket was hand-made by a Midlands company specially for James. The company did the work free of charge. Everyone wanted to do something, it seemed.

When the body was released by the coroner, Graham Clegg went personally to Broadgreen Hospital to bring James to his Chapel of Rest in Maghull, near Liverpool. 'His mum and dad and the family were not going to be able to see him, and I didn't want anyone else ,to be able to say "I saw him", recalled Graham. 'I sheltered my staff from things because I bad an inclination of how things would have been with him. It was worse than I thought. I cried most of the way from the hospital to the chapel. I placed him in the casket and sealed it so there was no way anyone could see him'.

Denise went back to the flat in Oak Towers and found James's favourite clothes, the Christmas outfit of cords and waistcoat he had been so pleased with. None of the women in the family could bring themselves to iron the clothes. Ray did the job, and passed them on to Graham Clegg.

'They also gave me a torch, a motorbike and a little teddy that had to be placed in the coffin with him,' recalled Graham. 'Ray gave me the things. He said, "James never went to bed without his torch". Ralph and Denise were so strong it would have been wrong for anyone else to break down in front of them. I said to Ray, "I've got to go now," and left quickly'.

Denise and Ralph had laid the plans for the funeral service with meticulous care. Every aspect was discussed and planned with them. Father Michael O'Connell, the greying, bespectacled local parish priest who had comforted and helped them in the dark days that engulfed them following James's death, knew how important it was that they should decide on the content of the service.

'Sometimes I feel that people have their control taken away when something like this happens,' Father Michael explained. 'They are told what is to be done and how it is to be done. But it was their baby who was being buried and it was important that they had an input into it. Everything was being done for Denise and Ralph. They were having to keep out of the limelight because the press were around. The police were organizing their side of things and Ray Matthews and other members of the family were doing things for them. The funeral was something Denise and Ralph would look back on in years to come and either feel satisfied or unhappy. One reason they might be unhappy would be that they didn't get the chance to say what they would like to have happen for their child's funeral. It was important to involve them so they could own it and to help them come to terms and face the reality that this very bad dream they were going through wasn't a dream.

'It was important that they felt they were doing something for James. They weren't able to hug him and hold him or dress him. By involving them in picking the readings, hymns and prayers and checking all the details, they were able to feel they were doing something for their son'.

The impending service also forced Denise and Ralph to make their first excursion out of their flat since the discovery of their son's body. Anxious not to be recognized, they chose to head for Southport rather than Liverpool to buy clothes for the funeral. The seaside resort with its elegant, up-market shops lies several miles north of the main conurbations of Merseyside. 'I didn't ever think I would be picking funeral clothes for my own baby,' said Denise. 'I didn't even want to go shopping, but I knew I had to. I never intended to be dressed up. It was a Wednesday because I thought the shops would be empty on a Wednesday. I got my hair cut first so people wouldn't recognize me'.

Unfortunately they were recognized in a shop even there. 'I saw two women looking at me and thought nothing of it at first,' said Denise. 'Then one of them spoke to my sister Sheila and asked her if I was the mother of James. I just left the shop then. We didn't buy anything in Southport in the end. We went to Skelmersdale'. Nobody had meant them any harm, but it was the kind of encounter they had hoped to avoid as they tried to steel themselves for the ordeal ahead.

Denise chose a simple black outfit. The most important accessory was the hat. Its wide black brim would afford her a measure of privacy from the cameras in her most difficult moments. By gently bowing her head, her eyes and most of her face were shielded from the public gaze. 'I picked the biggest hat I' could find with a wide brim, because I knew what the day would be like, and I didn't want any pictures taken,' said Denise. 'When we got home, I just went straight back up to the bedroom again'.

On the Saturday the Sacred Heart Church was a hive of activity with church-goers and members of the community rallying to decorate the church. Police officers brought some of the flowers that had been laid in the Strand. Parents from Sacred Heart School moved benches and chairs and women cleaned and polished the furniture and arranged the flowers.

Meanwhile Father Michael went with the family to the Chapel of Rest in Maghull, where they were able to see the casket. 'It helped them touch some of the reality so the Monday wasn't the first time they were seeing the casket. We had a few prayers, and it was the first time some of us had seen the flowers that were going to be there at the funeral. It was a time when they were very close together'.

If the Bulgers were preparing with infinite care for their son's funeral, the plans laid by the police were no less meticulous. Nobody could have accurately predicted in advance the numbers who were likely to turn up outside the church or line the route on the journey to the cemetery. The police had to be prepared for any eventuality, and officers were on standby to cope with the possibility of thousands of onlookers.

More predictable was the huge international media turnout. Inspector Ray Simpson from the Merseyside Police press office once again had to arrange to cope with the massive influx of press, television and radio crews. There was to be a limited rota access for the church itself. One television crew and one radio team would be permitted inside, along with five news reporters including myself, and one photographer, the Press Association's David Jones. Other newsmen would be allowed to position themselves at 'fixed point' locations outside the church and outside the house the funeral was leaving from. Passes were granted for each location on the understanding that all material gained would be pooled with any other media organization requesting it. Plans even extended to arranging with the Civil Aviation Authority to impose an air exclusion zone over the church and cemetery to prevent the intrusion of helicopter-borne photographers.

My first port of call that Monday morning was Kirkby Police Station, in the town centre a short walk away from the church. There Inspector Simpson briefed the media on exactly what would be permissible. He stressed that facilities at the church had been granted on the strict understanding that the media would respect the wishes of the family to keep the burial at Kirkdale completely private. It was agreed that journalists could view the floral tributes when the graveside ceremony had concluded and the family had left. I have known Ray Simpson for a number of years. His relaxed and friendly manner and endless patience have made him a popular figure with the journalists who have had cause to deal with him. His words carried all the more weight, therefore, when he announced, unsmiling, that anyone breaching the family's privacy at the cemetery faced the risk of arrest.

Ray had been to Kirkby with television journalists and technicians on the Thursday before the funeral, to arrange the coverage of the funeral. They had met with Ray Matthews, Father Michael and Graham Clegg, and discussed just what would be acceptable coverage for the family. 'We didn't want it to turn into a circus,' said Ray. 'It was a family funeral and we didn't want anything to get in the way of that'.

We were a subdued group as we wove our way along the short route to the church that morning. Journalists don't relish having to be present at occasions like this. By and large they feel uncomfortable about the intrusion their very presence represents, and are only too eager to go about their necessary business as the eyes and ears of the world in as discreet and unobtrusive a way as possible. This day was charged with so much emotion that everyone felt on edge and uneasy. Reporters have wives and kids too. They may shield themselves behind a veneer of cynicism, but in truth they are no more immune to tragedy than anyone else.

Sacred Heart Church is a large, grey, unattractive looking building from the outside, constructed, like much of the housing in Kirkby, in an era when function was all and "architects seemed to lose sight of the importance of living in visually aesthetic surroundings. Built in 1963, the church was already scheduled for demolition because of major structural problems which had caused parts of the walls and ceiling to flake away. We arrived a full hour before the service was to begin. Many of the photographers and television camera crews were already in position, but only a handful of local people had so far appeared.

On arrival we found our way into the church barred by two very determined stewards. Even the police press officers could not persuade their way past them. These men had their orders from the priest that only the 350 invited mourners with their special pink passes issued by him with the family's approval were to be admitted. The message that a limited number of media representatives were also to be allowed inside had not filtered through to them. Their resolute faces summed up the tension everyone was feeling, and the determination that nothing should be allowed to intrude on this day for the Bulgers. Messages were passed inside the church, and in a matter of minutes the situation was resolved amicably and we were allowed in, but it had been a salutary reminder of the way some of the coverage of the case had alienated the Kirkby community against the media.

The interior of the church was much more traditional in its design and welcoming in its atmosphere. Children's simple paintings and friezes decorated the walls of the long, relatively narrow nave, one bearing the message 'Spring is here'. Behind the high altar the predominantly blue and purple stained-glass window bore the word 'Peace' and a depiction of a white dove.

We were ushered up a stairway to seats in the front row of a choir loft, perched high up at the rear of the church.

Behind us sat a twenty-four strong choir, made up of volunteers from churches throughout the town of Kirkby.

A simple wooden altar table at the front of the church was draped with a white cloth bearing the words 'Renew Our Faith'. The altar was decorated with daffodils, carnations and other colourful spring flowers. A small stand covered in red cloth was placed in front of the altar, ready to receive James's little coffin.

Mourners with their special passes began arriving about forty-five minutes before the service was due to begin, led to their places on the wooden pews by ushers wearing white armbands. An organist softly played 'Pie Jesu', from Andrew Lloyd Webber's Requiem, together with more traditional religious themes.

Some of the faces were familiar, and one or two were famous. Albert Kirby, Jim Fitzsimmons, Mandy Waller, Jim Green and other members of the police Murder Squad were there, along with local dignitaries and council officials. Margi Clarke, actress daughter of a former mayor of the borough of Knowsley and a film star whose most notable success was the internationally acclaimed Letter to Brezhnev, sat quietly with her mother.

Outside a small crowd began to form. By the time the service began some 500 people had gathered, tearful mothers clutching the hands of their little children or hugging them against the cold, biting wind and occasion," gentle flurries of snow. Loudspeakers were to relay the service to them, and the television cameras were to transmit the service to millions more in their homes in Britain, and nations as far apart as Japan, Australia and the USA.

Television presenter and journalist Anne Diamond, whose Good Morning programme was providing live coverage of the funeral on BBC television, found it an especially poignant occasion. She lost her own baby son Sebastian to the tragic phenomenon of cot death in 1991. In an interview for the Liverpool Echo newspaper on the day of the funeral, she asked, 'How will they ever get over it? People have always said to me there is nothing worse than losing a child. Frankly, there is. Losing a child to a violent death is far, far worse'.

Simultaneous services were being held at London's Westminster Cathedral and at many other churches around the country. Other places of worship opened their doors for those moved to private prayer. A small crowd, of shoppers in the Strand Shopping Centre in Bootle stopped outside a Granada television showroom to watch the funeral scenes through the shop window on two large " television screens. Some were in tears.

Among those gathering outside the Kirkby church was one of Kirkby's best-loved sons, Phil Thompson, the former Liverpool soccer skipper and England international defender. Today he was just one of the crowd, a father of three young children, there like the others to show that he cared. 'I just felt I had to be here today for the Bulger family,' he said. 'I am a Kirkby lad and there has been some undeserved bad publicity about Kirkby over this. We don't want sympathy off anyone. We just feel for the family.

Denise and Ralph waited for the funeral cortege at Denise's mother Eileen's neat terraced house in Scoter Road, less than 400 yards from the church. Other close relatives arrived carrying flowers. Neighbours had their blinds and curtains closed in a traditional mark of respect.

Some ten minutes before the service was due to begin, a fleet of fourteen sleek midnight-blue limousines pulled up outside the house. With all the family allocated their seats there should have been thirteen cars. Graham Clegg was not happy with that idea. He had arranged for a fourteenth vehicle to carry the clergy from the church to the cemetery. Identical cars had been loaned from funeral directors in Blackpool and Leigh, Lancashire, to ensure that every car in the procession matched. Every detail had to be perfect that day.

The first three cars were hearses completely filled with beautiful flowers from all over the world. They were followed by the hearse containing the youngster's body in a small, white wooden casket with gleaming metal handles.

Flowers from his immediate family surrounded the casket. A large floral display picking out the word 'JAMES' had been placed alongside the coffin, together with a teddy bear in carnations. A few neighbours came out of their houses to watch, many of them weeping silently as the family prepared to leave on the brief journey. Denise and Ralph walked briskly out and climbed into the fifth car, immediately behind James's hearse. The rest of this large, devastated family made their way to the other cars and took their places, and the cortege made its slow, respectful way to the gates of the church.

As the family made their short ride, Father Michael briefly addressed the congregation and those waiting outside the church. 'I want you this morning to really sing your hearts out,' he said. 'We want you outside to be as much a part of our funeral Mass this morning as the people are inside. I would ask you outside to join with us in the hymns inside'.

The cortege arrived and funeral attendants opened car doors and helped the family form their procession. It only took four men to carry the tiny burden of James's casket. Ralph took the right, front corner of the white solid oak box on his shoulder for the walk to the doors of the church. Ray Matthews took the left corner, Gary Matthews and Philip Bulger supporting the rear corners. A dainty little posy of freesias rested on top of the gleaming nameplate. Father O'Connell and the other seven clergymen assisting in the service awaited them in the doorway in their cream and white vestments. Denise walked immediately behind her son's coffin, keeping her head slightly bowed. The congregation stood in silence as a red and white wreath was carried to be laid in front of the coffin stand. The entrance hymn was traditional and familiar. Everyone sang 'The Old Rugged Cross' with the gusto called for by the priest. It was a way of releasing some of the pent-up tension. The procession, led by the clergymen, made its way slowly to the front of the church, where Ralph and the other three bearers gently lowered the coffin into place. Ralph then moved to take his place in the front pew alongside his wife, as the rows behind them filled up with their relatives. Father O'Connell moved over from the altar to extend a few whispered words of comfort to Denise and Ralph as the hymn drew to a close. To the right of James's coffin his favourite little red armchair made for him by his father was placed on the altar. A teddy-bear and a cuddly rabbit, gifts to James from his grandparents, were seated on the chair.

After the hymn Father O'Connell spoke his words of welcome to the congregation, adding thoughts for those outside and watching and listening to broadcasts around the world. 'We offer our sincerest sympathy to Denise and Ralph and all the family on the loss they have suffered,' he said. 'The mass readings and hymns have all been chosen and prepared by Denise and Ralph and their family. I would ask you to listen really carefully to those prayers and readings and ask what is God saying to you and asking of us on this occasion. I would like you to be free to be moved by the Spirit, to allow yourself to feel free to sing, to cry, to grieve for Denise and Ralph and your own lost children, or even to give thanks for the gift you have in your home of your precious little ones'.

In his opening prayer, Father Michael said: 'God of all consolation, searcher of mind and heart, you know the burden of grief that Ralph and Denise and all of us feel at the loss of this child. Comfort us with the knowledge that the child for whom we grieve is entrusted now to your loving care. Take him into your arms and welcome him into paradise where there will be no more sorrow, no weeping nor pain, but only the fullness of peace and joy with your Son and the Holy Spirit for ever and ever. Amen'.

Ronnie Fulham gave the first Bible reading, and the congregation sang the 23rd Psalm. Then Albert Kirby moved to the lectern to deliver his reading, from the Book of Revelation. The detective, a church-going man with a strong moral code, kept his emotions firmly in check, his voice warm and reassuring as he read from the biblical text. 'I felt tremendously honoured as an individual and a police officer when the family asked if I would do a reading at the service,' he recalled. 'I immediately said yes. It was difficult to do it, but no more difficult than what everyone else was doing. The public saw a different side of the police force on this case, that we do care for people and aren't just machines doing a job'.

After his reading, Mr Kirby went back to his place among the congregation and the Rev. Bernard Schunemann, the Anglican curate of nearby St Mark's Church who had spoken so movingly on the nature of evil at the special service in the town on the Friday after James died, gave a Gospel reading.

Meanwhile, Father O'Connell prepared himself for he delivery of what must have been the most difficult homily he had ever had to give. We in the media had been asking the Roman Catholic press officer for days for an advance of the text of Father Michael's address but it had not been possible for the simple reason that he was still struggling to find the right words.

'A part of me was resisting sitting down and writing out a word for the homily because I would only be doing that for the press,' he recalled. 'The funeral was for the family, and if things were written down I would lose some of the freedom to be spontaneous or change things around depending what was happening in front of me and the vibes I was picking up from the family.

'The fact that I would have the eyes of the world on me entered into my thinking at an early stage and the option was that one could play to camera and preach to the world and have a cathedral-style service with all the frills that go with that. Or we could conduct it as a personal funeral for a family, and if the world wanted to look in then they were very welcome and if they wanted to partake in it then they were even more welcome. That is the way I decided it should be. It was a style that was comfortable for me and the way it would have been whether the cameras were there or not'.

Father Michael looked older than his thirty-six years as he stood up to speak. Listening and speaking to Denise, Ralph and the family in the days leading up to the funeral, he had drawn close to them. He and the other clergy he worked with had done what they could to help them. It had been a team effort from him and his colleagues, but for this particular day it was Father Michael who had the main burden to shoulder. He had not slept at all on the Sunday night. He had made himself a cup of coffee late that evening and carried it into the church, where he sat quietly in front of the sanctuary. 'That was my time of talking to God and saying, "What do you want me to do?"' he recalled. He had sat there, thinking and praying, until he was disturbed by the arrival of the first television technicians at 6.30 that Monday morning.

From whatever source, words did not fail him when his moment came. The words he delivered with his gentle Irish lilt visibly moved and I feel sure gave comfort to those struggling to understand this innocent little boy's cruel and inexplicable death. The priest knew well enough that millions of eyes were on him as he spoke, but showed no sign of it. He focused his words directly and simply on the bereaved family, speaking plain words of compassion and love.

'Everyone's heart absolutely goes out to you,' he said. 'We wish we could turn the clock back two and a half weeks. We wish we could make things better. We wish so much we could bring James back to you both and to all of us, but we can't. All we can do is often you our support, share with you our faith, acknowledge with you the loss you are feeling and the gift God gave us in James Patrick.

'Almost three years ago James was born. In that three years James shared so much with us. The only reason I can stand here this morning is because of my faith in Jesus Christ. God the Father loved us so much he sent Jesus Christ to show us that we can do it, that we can get through anything that we can survive, that we can conquer. Probably the greatest thing we fear is death. We can put up with sciatica and broken legs but we hate to hear the words leukaemia or cancer because of what they may signify. We can't bear to think about death'. But he added that Jesus Christ had showed by conquering death that it was not the end and did not have to be feared any more.

He said that James had experienced almost three years nine months of life, including the time he had been safe and warm in the womb. 'Then the time came for him to be born ... but how did that baby in that womb feel being pushed down a dark passageway? To that baby it might have felt like death but for us on the other side it was life -it was being born into this world. We live here and grow up here and we call it life and call it our world, and then the time comes again for us to die, to be born once more and for the final time into eternal life. That is where James is now, gone into that eternal life where there is no more pain and no more suffering'.

A baby started to cry in the congregation, the sound echoing around the church in a poignant counterpoint to Father O'Connell's words as he continued, speaking of the community projects and the good things started as a result of James's death. 'Even though we can't touch him, he is still influencing us, and having a power over us. His death is not in vain. Something in James Patrick has touched the whole world and maybe they will respond. It has brought something out of us deep down. The death of an innocent little child is causing us to do something about it and make life better.

'For three years we had James and in that three years from what I can gather he certainly developed a personality of his own, fond of his dancing, putting on his Michael Jackson music, someone who liked to make people laugh, someone who was always in good form, someone who liked his own chair, someone we are going to miss very much. James Patrick didn't waste life. He lived those three years to the full and put all his energies into it, staying up at night right until the last minute. Jesus Christ didn't turn the children away from him. James Patrick has his very own little chair up in heaven now. Maybe he has James Patrick on his knee. We are going to miss him every day for the rest of our life because we never forget and won't ever get over him. Time does not heal. Time just helps us to cope a little bit better. Let all he stood for, his innocence, love of life and music, his good humour and fun, his spontaneity, let all that continue to come to us now. Let us spread it out throughout the rest of Northwood, Kirkby and Merseyside. Life has changed, it hasn't ended. Let that change be as best we can make it, supporting one another in our tears and giving one another help and encouragement. Let us put our faith and trust in God and one another. Let this be a beginning'.

The power of these words left much to ponder over as some of James's aunts and uncles read prayers and took part in the offertory procession, bringing the gifts of bread and wine to the altar ready for the Communion rite. Two hymns were sung as the congregation took Communion. 'I Will Never Forget You' and 'Make Me a Channel of Your Peace' were the touchingly appropriate selections Denise and Ralph had made. Then, as the mourners resumed their seats, the organ music faded, to be replaced by a more contemporary sound. A recording of Michael Jackson singing 'Heal the World' was played. Many of his relatives must have been casting their thoughts back at that moment to images of bubbly James dancing to the stars music in happier days. At any rate, the song served to release the emotion many of those present had been struggling to hold back. Suddenly handkerchiefs were out. Men, women and children sobbed and dabbed their eyes. Denise and Ralph clung closely to each other in the front row as they had throughout, sometimes he with his arm wrapped round her, at others she holding on tightly to his arm as they drew their strength from each other.

Before the day was out news of the song being played at the service had reached Jackson in America. He sent a message of condolence to the family through the UK office of his Heal the World Foundation, saying he was 'grief-stricken' by the news of James's death. We must all unite and work together to heal the world on behalf of our children to ensure they are able to live in the safe and caring environment to which they are entitled,' he said, in a message conveyed to the family by Merseyside Police. A bouquet of flowers from the star followed the next day.

When the tape ended the various clergy led the congregation in a series of prayers of commendation. Incense was spread around the coffin during the final blessing; its sweet smell hanging heavy in the air during the closing hymn.

As the funeral procession formed up to leave the church, another taped contemporary song was played. 'Tears in Heaven', Eric Clapton's Emmy award-winning song for his five-year-old son Conor, who fell to his death from a New York skyscraper in a tragic domestic accident, could almost have been commissioned for this occasion. It certainly brought the tears pricking back into many swollen eyes in the sombre church. As the music played Ralph and the other bearers collected the coffin again for its last journey. His face was a frozen mask of suppressed pain, his red-rimmed eyes staring straight ahead. Denise followed close behind the coffin, her head bowed, the brim of her hat doing its job for her. As they made their way down the central aisle of the church I could only marvel at the astonishing reserves of dignity and self-control the couple had drawn on to get them through this ordeal. They had passed their test of courage.

Then they were gone, the funeral cortege making its slow and respectful progress towards the cemetery where, thankfully, the much maligned media kept their part of the bargain and left the Bulgers to say their last goodbyes to their son in private. A message of thanks was later passed on by the police.

Father Michael accompanied James on the journey, sitting in the hearse. For the first time, he allowed himself the luxury of tears. 'In the church you are there not for yourself but for others. If you need something for yourself later you have a duty to pick it up at some other time. That funeral was their time and my part was to be the channel.

'When I came out in the car I saw all the people standing there outside and we got to the top of the road and turned left and all the people were lining the streets. I cried then, till we got to the cemetery. That was my time to cry. I was alone then.

'I thought of all the things that certain press people had written about Kirkby and I thought, "How could they write those things about such fabulous people?" I have been in Kirkby for eleven years. Everybody knows everybody there, and they are 'a community that support each other fantastically in times of need. They rise to occasions. They share everything'.

The route to Kirkdale cemetery was lined with people. Traffic came to a halt as motorists paid their respects. An RAC patrolman stopped his van, climbed out and bowed his head as the long cortege cruised slowly by.

In the privacy of the cemetery the family got out of their cars and were handed bags of rose petals by the funeral attendants. Graham Clegg had asked florists in the area who were preparing tributes for the funeral to provide rose petals, and the response had been massive. The other invited mourners gathered around the grave. They had been brought from the church by coach and were then ahead of the family. Among them were some of the police officers who had been at the scene when James was found. 'I think that anyone very much involved was helped by seeing that he was at rest after what he had gone through,' said Graham. The family had been pleased to grant their request to attend.

Ray Matthews gave Mandy Waller a warm embrace. Then one of the policemen who had been at the scene, a big man with a beard, put his arms around Ray and shook his hand. The officer broke down crying. 'I wish we could have done more for you,' he said.

At the conclusion of the graveside ceremony, Denise, Ralph and their closest relatives placed single red roses on James's casket. The other mourners sprinkled rose petals down into the grave.

'I hate to see soil thrown into a grave, and it was especially so in James's case,' said Graham. 'I felt he had had enough thrown at him. His grave had to be as peaceful as it could be. The white casket with a multitude of colourful petals made somewhere so dark look bright. He was in a bed of roses.'

'Denise and Ralph were exactly the same as they had been at the church. I don't know where they got their strength from. They are just amazing people really. Everyone conducted themselves the same way. I don't think anyone wanted to let Ralph and Denise down. There were tears in everyone's eyes, mine and my staff's included, but there was so much dignity.

'As the family went back to the cars I spent a few moments looking at the grave. I thought, "He has gone through a lot, that little boy. Now he is at rest." '

By the time I was able to make my way out of the packed church the cars were already out of sight on the journey to the cemetery. The chill wind bit instantly through my warm overcoat. If anything the temperature had dropped further, and I found myself shivering. Yet it was a relief to be out there in the fresh air, breathing deeply, clearing my head after the charged atmosphere of the seventy-five minute mass.

Sean Sexton was waiting there to pass on the family's thanks for the 'absolutely magnificent' support the public had given them. 'The family wanted the community here to share with them in their grief and that is what has happened,' he said. 'It is amazing how the family are coping and the dignity they have shown is remarkable'. Nobody could dispute those sentiments.

All that was left for me now was to file my immediate story quickly and go to a nearby hotel to compare notes with Peter Beal and Stephen Guy, two colleagues from the Press Association's Manchester office who had been covering the scenes outside, and prepare a more considered piece for morning papers. It was a day I had been dreading, and it was a huge relief to have it over and done with.

For the Bulgers, of course, it will never be over and done with. After watching their son's little coffin finally laid to rest they returned to Kirkby to a quiet, subdued reception for close family and friends in the church hall. The police officers stayed away, feeling it was a time for the family. Denise was to tell Mandy Walk the next day that she and the others would have welcome. When it was over they went back round the corner to Eileen's house, with just their own recollections and a few photographs to remind them of their poor little child.

Alongside his grave they had left a floral arrangement depicting the gates of Heaven. With it was a card with a brief verse. It read: 'James, our beautiful baby son. We didn't get to say goodbye and that really makes us cry. You brought so much love in our lives, That love for us will never die. The only thing that we can do is sit and pray for you. In our hearts you will still be there, locked inside our loving care. God, look after him as we would do for we are sure that he is with you. Goodnight and God bless James Patrick. All our love, Hugs and kisses, Mum and Dad'.

There were four kisses at the foot of the card.

Chapter Twelve

So James Bulger had finally been laid to rest. Ahead, for his parents and family, lay a long and painful grieving process. For the police and the lawyers, the months that followed were to be a time of meticulous planning to play their part in what all knew would be a historic murder trial. For the politicians, the pundits and the public at large, it was a time to search the soul of the nation.

What Robert Thompson and Jon Venables did frightened Britain in a way no other crime had done in a long time. This was not some sick adult serial killer or deranged terrorist group. It was two children of an age automatically associated with innocence. The effect on the national psyche is well illustrated by a survey of 1000 parents around Britain carried out by the charity Kidscape in July 1993. It found that 98 per cent of parents now said that abduction of their children was their biggest fear, overshadowing worries about road safety, drug abuse, video nasties and television violence.

Almost from the moment James's body was found on the railway line, the first simmerings of a huge political debate began. The middle classes of Britain had been uneasily aware for a long time of a growing juvenile crime problem that was encroaching increasingly on their lives. Whether it was teenagers hanging around in large, bored, intimidating groups on street corners, the ugly aggression of the 'yob culture' that could make even a visit to the local pub anything but relaxing, or the experience of a personal encounter with the kind of casual violence that it seemed could erupt so startlingly and unpredictably almost anywhere, we all knew that these were worrying times.

But this sudden, shocking crime galvanized popular opinion. If we were now in a society where ten-year-olds could kill a two-year-old child for kicks, there had to be action. It was time to turn the tide.

Home Office crime figures show that one in three men (33 per cent) and 8 per cent of women born in 1953 had been convicted of an offence by the age of thirty-five, excluding motoring offences and minor matters like drunkenness. In 1970 1.6 million offences were recorded by police in England and Wales, a figure that has grown steadily by an average 5 per cent a year until in 1992 the total reached 5.6 million. Over 80 per cent of known offenders were male, 46 per cent were under twenty-one and one in five under seventeen. Official figures showed a fall in juvenile offending over the last ten years, but a combination of a demographic reduction in the juvenile population and changes in police policy towards issuing more unofficial cautions to juveniles hides statistically what experts believe is in truth a substantial increase in offences.

Juvenile crime, and the seeming inability of the judicial system to combat it adequately, became the hottest issue around in the weeks following James Bulger's death. The newspapers carried a seemingly endless catalogue of cases of young delinquents who seemed beyond any control.

In March Mr Justice Holland, dealing at Durham Crown Court with a fourteen-year-old boy sex attacker he described as 'an outlaw', admitted he was powerless to place him in custody after he had pleaded guilty to indecently assaulting a fifteen-year-old schoolgirl pinned down in a churchyard and raped by another youth. Persistent juvenile offenders can be sent to detention centres at age fifteen, but below that age courts can only commit them to a secure unit if they commit grave offences like murder and rape, carrying a maxim penalty of fourteen or more years. All the judge could do was return the boy to care, and within a month he absconded twice in a matter of hours from the unlocked children's home - taking his total number of times 'on the run' to twenty-five in two years. The boy, with forty-three previous convictions, faced Gosforth Youth Court in Newcastle-upon-Tyne on 31 March and admitted eleven offences including car theft, burglary and carrying an offensive weapon. All the magistrates could do was place him under the supervision of the local authority once again. Magistrate Edna Maier said, 'We feel very strongly, as does the public, that these offences warrant a custodial sentence. However, our hands are tied'.

The same court found itself dealing with a thirteen-year-old so-called 'Rat Boy' who lived in makeshift hideouts in a maze of ventilation shafts in the Byker Wall housing complex in Byker, Newcastle. The boy, who had absconded from care or run away from home more than thirty times, admitted four burglaries, three of them on the homes of elderly women, and butting a policeman in the face. A one-year supervision order was his 'sentence'.

Two twelve-year-old girls were cautioned after soliciting in red light districts around Walsall in the West Midlands within a few days of each other. One had run away from home and the other from her foster parents' home.

On 8 March, two seventeen-year-old girls, Maria Rossi and Tina Molloy, were ordered to be detained indefinitely by Cardiff Crown Court for the murder of seventy-one-year-old, partially blind spinster Edna Phillips, who was choked with her dog's lead, slashed thirty-five times with a carpet knife, stabbed, stamped on and battered in her home in Penywaun, Mid-Glamorgan, in July 1992.

On 19 March, fourteen-year-old Sally Ann Cattell died at the wheel of a high-powered Austin Metro car she had taken after overturning it in a 70-mph police chase in Birmingham.

The stories continued. Every day's headlines seemed to contain another outrage or another tragedy brought on by the seemingly unchecked explosion of youth crime. And this was not just a problem of the 'underclass'.

The hierarchy of the judiciary was only too aware of the need to respond to public opinion in the levels of punishment it was able to impose. The Lord Chief Justice, Lord Taylor, told the annual conference of the Law Society of Scotland on 21 March that the 1991 Criminal Justice Act had forced judges into 'an ill-fitting straitjacket 'by restricting the sentences they could impose. 'I believe the fundamental error underlying the Act is a misconceived notion that sentencing should be programmed to restrict the discretion of the sentencing judge,' he said. 'It is of prime importance that sentences passed should not be so far out of touch with the expectations of ordinary law-abiding citizens as to create discontent'.

'However forward-thinking the penologists, criminologists and bureaucrats in government departments may be, their views should not be allowed to prevail so as to impose a sentencing regime which is incomprehensible or unacceptable to right-thinking people generally. If that happens, there could be a real risk of aggrieved parties taking the law into their own hands'.

Prime Minister John Major gave an early political lead on the issue. He said in a Mail on Sunday interview on 21 February: 'I would like the public to have a crusade against crime and change from being forgiving of crime to being considerate to the victim. Society needs to condemn a little more and understand a little less'.

The same day, Britain's then Home Secretary Kenneth Clarke spoke on BBC Radio Four of a loss of values and sense of purpose among the young, and a feeling that they could get away with anything. 'I do believe the courts should have the power to send really persistent nasty little juveniles away to somewhere where they will be looked after better and where they will be educated,' he said. Turning to social workers, he added: 'They have to accept they are not succeeding at the moment with children. It is no good mouthing political rhetoric about why children in their care are so delinquent. John Major and I believe it is no good that some sections of society are permanently finding excuses for the behaviour of the section of the population who are essentially nasty pieces of work. You have to be able to arrest them, convict them before properly conducted courts and then have a regime of punishment in prison which is so organized that it might make them capable of reform'.

On 12 March Mr Clarke returned to the theme when he addressed the Conservative western area conference at Weston-super-Mare. 'I want more emphasis on the fear of deterrents than the fear of crime,' he said, promising a crack-down on persistent, out of control juvenile offenders. 'This requires a new regime and above all, new custodial powers for the courts to lock up twelve-to fifteen-year-olds which they do not currently have,' he added.

Mr Clarke announced a £75 million plan for five secure centres, with forty to fifty places each, where boys aged twelve to fifteen who had already been convicted of three imprisonable offences could be detained under a new sentence called a secure training order. Unlike the harsh, disciplined regime of the old Borstals, boys at these centres would be given high standards of care, including education and training as well as discipline, to build their characters. They would stay for an average of six months to a year with close supervision afterwards.

Social security secretary Peter Lilley wrote in the News of the World on 7 March that the break-up of families was to blame for the spread of serious crime 'like a plague' through Britain's young people. He said that in thirty years the number of divorces had risen six-fold while the proportion of children born out of wedlock had grown five-fold. Mr Lilley said this problem was at the heart of the upsurge in criminality.

The opposition benches of Britain's parliament were not slow to enter the discussion, with Labour's Shadow Home Secretary Tony Blair speaking out resolutely on the need for action. In a Daily Mirror article on 22 February he wrote: 'There is something very wrong and very sick at the heart of our society. I believe it is time to rebuild Britain as a community where there is respect for others, common decency and a shared sense of values, where we feel - and are - part of the same country'.

He criticized the government for complacency, and said criminals of ten or eleven did not just happen. Broken homes, bad housing, poor education, no job or training, and a lack of hope or opportunity all affected the way a child developed, he argued. But his line was anything but soft on young offenders. 'Those young kids who had become a real danger to society, who are out of control, will have to be put in some sort of secure accommodation. That is the tragedy - but there is no other realistic option if the public is to be properly protected'.

From professionals in many areas connected directly with tackling the problems of youth crime, there seemed to be a genuine degree of consensus emerging, at least in identifying the nature of the problem society faced.

Masud Hoghughi, fifty-five-year-old director of the Aycliffe Centre for delinquent and disturbed children in County Durham, one of the few centres at the time which included secure accommodation for serious offenders, commented in the Sunday Times magazine: 'James Bulger's murder was a watershed for the country: it made the nation wake up to the fact that young people at the margins of our society are out of control. Why? Everything which gives us a sense of self-worth is deteriorating. We are creating a society of envy where the prevailing value is how much money you have, not your worth as an individual'.

John Findlay, of local government union NALGO, which represents education welfare officers, claimed in the Daily Mirror that juvenile crime could double in five years unless there was a crack-down on the half a million school children estimated to be playing truant every day. He said 5-10 per cent of youngsters are absent from school every day, and the country needed an extra 900 education welfare officers to keep the lid on the crisis. 'Children playing truant are not necessarily going to become criminals. But they are more likely to be on the streets and exposed to juvenile crime. Many are sucked into it,' he said. 'Unless there is change, there is going to be a massive explosion in juvenile crime. We fear shoplifting, drugs, car thefts and vandalism by juveniles could double in five years'.

Merseyside's neighbouring county of Cheshire suffered an increase in crime of 2.3 per cent from 1991 to 1992, with one in five detected offences committed by under-thirteens. Reflecting on the problem in his annual report, Chief Constable David Graham said: 'This clearly raises questions about parental responsibilities. One wonders if the values and standards of past generations are being eroded to such an extent that an increasing number of young people are left drifting helplessly to determine their own values and standards in an increasingly materialistic society'.

The lack of moral guidance available to many children became a recurring theme in the debate. Parents, and particularly single parents, often lacked the time or the patience to drum into their children the values of right and wrong. Many modern schools also failed to provide proper moral guidance to their pupils. The prevailing political ideologies of the progressive Left of the 1960s, when the 'nuclear family' became derided and devalued, and the 'winner takes all' self-interest of the Thatcher years in the 1980s placed little value on the importance of a strong moral framework.

The Archbishop of Canterbury, on a visit to Merseyside on 24 March, said: 'For children, the family is by far the most important influence for good or ill, though by no means the only one. It is extremely difficult to learn to be good without the love, support and guidance of parents. As I have said elsewhere, it can be the easiest thing in the world to become a parent, but being a good parent is difficult and requires sacrifice and unconditional love. As the extended family unit becomes less common, young parents need other sources of help in their demanding task. If we want to stop young children roaming the streets causing harm to themselves and others, it is above all the parents who must be challenged and helped'.

The Archbishop warned that a vision based on shared commitment to a moral society was needed for all the souls of the country. 'If morality continues to become a mere matter of individual opinion, our society will continue to disintegrate. I sense a gathering current of opinion which holds this individualization of belief and morality to be a public disaster of gigantic proportions, at the levels of individual, family and wider collective behaviour. If right and wrong become merely relative to each person's individual instincts and calculations, society loses its cohesion'.

Given that the 'underclass' of marginalized, alienated people trapped by desperate circumstances at the margins of our society is very much a reality in the 1990s, bringing about a moral revival on the scale required to put society back on track will take something more fundamental than locking up the extreme young tearaways in an environment that will genuinely help them, important though that is. The problem looks so overwhelming that it can almost make you despair. But a start has to be made somewhere.

At the end of June, the Family Policy Studies Centre, Crime Concern and NACRO published a report entitled Crime and the Family—Improving Child Rearing and Preventing Delinquency. Its three authors, David Utting, Jon Bright and Clem Henricson, conducted an in-depth review of criminological research in Britain and the USA connecting family circumstances to the risks that children would turn to crime. What many others had concluded, based on 'gut instinct' about the causes of juvenile crime, this report verified through hard evidence. It was also able to go on and make some of the most constructive suggestions to date about fundamental ways of preventing juvenile crime.

The report said that poor parental supervision, harsh, neglectful or erratic discipline, parental discord, and having a parent with a criminal record, were among the main childhood factors consistently and significantly linked to later teenaged offending. Other factors it identified included low family income, social disadvantage, including coming from a large family, low achievement in school and aggressive and troublesome behaviour. Several of these factors were clearly at work in Robert Thompson and Jon Venables. Aggression in young children has been linked to deficient relationships with their parents when they were as young as twelve or eighteen months old, the report adds. Deprivation and inadequate care in the home experienced by five-year-olds had similarly been linked to later offending.

Author David Utting, a research fellow at the Family Policy Studies Centre, said: 'It would be ridiculous to lay all the blame for rising crime at the feet of parents. But there is reason to believe that raising children has become a more difficult task which today's parents carry out in greater isolation from support that was once available from the extended family. Whether we are talking about children living with two parents, one parent or in stepfamilies, it is clear that affectionate parenting and consistent discipline helps protect against acquiring a criminal record'.

The report finds that some studies in Britain and America suggest that children who experience divorce are at greater risk of delinquency. A comparative analysis of results from fifty different surveys concluded that delinquency might be 15-20 per cent more prevalent among children from broken homes. The correlations were stronger with truancy and under-aged drinking and smoking than with serious crime. It was thought that the discord that surrounded separation was what caused these harmful types of behaviour rather than the act of divorce. Homes that were intact but neglectful and unhappy were more likely to produce delinquent children than broken homes where children were nurtured and loved.

The report said that a national initiative should be launched to tackle the roots of delinquency through improving parenting skills and supporting vulnerable families in the task of raising children. It argues that all parents and children should have access to parent education programmes, pregnancy and post-natal care guiding new parents into networks where support and advice are available, and courses for improving parental skills. It calls for good quality, affordable childcare for working parents, 'effectiveness' programmes in primary and secondary schools to ensure minimum reading and mathematical skills and to maintain liaison with parents, and family planning and 'preparation for family life' education as part of the national curriculum in secondary schools. The report says the schools should forge an effective partnership with parents to tackle education under-achievement and specific behavioural problems like bullying. The report also recommends that families in disadvantaged, high-crime neighbourhoods should have increased support. 'This, it says, should include more open access family centres with services ranging from parent and toddler clubs to education in parental skills and family therapy. These centres should be opened to the whole community to avoid stigmatizing families under stress.

Other measures advocated include remedial design work for high-crime estates, community policing to include preventive work with families, and after-school clubs and holiday activities for children and young people.

Families under severe stress who have already come to the attention of social workers or the police, should, says the report, have family support volunteers to help parents and children in their homes, and intensive 'family preservation' services to prevent family breakdown when children are at imminent risk of being taken into care. Two innovative examples cited in the study are the Newpin voluntary agency set up in South London in 1981 and now working in London, Gravesend and Bristol, and the Families First programme in Michigan, USA.

One other recommendation which the report says would be of particular benefit would be the more widespread provision of pre-school education. About half of all three to four-year-olds in Britain attend at least one pre-school playgroup session a week, but those from disadvantaged backgrounds are the least likely to be among the 46 per cent of three-to five-year-olds who go to nursery schools or infant schools. An American research project in Michigan following the fortunes of disadvantaged black children who had a pre-school education more than twenty-five years ago showed that it was estimated to have saved the American taxpayer 7 dollars in real terms in reduced crime and other social costs for every dollar invested.

This positive and imaginative programme of improved services and facilities would clearly cost a great deal of money, at a time when public spending in Britain is under even greater than normal constraint. Before these ideas are dismissed out of hand on financial grounds, though, the report also points out that the criminal justice system in England and Wales alone costs over £9 billion a year to administer. David Utting said: 'If only a modest proportion of those resources could be devoted to preventing the social cancer of crime, we believe the savings in public health and wealth would more than justify the initial costs'.

Whether any of these measures, had they been available to the Thompson or Venables families, might in some way have prevented Robert and Jon from reaching the point of committing their crime, it is impossible to say. In the final analysis, it is worth reminding ourselves-reassuring ourselves, perhaps-that we are dealing with an incredibly unusual set of circumstances here. The crimes of Robert Thompson and Jon Venables are not so much part of a trend as a dreadful extreme, an aberration.

Until now, Britain's most notorious child killer was Mary Bell, who was eleven when she killed Martin Brown, four, and Brian Howe, three, in Newcastle. She was convicted of manslaughter in 1968 and sentenced to life. At the trial psychiatrists remarked on her 'lack of feeling', and one, Dr David Westbury, later described her as a 'manipulator' and a 'psychopathic personality suffering from an abnormality of mind arising from a combination of genetic factors and environmental influence'. Mary Bell was released in January 1980, just before her twenty-third birthday. She remained on 'life licence', which meant she had to keep in contact with supervisory authorities.

A boy of eight was accused of killing his seventeen-month-old baby brother in the 1950s after the child's crying disturbed him as he did his homework at the family home on the Isle of Wight. He hit him on the head with a feeding bottle. The prosecution eventually offered no evidence because it could not sustain an argument against the strong presumption of innocence of intent in a child so young. The case was dismissed and the boy went home to his parents. The minimum age of criminal responsibility was then eight, but in the wake of this case was raised to ten in the 1963 Children and Young Persons Act.

In October 1988, in a case with some chilling parallels with the killing of James Bulger, Ciaron Collins was convicted by Chelmsford Crown Court of the abduction and murder of Sharona Joseph. Collins was twelve when he lured Sharon, two years seven months, from her sister Daniella's ninth birthday party at the Aberford Community

Centre in Borehamwood, Hertfordshire, on 22 February that year. He took her to a grassy embankment by the St Pancras-Sheffield railway line, pushed her face into the ground and suffocated her. Sentencing the boy to be detained at Her Majesty's pleasure, Mr Justice Caulfield said, 'You have carried out a most wicked act against a little girl who could not possibly harm anybody, and even after death the evidence shows that you desecrated her little body'. The court had heard that Collins's parents had divorced after his natural father had been jailed for drug offences soon after his birth. Two other relatives he had been close to had died. Once he moved to Borehamwood and the divorce went through, he descended into delinquency. His mother set up home with another man who tried to discipline him but was convicted of common assault against the boy in 1985. He had run-ins with the law for minor thefts and arson, repeatedly ran away from home and was made the subject of a temporary order to Rufford House Children's Home in Watford. Collins had absconded from the home at 5 a.m. on the day of the murder.

Professor Ken Roberts, Professor of Sociology at Liverpool University, said: 'These cases, when they happen, are one-offs. They get latched in the memory. It is so unusual that you still remember these names years and years after -like Mary Bell or the Moors murderers. Throughout history there have been these one-off cases of horrific crime, which are not part of any general trend'.

Professor Roberts was quick to dismiss media suggestions that the crime was in some way representative of the particular problems of Merseyside. 'The coverage it attracted is because of Liverpool and its image,' he said. 'The general perception is of an area in decline with a lot of bad areas and a lot of crime.

'There are large areas where life is rough and kids are out of control. Liverpool is an extreme case. The way Britain as a whole is heading. Liverpool is where it is going to. The economic base in Liverpool began to decline at the time of the First World War and has been declining ever since. In other parts of Britain, dependent on manufacturing, it has been happening since the 1960s.

'Economic decline and persistent unemployment interact with a weakening of family life -but that isn't just a Liverpool problem. In poorer parts of Britain, in the past you at least had the family and the community, but now that is no longer true. The working class is now much more fragmented and individualized and households are privatized'.

He said the economic decline had broken up Liverpool's strong historical community ties, but the dramatic redevelopment programme to move people out of the city accelerated that process. 'You now have more children being reared by single parents but who have long periods in households existing on the minimum state level. If you go to working-class areas in Liverpool now, the children being brought up in the Bulger way, where everything is stable and they are close-knit, have become much more rare. Families are affected by unemployment, and children are being reared by single parents or living with step-parents. These trends between what it was and is now are particularly stark in Liverpool-but I don't think that explains the killing of a child.

'As I said, you get occasional, one-off child murders everywhere. Maybe it is because it was Liverpool, with its extreme examples of the way things are moving, that people try to make a connection. Wider public opinion sees this as one more example of the way society is heading, with Liverpool as a clear example -general threats to order, rising crime, riots, and now taking infants out of shopping centres and killing them'.

In fact, Professor Roberts takes the view that the overall level of violence is lower today than it has been in the past. He cites the 'golden age' argument that people always look back to the past and convince themselves that things are getting worse. His analysis of the nature of violence today is fascinating.

'There is a long-term rise in property crime, petty thefts from shops and houses. But I doubt whether overall society is becoming more violent. People are generally less tolerant of violence. In the early twentieth century Britain was quite a violent place. Streets were places where you had fights. There were fights outside pubs every weekend. Even when I was at school fighting was an acceptable form of recreation for lads. You were expected to stand up for yourself.

'Now society has become less tolerant of this. Rowdy behaviour hasn't increased, but there has been a change in what society is prepared to tolerate. People won't tolerate gangs running round and children fighting in the playground or in the streets.

'The result is that what violence there is is less socially regulated. This may sound strange, but people fight according to rules, even informal ones. Although people might be rough and punch and shove each other and call each other names, it normally doesn't lead to anybody getting hurt. In the past, where there was a lot of violence it was regulated in the main so that people didn't get killed or seriously injured. When fighting was a normal recreation for children in the street it was controlled by peer groups who were around and watching. Apart from being spectators and sharing in the excitement, they regulated what was going on and nobody was going to get seriously hurt.

'As society became less tolerant of violence, the rules of violence tended to disappear, so more of the violence is unrestrained. In the early 1950s in Liverpool young boys got into crime but there were limits. It was okay to pinch from Woolworth's but not from the corner shop. One thing that has gone is that moral framework which in some communities condoned some kinds of crime but put limits around them. That applies to crimes against property and also to violence and aggressive behaviour towards other people. Wider society increasingly condemns all violence. Teachers hitting children in class and even parents hitting their children is considered wrong. So the moral framework that used to control violence becomes wider. What violence there is is more likely to get out of control'.

The lack of intervention by the public as James was led away by the boys came as no surprise to Professor Roberts. 'Public places are less regulated today because they are less controlled by people who know each other. When people are out in public they are amongst strangers. The stranger in the area doesn't stand out because they are all strangers to each other. People were about when James was taken and didn't see anything unusual in children taking a child off. The Strand was not the type of area where everyone would be recognized except these two from outside who everyone would know should not be taking a child. Also there is a tendency now for people to mind their own business. Life is more privatized and people tend to regard it as not their business, whatever else is going on'.

Professor Roberts was not encouraging about the prospects of the government reversing these worrying trends in society by any specific actions. 'I think possibly in the longer term all trends end at some point and then things tend to move in a different direction. It is possible that at some point in the future there can be a sort of moral revival. But I don't see it at the moment. People were saying after James Bulger was killed that this could shock society into pulling itself together'. He shook his head and smiled sadly. 'No. It is already yesterday's news for most people'.

Peter Kilfoyle, Labour MP for Liverpool Walton, is the father of five children, one of them a year older than James, another just a few months older than Robert Thompson and Jon Venables. Robert's family live in his constituency, which also covers the scene of the killing. He was as shocked and as deeply moved as anyone by the tragedy. 'The video pictures of the little boy putting his hand up were so poignant,' he said. 'Kids look for protection and they are trusting. It left me with an image of this trusting little hand going up to other kids and that little boy ending up being killed'.

Mr Kilfoyle believes the potency of that image combined with the natural attention Liverpool seems to attract explains the huge degree of attention the case attracted. He is deeply sceptical about the way it was linked to the general debate about juvenile crime, and about whether the problem itself is as big as many people suggest.

'The image that is portrayed and manipulated by some politicians is that there is a massive problem with juvenile crime, whereas more cautious voices say every generation looks back and says, "We were pretty good, this generation is awful". Exactly the same thing happened in the Teddy Boy era,' he said.

Mr Kilfoyle had the gravest of reservations over two boys of ten being brought before a court to stand trial for murder. He actually approached former Home Secretary Kenneth Clarke through Tony Blair to question if there was some way the boys could avoid being taken to a courtroom.

'I am not a lawyer and I really don't know why children of ten should have to go through the process of law, no matter how horrific the act, and I emphasize that it is a horrific act to take the life away from a toddler like James Bulger. Does justice require that children have to go before the full panoply of the law which can be tremendously intimidating for adults, never mind children? Do children facing that legal process understand what is happening?

'When Dickens wrote Oliver Twist there was capital punishment for all sorts of what seem minor crimes. These were children in an age that didn't really recognize children at all. That book had a major influence on attitudes in Victorian England. Have we progressed so little that we don't realize it is a different world for children and that their perspective is wholly different from the world of adults?'

Mr Kilfoyle said the only two elements worth considering in criminal justice were deterrence and punishment for its own sake. He accepted that every precaution had to be taken to ensure such a terrible act as the killing of James did not happen again, but questioned just what was being served by making children sufficiently emotionally crippled to have done such a thing stand trial in open court. 'It isn't something children will go out and copy tomorrow morning. That is evident. By the time this comes to court you will probably find that most children will have forgotten about it. Even despite the coverage they won't rationalize it and say, "This child has got away with it. I will have a go".

'There has got to be a better way than going through the courts. When you have these aberrations you have to have some different way of dealing with it. It brings into question how you handle crime and anti-social behaviour by very young children. I believe a panel, perhaps of a judge, a psychiatrist and a social worker, could arbitrate on these cases. In a primitive society one day you are a boy and the next day you are a man. In our society we don't do that. There is no such thing as an automatic cut-off point. All men remember in their schooldays a point where there were lads who seemed to be men and others little boys, all of the same age. There is no defining point where you become adult. I cannot believe that at the age of ten you can say someone is criminally responsible. Why not nine, or eleven? It seems to be purely arbitrary. Every individual case should be taken on its merits and there ought to be someone who can assess every individual case.

'I find it impossible to believe that a ten-year-old can really understand what it is that they have done in this instance. I don't care what psychologists or criminal lawyers tell me. They may in terms of the law be deemed responsible for the act and be tried accordingly. No one can tell me they begin to understand the enormity of what they have done. All my instincts tell me I cannot see ten-year-olds understanding what they are doing in killing a little two-year-old boy. The only explanation - which I reject out of hand - is that you get people who are inherently evil from a very young age. I don't believe that is true. I believe there are people who have had terrible influences brought to bear on them which make them what they are, and in later life they can make choices and change that, but not at ten. I cannot believe anyone that age really understands right from wrong. They can be conditioned into understanding over a period of time. They can learn over a period of time what within a certain moral code is considered right and wrong. I am sure that even a ten-year-old would know it is wrong to kill but I just find it impossible to believe that a ten-year-old can understand the significance of what they did.

'James Bulger is the obvious victim of this crime. Just after him you have his parents and family. But there will also be the families of the two children accused of the crime. There are so many victims in all this. You have to think of the interests of all of them. There is a lot of truth in the Jesuit maxim. "Give me the child to the age of seven and I will give you the man". Those events early on affect the rest of your life. They don't just affect you as an adult but as a child'.

Mr Kilfoyle is convinced that a socio-economic under-class has developed, in Liverpool and elsewhere, institutionalized in terms of the welfare state and with no stake in mainstream society. He also sees much more alienation in society, brought about because of the emphasis on individualism at the cost of the communal by various political movements during the last thirty years. But, like Professor Roberts, he cautions against interpreting the James Bulger case as a necessary conclusion of the social trends of the country or the area.

'Whether within this constituency or without, it would be illogical to say there would be a certain pattern of behaviour from which you would expect this kind of aberrant behaviour to come. It is a combination of a variety of factors. We don't know for sure the circumstances surrounding what either or both of the boys did. What I am sure of in my own mind is that there is a change taking place in terms of family relationships. That is self-evident. There are far more one-parent families. There is a change in the relationships between individuals and the various social, religious and political institutions in the country. Whether that is good, bad or indifferent, others are probably better placed to judge. Any society is a dynamic organism, not static. It is very dangerous to try and make generalizations based on an isolated case.

'Accepting that there is a lot more alienation is a far different thing from saying that every abhorrent and aberrant criminal act is to do with a breakdown in social order or in one group within that order.

'There are many elements which came together in this case. People try to rationalize things in simple ways, but there are many questions for which there is no answer. We ask ourselves why and we just don't know. We may know how James Bulger died and who actually committed the act. I don't think we will ever really know why. 'That is what makes it such an aberration. That is in part what makes it so horrific, the fact that there doesn't seem to be any logic to it'.

Detective Superintendent Albert Kirby says the lessons he took from this case confirmed his views of society, and the importance of family, individual and religious beliefs. 'What you get out of a family is people being taught the difference between right and wrong, how to love and respect other people and respect their property. If you put all those factors together it highlights a lot of the fundamentals of basic decency.

'When you look at Ralph and Denise Bulger and the family there is not one person who has bad dealings with them who can show anything but utter admiration for them. I see all those values put together in one family and it is a tremendous credit to them, the way they held themselves together and the dignity they have maintained throughout this case. It reinforces my views as an individual of how all those things come together. If you looked at the Bulger family and could try and convince people that was the way they should conduct their lives I believe it would make society a much happier and safer place to live in.

'The families of the two boys certainly aren't the worst families in the world, but they are lacking some of the fundamentals many children have in their upbringing. The boys came from split families, which is very sad. It is very difficult for parents to exact control in that situation. Single mothers aren't superhuman and you come to the stage where you become so tired you can't possibly give towards your children the loving and care and support that two parents working together within a family would give'.

Albert Kirby's strong views on the importance of family life are based on much more than his perspective as a senior police officer faced with the upsurge of juvenile crime. His father, a harbour-master in Barrow-in-Furness, died on Albert's fourth birthday. Then, when he was nine, his mother took ill and died, leaving him an orphan. An elderly aunt rallied round to take charge of his upbringing, and he went away to boarding school where he was one of 400 boys all of whom had lost at least one parent. 'I was exceptionally fortunate to have a relative with such commitment,'" he said. 'Family life is something I feel very strongly about, and my own childhood gives me a foundation for my views. I can see and have always seen over the years the strengths that are gained in a very close family environment'.

He believes the public must be protected from juvenile crime and supports the need for the courts to regain the power to lock up youngsters who re-offend over and over again, laughing in the faces of authority.

'Juveniles are now the biggest source of crime in the UK,' said Albert Kirby. 'The law has had its day of patting these children on the head and saying, "Don't be a bad boy". Juvenile offenders have to be arrested, convicted and punished or there will be more trouble. I hope that this case will have highlighted the fact that children of this age are capable of serious crimes. Those two boys went out that day to commit murder'.

Chapter Thirteen

Robert Thompson and Jon Venables went on trial for the murder of James Bulger at Preston Crown Court on 1 November 1993. In its awful way, it was a moment of history. They were eleven years old by now, but they remained the youngest children to stand trial for murder in Britain this century.

It was almost nine months since James had been killed, not a particularly long time for a murder case to come to trial in the English courts, but an eternity for Denise and Ralph Bulger and their family.

The murder squad had been far from inactive in the interim. Preparing a case for a trial of this complexity is a long and painstaking task. One of the first jobs was to arrange identity parades for the many witnesses to try to pick out the two defendants. The parades were to be held in Manchester, and a coach was provided to take the witnesses. There was concern when it emerged that at least one newspaper had been tipped off, and the parade was postponed when Jon was too upset to go ahead with it. Robert's parade eventually went ahead, but Jon's was called off again because he was still too distressed to proceed. He protested that he had admitted what he had done and could not understand why he had to go through the process. It was a difficult concept to explain to a child of ten. Eventually a compromise was reached by which video footage was taken of Jon and other youngsters walking with a social worker, and the witnesses attempted to identify him later by viewing the tapes.

Jon's Solicitor Laurence Lee recalls meeting Robert at one of the identification parades and being spoken to directly by the boy for the first and only time. 'You're an ugly sod!' Robert told him.

Mr Lee had been called in by the police to represent Jon, and had reservations about taking the case at first. 'At the beginning it took a lot of soul-searching. It was very harrowing and upsetting both to me and my family. Then I realized I was a professional and I had to take it. We only got one nasty phone call. Most people appreciate that ten-year-olds have got to be represented. If war criminals can be represented then these boys can'.

Mr Lee's first problem had been to form a working relationship with a boy who had such a mental block about the case that he would break down into uncontrollable tears every time it was mentioned. 'He didn't know me from Adam,' said Mr Lee. 'The difficulty was, how does he build confidence with a complete stranger? How does he gain confidence in a middle-aged twerp like me'.

It was to be Mr Lee's own penchant for Nintendo Game Boy computer games that came to his rescue. 'I saw him almost every week. For the first four or five times I didn't even mention the case-I just tried to form a relationship and gain his confidence. I took my Game Boy in with the basic Tetris game involving building squares and blocks to try to get a rocket ship. Jon was amazed at how good I was at it. He has his own Game Boy'.

Later junior defence counsel Mr Richard Isaacson, an even more skilled Game Boy exponent, would also bring his game in, and they would play the games together as Mr Isaacson asked questions. Mr Lee would make notes between games. 'It worked like a charm. We got as good instructions as we could have got,' said Mr Lee.

'We also talked football. When he said he didn't want to answer a question I kept telling him 1 November was his Cup Final and if he wanted to win the cup he had to train and be put through his paces, and the only way to train was to answer hard questions. My game plan was that by the time the case was committed I would have formed a working relationship with him'.

The boys went nine times to South Sefton Youth Court before being committed to Liverpool Crown Court, where they made their first appearance before the Honorable Mr Justice Morland, presiding judge of the northern circuit, on Friday, 14 May.

They both looked genuinely scared. The media seats for this hearing were in the jury box at the far side of the court, and we had to walk past the front of the dock, passing within four feet of the two boys, to reach them. Thompson in his familiar blue, green and red track suit top, kept his head bowed, his eyes down towards the floor, occasionally darting upwards to take furtive glances at the passing journalists. His mouth was set in a grim frown. Venables, in a green, black and white patterned tee shirt, appeared on the brink of hysteria. His eyes were wide and staring, like those of a cornered animal. A blonde woman social worker had an arm around his shoulders, making him perform deep breathing exercises as he fought to keep control of himself.

We all stood as the judge in his red gown and white wig entered the court and bowed briefly to the assembled barristers before taking his seat, businesslike and brisk. It quickly became clear that the real business of this morning had been discussed and decided before the court was formally assembled. The judge made the expected order under section 39 of the Children and Young Persons Act of 1963, barring any reporting which would identify the two defendants or any child witnesses in the proceedings. Then the boys were formally arraigned by the woman clerk. It was to be the first time the charges had ever been read out to the boys in open court, and probably the first time they had heard them since they were first charged by Jim Fitzsimmons almost three months earlier.

The boys were told to stand and the clerk asked, 'Are you Robert Thompson?' Thompson nodded. She then said, 'Are you Jon Venables?' The boy had recovered from his earlier apparent panic. His voice was clear as he replied, 'Yes'.

The clerk read out the first charge, of attempted child abduction on 12 February, and asked the two boys in turn for their plea. They both replied strongly, without hesitation, 'Not guilty'.

The clerk then said, 'In count two you are both charged with child abduction, the circumstances being that on 12 February 1993 you took James Patrick Bulger, a child under the age of sixteen years, without lawful authority to remove him from the lawful control of Denise Bulger'.

Thompson: 'Not guilty'. Venables: 'Not guilty'.

'In count three you are both charged with murder, in that on 12 February 1993, you did murder James Patrick Bulger'.

Thompson: 'Not guilty'. Venables: 'Not guilty'.

The judge then immediately began reading a list of ten orders. The first and most important was that the trial of the two boys was to be held at Preston Crown Court, beginning on Monday, 1 November 1993. Most of the other orders were technical, having to do with the serving of evidence papers in the case by the prosecution and defence. The judge also ordered that the boys be remanded to Liverpool City Council care and authorized the council to keep them in secure accommodation.

Counsel for the prosecution and defence consented to the orders without discussion. We all stood again as the judge left the court and the two boys were led to the secure area behind the dock. The entire hearing had taken just six minutes.

The weeks and months slid by inexorably until we reached the first week of the trial, a grey, cold, autumnal week sandwiched between Halloween and Bonfire Night. There had been no members of the public at the Liverpool Crown Court appearance, and now only a handful of curious passers-by paused to join the huge media contingent from several countries awaiting their arrival in Preston. The boys arrived about an hour before the trial was due to start, travelling in close convoy in two separate police Ford Transit vans, their windows completely blocked up with boards that were brown on the outside, but a friendlier white on the inside. The police were still anxious not to create any more of an intimidating atmosphere for the children than was inevitable given the circumstances. A police motorcycle led the two vans, and another followed close behind. They whisked up to the tall black rear gate of the court complex and disappeared inside swiftly with the minimum of fuss, as dozens of news cameras clicked.

Court number 1 at Preston is one of the old-fashioned courtrooms, redolent of legal history and atmosphere, that are becoming an increasing rarity as more modern, functional court complexes spring up around Britain. The large, oblong room is decorated all round with mottled green tiles, topped with ornately carved dark oak panels.

Oil paintings of past legal luminaries stare down severely out of their gilt frames as if to remind anyone who could dare to forget of the solemnity of the occasion. The high ceiling features a pannelled stained glass skylight allowing a glimmer of natural light, surrounded by white plaster detailed with all the splendor of an Adam fireplace. Only the microphones rigged up for an audio link and the television monitors positioned to show the security video-tapes to the court served to remind you that this was a court case being conducted in the last decade of the twentieth century.

The Press Association had been granted one of the six main press seats in the court, and that was to be the position from which I would cover the trial over the coming weeks, sitting at a bench directly in' front of the jury, facing the witness box across the clerk's desk.

Another twenty-eight journalists had been allocated seats to the sides and rear of the well of the court, and the judge had allowed the case to be transmitted by infra-red audio link to an eighth storey room in a nearby office block where the rest of the media could listen as the case unfolded. On the first morning though, all the media covering the event were told to attend an informal 10 a.m. briefing in the main courtroom.

The judge and counsel did not wear their wigs and gowns for this session, and Mr Justice Morland's tone was friendly but firm as he welcomed the media. 'The story you are covering will make very sad listening and viewing,' he said. He then outlined the rules governing the reporting of the trial and we were given a printed list of the 'do's and don'ts', and asked to sign that we were aware of them. In case anyone regarded this as friendly advice rather than instruction, there was a footnote reminding us all that anyone transgressing these instructions faced a lengthy period of imprisonment and a fine.

The judge retired, the journalists without seats in court were asked to leave, and the last tense moments until the start of the trial ticked away. The barristers robed up and donned their wigs while the rest of us milled around, chatting nervously. The tension in the air, the sense of something momentous about to happen, was palpable.

At 10.30 we were all back in our places, the court now packed with people. The group of people from whom the jury would be picked, known at this stage as the jury-in-waiting, occupied some of the seats which would later be taken by the media. A few enterprising journalists had worked their way in among the forty members of the public allowed in the gallery at the rear. One row of seats, at the front of the gallery, remained empty. These had been reserved for the Bulger family.

The judge entered court, carrying the little piece of black cloth that is now ceremonial but in days past would be placed on his head above his wig only when he was passing sentence of death. His tone was stern as he said, 'Let the defendants be brought up'.

I hardly dared breathe in the moments that followed. Eventually we heard footsteps and the two boys climbed the twenty-three steps from the holding area below the court into the dock. I had heard that they had put on weight since I had seen them last, but the sight of them still came as a shock. Jon, once a thin-featured and slight six-stone, was now chubby and round-faced, having put on two stone since his arrest. Robert, always inclined to look overweight, had ballooned still further. They were both smartly dressed in collars and school ties. Jon wore a pale blue shirt under a black blazer. Robert wore a white shirt and a black pullover. Jon stood to the right of the dock. To his left was a burly, kindly-faced social worker. Next to him was Robert, his close-cropped hair longer now but still shorter than Jon's. To Robert's left stood the same tall, thin social worker who had accompanied him throughout his youth court appearances.

They were allowed to sit down on four grey-padded wooden seats positioned on a specially raised dais to allow the little boys to see over the brass rails that surrounded the dock. Both boys were blowing air through their plump cheeks apprehensively, brows furrowed as they glanced around them.

The surroundings at least were familiar to them. Police had brought them to the court three weeks earlier to see the room where they would stand trial. It had been meant to be a discreet, low-key visit, but the Sun newspaper found out about it and the boys had once again become headline news, their pictures, with faces blanked out, appearing on the paper's front page.

The judge asked: 'Are you Robert Thompson?' Robert raised a hesitant left finger by way of response. 'Are you Jon Venables?' Jon just nodded.

The nine men and three women who were to try the case were chosen by ballot from the waiting potential jury and one by one took the oath before settling in their seats just behind me. Robert and Jon watched in quiet fascination, frowning and taking deep breaths. Then the clerk read out for the jury the three charges both boys faced. Jon crushed a small white tissue in his hands. His mother and father sat near their son, just to his right, below and behind him in the well of the court outside the dock. Occasionally he would glance back towards them but they kept their heads bowed low, never meeting his gaze. Mr Venables's eyes were red-rimmed, his face haunted and pale. Robert's mother was not in court.

The formalities concluded, the judge told the jury: 'This is a case which has generated a substantial degree of media attention. You must remember to decide this case solely on the evidence produced in court and only on that evidence. If you have heard anything on the radio, seen on television or read in the newspapers and if you do so during the trial remember-put that out of your mind. You decide this case from the evidence you hear in court'.

That was as much as the jury were to hear for several hours. They were invited to retire while Mr David Turnet QC, defending Thompson, made an application to the judge. This application was nothing less than an attempt to have the judge grant a 'stay' due to 'abuse of process'. This would effectively have ended all proceedings against the two boys for the crimes for which they stood accused. Mr Turner's case was that a fair trial of the two boys was no longer possible because of the massive publicity it had provoked.

Mr Turner's detailed arguments included quoting newspaper cuttings across the spectrum from The Times to the Sun in support of his case. When he had finished he said: 'We submit that against such a barrage of publicity on a national scale it is impossible or at least there is a risk that it is impossible that these defendants can have a fair trial. On that basis we ask you to order a stay'.

At this point Mr Brian Walsh QC, defending Venables, rose and supported Mr Turner's submission.

It was not the first time in recent years that the media suddenly found themselves on trial in a major criminal case. Sitting on the press benches at such a time you feel as if you are bearing the brunt of the collective blame for the behaviour of everyone in the industry.

Mr Richard Henriques QC, prosecuting, rose to oppose the application, but made it clear from the first that he was not defending the media. 'We oppose the application but we don't condone the tone of some of these reports,' he said. 'If their minds have been poisoned their minds can be cleansed by a powerful direction not to be influenced by what they have read. Never in the history of criminal trials has any trial been stayed on the basis of adverse publicity prejudicing a fair trial,' He said that the real issues in the case were not affected at all by the publicity, as the real issue the jury would have to try was between the accounts of the two defendants. 'There is nothing which poisons the case of defendant A over B or vice versa. There does come a point when lambasting by the press can almost be counterproductive, and we apprehend that twelve fair jurors seeing two eleven-year-olds in the dock will deal with the case as juries always do - on the evidence'.

The argument bounced back and forth for several minutes, and having heard counsel at length, the judge immediately delivered his ruling. After summing up the legal precedents he said: 'In my judgement as a matter of general principle if there cannot be a fair trial because of the serious prejudice suffered by a defendant because of the extent and nature of adverse publicity before the trial, that can be a ground for granting a stay of criminal proceedings'.

It was an uncomfortable moment. Confidence in the justice system had been shaken by a series of remarkable reversals in recent times. Were we now to see the case against the alleged killers of James Bulger dropped before it ever got to trial?

The judge-continued, accepting that there had been 'saturation' coverage of the case and that while the investigation was proceeding coverage had gone well beyond what was normal before a defendant was charged and before a trial on indictment began. He said he found 'much strength' in Mr Turner's argument that editors had suggested by innuendo that the defendants were guilty. However, he continued 'This is not a case where either of the defendants is raising a defence of alibi. The issues in the case which in my judgement are material factors for me to take into account in considering the defendants' application appear to be whether the Crown can establish a joint enterprise, whether one or either of the boys is proved to have been the killer of James Bulger, and whether one or either of the defendants has proved against him the necessary intent for murder to be established. Having considered all these matters I am not satisfied on the balance of probability that there cannot be a fair trial. The jury have already been warned and they will be directed in the clearest terms when they retire to put out of their minds anything that they may have read or seen or heard outside this court about this case or its background. For those reasons, this application is refused'.

Albert Kirby and Jim Fitzsimmons bad been sitting impassively throughout the arguments and the ruling, on the front row of the seats reserved for police officers on the far side of the court from me. Their faces betrayed no emotion now, but I could well imagine their sense of relief.

Robert and Jon had sat in the dock, occasionally fidgeting, eyes darting restlessly about the room. Most of the complex legal argument and its significance must have been lost on them. Jon looked nervous, Robert more bored than anything. Now it was time for lunch, for them and the rest of us. It was to be the afternoon before Mr Henriques would open the case for the Crown.

Getting out of the building was simple enough, but getting back in for each session was a test of patience, confronted by the tightest security I had ever encountered in a court. The press and the public stood in long queues to pass through an airport-style metal detector. Bags and all metal objects had to be handed to security staff at a desk alongside the detector for checking. Once through the machine, whether it had 'beeped' or not, another security officer gave everyone an electronic frisking with a second, hand held metal detecting device. The ability of mint wrappers to set off these devices gave testimony to their sensitivity.

When we returned to court, Robert was in shirtsleeves, his pullover removed. The room had no air-conditioning and as the day wore on the close proximity of so many people packed into the court made it increasingly stuffy and airless. The heating was not turned on, but sitting in that court it was difficult to believe that it was a chilly November outside.

Ralph Bulger got his first glimpse of the boys that afternoon. Mandy Waller and Jim Green had brought Ralph, brother Jim, Ray Matthews and other members of the family to court in a police vehicle to hear the start of the trial. They took their reserved seats in the front row of the public gallery and prepared to listen to the opening of the case. They had a good idea what was coming. Albert Kirby had had a meeting with Ralph a few weeks earlier and patiently took him through the details of what had happened to his son. Ralph, understandably, found it difficult to pass on what he had heard, and a second briefing was later arranged for other relatives.

Denise was not in court. The one real ray of hope for the future through the agonized limbo of Denise and Ralph's summer had been the news that she was expecting another baby. She had wanted to be at Ralph's side in court but she was now heavily pregnant and Ralph would take no chances and persuaded her to stay away.

Ray Matthews, sitting alongside Ralph in the gallery, recalled his reaction to seeing the boys who had brought so much pain and grief to his family for the first time. 'A cold shiver went down my spine,' he said. 'I expected them to be taller and broader. I couldn't believe it. Ralph's self-control was incredible. The whole family gave him credit for not standing up and shouting. He was only ten feet away from them and there was only a three-foot barrier separating them'.

It was to be outside, afterwards, that Ralph would finally express his feelings to Ray in three short words. 'Evil little bastards'.

When the court resumed there was more brief legal discussion before the jury was called back. Mr Turner asked that some of the photographs they were to be shown by the prosecution, depicting James's tiny head on the railway line, should be removed. 'Even to those of us in these courts regularly these are emotive and distressing photographs,' he said. He accepted that they might eventually have to be shown to the jury but added: 'We submit that a jury could be emotionally involved by these photographs and we submit that they are removed'.

Mr Henriques said: 'Very great consideration was given to what photographs should be in this bundle. Many were much more distressing than these. The cause of death was multiple blows to the head and this is the sight that the inflictor of those injuries would have had at the time.

The judge ruled shortly: 'Mr Turner, I am against you on the photographs'.

The jury were called back, and at 2.30 that Monday afternoon Mr Henriques rose and began making a speech that was to send shockwaves around the world. His words were simple and direct, his approach matter-of-fact. There was no need for elaboration or lofty adjectives. The facts spoke for themselves.

'James Bulger was two years and eleven months old when he died. He was the only child of Ralph and Denise Bulger and they live in Kirkby. They always called him James and we will refer to him as James throughout this trial. He died on Friday, 12 February this year. In short, these two defendants abducted James from his mother in a shopping precinct in Bootle. They walked him some two-and-a-half miles across Liverpool to Walton, a very long and distressing walk for a two-year-old toddler. James was then taken up on a railway line and subjected to a prolonged and violent attack. Bricks, stones and a piece of metal appear to have been thrown at James on that railway line. He sustained many fractures of the skull. Death resulted from multiple blunt force injuries to the head. There were several lacerated wounds. At some point James's lower clothing was removed. His body was placed across a rail on the railway line and some time later his body was run over by a train which cut his body in two. The pathologist concludes that death occurred prior to the impact of the train. The prosecution alleges that the two defendants acting together took James from the precinct and together were responsible for causing his death.

'Both defendants are now eleven years of age. On Friday, 12 February they were both ten years six months old, both born in August 1982. Notwithstanding their ages it is alleged that they both intended either to kill James or at least to cause him really serious injury and they both knew that their behaviour was really seriously wrong. Not only is it alleged that they both abducted and murdered James, but that they attempted, prior to abducting James, to abduct another two-year-old boy. He was in the same shopping precinct three hours earlier. That attempt failed because the boy's mother saw one of the defendants beckoning to him to follow him. She called to him, thus preventing the abduction'.

Mr Henriques then began relating the detailed events of that day. He told how the boys had played truant from school, gone to the shopping precinct and spent much of the day up to mischief around the shops. He explained the attempted abduction, and the time-table from the security video cameras showing James being led away.

At this stage it all became too much for Jon. He began to sniffle, and was soon crying openly, hugging the arm of the big social worker alongside him, who tried to reassure him. His parents kept their heads down, eyes fixed on the back of the bench in front of them.

Robert grew increasingly restless, slumping back in his chair further and further, occasionally flexing his fingers or kneading them together in his lap as he stared at the high ceiling or glanced around the room.

Few others took their eyes off Mr Henriques as his story unfolded, detailing the accounts of the many witnesses who saw the boys on the long march to the railway track. 'It was between 5.30 p.m. and 6.45 p.m. that James was stoned and beaten to death before being placed across a railway line,' he said. He described the discovery of the child's body and gave details about the scene of the attack, and the sickening catalogue of injuries described by the pathologist.

He revealed that blood found on Jon's shoes had matched the DNA profile of James Bulger's blood, allowing scientists to conclude that it was 'extremely unlikely' that the blood came from any other person than James Bulger or a close relative of his. 'That is strong evidence indeed linking Jon Venables to James Bulger,' said Mr Henriques.

The blood on Robert's shoe matched James's group but also 23 per cent of the population, and there was not enough blood for a DNA test. However there was 'a close correspondence' between marks on James's face and the upper and side sections of the shoes worn by Robert.

Mr Henriques concluded for the day by giving an account of the paint which stained James's body, clothing and left hand, and of the tin of Humbrol modelling paint discovered nearby. He said that the two boys were arrested at their homes on Thursday, 18 February, and were interviewed by police. He would give details of the interviews the next day, he said.

The court rose for the afternoon amidst palpable sighs of relief. Robert and Jon were led down from the dock, Jon's social worker steadying him by the shoulders as he trudged back down the steps. Outside, a crowd a couple of hundred strong had gathered, attracted by the television and stills cameras. Many of them were shoppers from the covered market alongside the court complex. Some stood on a monument opposite the rear gates of the court to try to get a better view. The vans carrying the two boys left as quickly and smoothly as they had arrived. There was a low mutter from a few people in the crowd, but nothing even approaching a disturbance. As the vans disappeared, the spectators quickly shuffled away, many looking a little shame-faced at their own curiosity.

That night, as was to become the pattern, Ray travelled home with Ralph and the others to report back to Denise and other relatives on the day's events. 'That opening speech put me in a good position to go back and tell the other members of the family what happened,' recalled Ray. 'I was able to relay it to my Mum and also to Denise. I would go with Jim Green and Mandy Waller to see Denise each night when we got back, and tell her what had happened, leaving out the graphic detail.

'Denise would just sit in silence and listen. She was nearing the end of her pregnancy so we had to be very careful in what we said. Luckily we had Jim and Mandy's support to help us through. She would break down crying sometimes when we told her certain things. She did not read any newspapers or watch television news, though one night she came downstairs at my brother's house and caught an ITN report which upset her a lot'.

The next morning the court reassembled punctually at 10.30 and Mr Henriques continued his account. The tense, close atmosphere enveloped the courtroom again almost instantly. It was as if we had never been away.

He began by reading extracts from the transcripts of the interviews with the two boys. First he recounted Robert's various accounts of the attack, firmly placing the blame on Jon. Jon's face was a picture. His mouth dropped open and he looked along towards Robert with what was clearly astonishment. He could not really see the smaller boy round the large figure of the social worker between them. It was probably as well. Occasionally Jon whispered urgently to the official. Robert looked in every other direction except towards Jon.

Mr Henriques revealed that by the third interview Robert was telling police: 'You will find out in the end it was him that took the baby'. He agreed eventually to being at the reservoir in Breeze Hill with them and said James had been 'crying for his mum'.

In the fourth interview he admitted they had taken James to the railway line and-said" Jon had thrown paint from a stolen tin of model maker's enamel in the toddler's eye, making him cry. In the fifth, brief session, he said: 'Jon might have hit him in sly, because Jon is sly'. In the sixth he was insisting: 'Ask Jon. I never touched him. Why would I want to hurt a little boy? How do I know what Jon done?'

Later in that interview he said Jon might have kicked him 'in sly'. He added: 'Jon threw a brick in' his face and he just fell on the floor! Asked why he didn't stop him, Robert had said: 'I was trying and then he just threw it. When the brick hit him in the face he started bleeding'.

Then Robert had declared: 'I never touched the baby. I wouldn't touch him'.

'Mr Henriques paused in his account here and said to the jury: 'When you are considering the question of whether he knew hitting a baby was seriously wrong you will bear in mind the words "I never hit the baby. I wouldn't touch him." '

Resuming the account, Mr Henriques read that Robert then said: 'Then he hit him again. He picked up a big metal thing that had holes in and hit him again with a stick and then threw that in the nettles. He hit him with a stick in the face'.

By the seventh interview Robert was saying: 'James was knocked out and wasn't moving. He was lying on his back over the railway track. I was trying to see if the baby was still alive and he wouldn't move. I got my ear against his belly and he wasn't moving'.

In his eighth interview Robert had said: 'I didn't touch the baby. I tried to get him off the railway track. I lifted him up round the belly. Then I put him back because I was going to get full of blood'.

Mr Henriques paused here. 'By then, you will conclude, he had realized there would be blood to link him with the crime. He is now adopting a version of the facts designed to explain away the blood on him'.

Robert had then claimed James still had all his clothes on, which Mr Henriques said was clearly untrue. The boy's account had continued: 'Jon threw bricks at him and hit him with a stick. He threw a battery at James and hit him in the face'. Asked why, he had replied: 'Because he felt like it. I told him I was going because he kept on hitting him'.

Robert stuck to his version that he only touched him to see if he was breathing. 'So I have nothing to bother about,' he had said, adding, 'If I wanted to kill a baby I would kill my own, wouldn't I?'

Mr Henriques concluded his account of Robert's interviews by telling the jury: 'You will have noted how the interview progresses to leaving him at the reservoir, then to taking him to the railway line but not touching him, and finally admitting touching him but placing all the blame on Jon Venables'.

He turned then to an account of Jon's interviews, which began as we have heard with flat denials. At one stage he turned to his mother; and said: 'We never got a kid away. Mum, we never got a kid'. He had cried and added: 'You think we did. We never'.

The next day, after being told Robert had admitted seeing James in the Strand, Jon had again insisted, 'We never. We never'.

His mother had then asked him: 'Is that God's honest truth, son?' Jon had replied: 'I'm telling you we never'. Eventually Jon admitted that Robert had taken James and left him in the road. 'I never touched the baby, Mum, I never,' he said.

Later Jon was to claim: 'I left Robert on his own till he came He was asked: 'Tell me the truth now, please, Jon'.

His response was: 'I never killed him, Mum. Mum we took him and left him at the canal. That's all'.

Mr Henriques then described how Jon had admitted with the tape machine off that he had killed James, and repeated it later on tape. He said it was Robert who had said: 'Let's get this kid lost'.

He said they walked through T. J. Hughes's with James following. 'Robert went "come on, mate" like that,' he continued, adding: 'The boy followed us downstairs. I know Robert said: "Let's get him lost outside so when he goes in the road he'll get knocked over". I said: "It's a very bad thing to do, isn't it." '

Here Mr Henriques paused significantly once again and said: 'Perhaps you will bear in mind when you consider if he knew what he did was very seriously wrong, those words: "It's a very bad thing to do, isn't it." '

Jon had told police then that on the canal bank, Robert had picked James up and slammed him down and put a bump on his head. He then told how they got to the railway track where Robert bad thrown the paint in his face and then picked a brick up and threw it in his face. He claimed he had thrown little stones because he didn't want to throw bricks, and had missed James with some of them. James had fallen down but kept getting up again and Robert had hit him with a steel bar. He said he had pulled James's shoes off but Robert had pulled off his underpants 'at the end when he was knocked out'. Robert had put the underpants on his face and then threw them 'back where there was all blood'. In a later interview Jon said they had put bricks on his face. 'I think he was moving because the bricks were moving about,' he added. He agreed that he had kicked James in the face on the railway line.

Jon's mother and father both wept as they listened to the words of their son's confession to the police. Jon kept looking around at them from the dock but they could not meet his gaze.

Mr Henriques told the jury that one factor they must be sure about was that because the boys were under fourteen they knew that what they were doing was seriously wrong, as opposed to something naughty or mischievous. He said it would be obviously seriously wrong 'not merely to a ten-year-old but to a child half that age or even less'. He added: 'It will be the prosecution submission that you can properly be satisfied that each of them knew it was seriously wrong to take a child from his mother and use extreme violence on a child of such tender years'.

The jury were then handed copies of a bundle of photographs and Mr Henriques guided them through them one by one. The first pictures were innocuous enough but there was an air of terrible suspense in court as the jurors viewed pictures of various significant scenes at the Strand shopping centre and on the way to Walton. Before asking the jury to turn to photograph 45, Mr Henriques became grave. 'Members of the jury, the remaining photographs are unpleasant to look at and I invite you to steel yourselves. You will see as few as you can properly be shown consistent with our duty to present this case. It is right you should not be taken by surprise so it is right that I should warn you now that you are now going to see pictures of the scene after James's body was found'.

Robert and Jon had been peering down over the shoulders of the lawyers from their raised vantage point in the dock to view some of the earlier photographs. Now the social worker with Robert whispered to one of the barristers who nodded and promptly moved the bundle he was studying from the young defendant's field of vision.

The jurors somehow remained largely impassive as they studied pictures of a scene it would be difficult to summon from the darkest recesses of the human imagination. One middle-aged woman recoiled for a moment as she turned to a close-up photograph of the injuries to James's face. She recovered her composure quickly enough, but when the viewing of the photographs was concluded she removed her spectacles and dabbed at her eyes with a handkerchief.

With his opening remarks complete, Mr Henriques now began calling the first witnesses who had seen Robert and Jon in the Strand in the hours leading up to James Bulger's abduction. During that afternoon it was time for Diane Power to tell her story about how two boys had tried to lure away her son. Smartly dressed for the occasion in a black and green check suit with gold buttons, Diane made a fine witness. Clearly nervous, she still spoke up strongly as she gave her account of the moment she nearly lost her son. Jon Venables cried in the dock as he listened to her. Robert Thompson sucked his thumb.

When David Turner began to cross-examine her she responded indignantly, bristling at any suggestion that her account could have been coloured by subsequent publicity. There was a moment of badly needed light relief when she struggled to follow his questions about a map of the precinct and the judge rose from his seat and walked along the bench to lean over and explain the diagram to her in the witness box below him. She smiled gratefully at the judge and then turned to Mr Turner and asked, in a Liverpool accent you could have cut with a knife: 'Now what did you want to know?'

It was a brave performance but the occasion at last overcame her. When Mr Walsh asked her if it was true that she thought the boys had been 'playing tig' she answered 'yes' but then her voice faltered and she started to weep. An usher offered her a tissue from a box and she was allowed to sit down and compose herself before Mr Walsh gently concluded his last couple of questions. As she left the box you felt that she must have won the hearts as well as the minds of the jury with her straightforward honesty.

Ralph Bulger was once again in court throughout the second day of the hearing, but on day three - Wednesday - he was absent. Denise had a hospital appointment for a check-up on her pregnancy, and his place was clearly with her. Happily the news was good, mother and baby still doing well.

In court that Wednesday we heard from more witnesses leading up to the moment of James's disappearance, and eventually junior prosecution counsel Mr Henry Globe read the statement Denise herself had given to police early on the Saturday morning while the frantic search for James was still going on. She told of taking James on the outing with Nicola Bailey because he liked car rides. 'James likes anything to do with trains, planes, police cars, taxis anything that moves really,' she wrote. She told of James getting hit on the head by a babysuit thrown down by an assistant in a clothes shop, laughing and starting to throw more babysuits around the shop. In Tesco James had taken and eaten some Smarties, and kicked a cardboard box about.

Turning to their fateful visit to the butcher's shop she told of getting served and turning to look for her son. 'He wasn't in the shop. He'd been al my side while I was being served, but as I looked down he'd gone. I panicked. I ran out of the shop, ran to the security office, looked around. I couldn't see him. I went into Superdrug and a stationery shop but couldn't find James. I started asking people if they had seen him. Nobody had. I then went to the security office and reported him missing'.

The first part of the afternoon session passed in total silence as the jury studied intently the blurred security video shots showing James being led away. Special monitors had been set up in court to allow the judge, jury, lawyers and defendants to see the images. A white arrow had been superimposed on the pictures to help highlight the relevant figures. The jurors asked to be shown the final section of the video, from the moment just before James appeared with Denise on their way to the butcher's, for a second time.

Ray Matthews was present throughout the trial, listening to every awful world of what happened to his beloved nephew. But when that video-tape was shown, he had to leave the room. 'I forced myself to sit and listen,' he explained. 'But James started to die from that moment when the camera caught him in the Strand. It was two-and-a-half hours of slow and tragic death. I couldn't watch'.

When the tape was concluded, Mr Globe read Nicola Bailey's statement about James's disappearance, before moving on to further witnesses.

For five full days the jury heard from a succession of witnesses who told of seeing two older boys and a toddler on the fateful afternoon. Some wept or shook with nervous emotion, many of them no doubt tormented by the wish that they had made the one vital intervention that would have saved James's life. A case like this is full of terrible 'if onlys'. None of these people was blessed with the gift of hindsight that day, and anyone who seeks to criticise any of them should try to imagine themselves in their shoes and ask if they could confidently say they would have acted differently.

It became too much for Ralph by the first Thursday afternoon. Clearly upset by the accounts he had heard that morning, he did not return after the lunch adjournment.

Other members of the family stayed in court but the police laid on a car to take Ralph home to Kirkby. He did not appear the next day and on the Saturday morning I received a telephone call from Sean Sexton, asking me to put a statement out through the Press Association on Denise and Ralph's behalf, saying that neither of them would be attending the court from now on. 'Ralph has had enough. He felt it was his duty to be there but he just can't take it any more,' said Sean. 'Neither he nor Denise will be going to court again, even for the verdict'.

Said Ray Matthews: 'Ralph found it very difficult. You could see it in his face and by his actions during the breaks. He did try to see the case through, but it was just far too much for him'.

The pattern of the cross-examination of the witnesses along the route became familiar, Mr Turner and Mr Walsh picking them up on discrepancies between their original statements and their stories in the witness box. Had they been influenced by what they had read and heard of the case? Could the months have dimmed their memories? Witness after witness indignantly dismissed such suggestions. It was a thankless task for the defence. The overwhelming impression that came through was of a series of honest people doing their public-spirited best to tell the truth as they had seen it.

Among the most poignant was the account of Mrs Elizabeth McCarrick, who was with her seven-year-old daughter when she had almost stopped James from walking off with the boys close to a subway entrance in Walton. They had told her they had found him by the Strand and they were taking him to Walton Lane Police Station. 'I managed to make the chubby one let go of the toddler's hand. At that stage I was going to take the little boy myself,' she said. 'The little boy did not make a sound. I thought he was tired. His head was down. I managed to get my little girl to hold his hand but the taller one said: "It is all right. We will take him to the station." '

She said they had been adamant about taking him. 'The chubby one turned round as if he was going to run away. The taller one called the chubby one back and the chubby one grabbed back hold of the little boy's hand'.

Mrs McCarrick told the boys the best route to the police station and asked James if he was all right, because he looked tired. 'He looked up at the chubby boy when he grabbed his hand. He did not say anything,' she said. She had then seen the three boys across busy County Road before losing sight of them.

The last of the witnesses to see James alive can only be named on the orders of the judge as Miss H. By the time of her appearance in the witness box she was fifteen. She sobbed as she gave her evidence, describing her fleeting ten-second glimpse of James being pushed towards the road by the railway bridge in Walton Lane, and how after spotting her one of the boys had picked him up and carried him horizontally across his body, 'like a baby' towards the embankment.

The judge asked her: 'Could you see what state the little boy was in when he was carried?'

'I could only hear laughter,' she replied.

The Bulger family are only too aware of the remorse and guilt of many of these witnesses, who still blame themselves for not intervening. 'We can't hold anything against those people,' said Ray Matthews. 'At the time they didn't expect the outcome to be what it was. To see two ten-year-olds with a small boy you take them for brothers just looking after a small child for the day. It is for ever on their consciences, obviously, but we have got nothing against those people. I know Denise and Ralph feel exactly the same way'.

We next heard from staff at the video shop about Robert and Jon arriving there after killing James. They had actually gone on an errand for the shop, before being found by Mrs Venables and dragged out of the shop. The next evening Robert, his brother and two friends went back to the video shop and spent about three hours there, watching cartoons and helping the young brother with his homework. Robert's behaviour seemed quite normal to the witnesses.

As one of the video shop staff sat at the rear of the court after giving her evidence, Robert got up to leave court at the end of a session. Ray Matthews, sitting behind the dock, clearly saw Robert smile and wave at her. 'That amazed me,' 'Ray recalled. 'The reaction of an ordinary ten-year-old would be to put his head down and get out quick. They are only ten in age but fifteen or sixteen in the head. They are so streetwise - more streetwise than I've ever seen any kid that age before. They just seem so cool and calculating. To think Thompson actually took flowers and saw James's photo among the tributes ... to actually lay flowers ... that isn't the action of a ten-year-old'.

A series of exhibits was now produced for the jury. They were shown clothing that James and the two boys had been wearing, and plastic bags containing bloodstained stones and bricks recovered from the crime scene. One exhibit, the rusty 'fish plate' metal bar used in the attack on James, was handed to the jury for inspection. It was two-and-a-half-feet long and weighed twenty-two-pounds, a blunt instrument clearly capable of inflicting the most terrible damage. The judge remarked on its weight before handing it on to the jury, and one woman juror gasped at its heaviness when she held it. Another young woman juror shook her head, refusing to touch the bar when it was offered to her.

Having seen the implements, it was time for the jury to be told of the damage they had caused. Home Office Pathologist Dr Alan Williams produced sketch diagrams for the jury and spent an afternoon in the witness box describing in precise, graphic detail the injuries James had suffered. There had been a total of forty-two injuries apparent on his external examination of James's body, fifteen of them on the front of his face alone. There were extensive skull fractures.

'In my opinion the cause of death was the result of multiple head injuries,' he said. 'There are so many injuries to the scalp and skull one cannot single out one particular blow to the head and say that was the one that was fatal. I would estimate there were at least thirty separate blows to the body. The majority were due to heavy blunt objects and given the amount of brick dust at the scene I consider bricks to be a likely implement'.

Dr Williams said the pattern on James's face appeared to have been caused by stamping or kicking from a shoe.

Mr Henriques asked him: 'Were you able to determine whether the child died before or after being transected by the train?'

'I am certain that death was caused by the head injuries and not by transection by the train. I have no doubt about that,' he said.

Mr Henriques asked if James would have been alive after the attack, and Dr Williams said there was no vital reaction to suggest any protracted survival, though there was evidence to show he did not die immediately. 'It suggests there has been a short period of survival after the fractures. It may only be minutes,' said Dr Williams.

It had been a grim afternoon for all of us, and in particular for the Bulgers. 'It has been very traumatic to have to sit and listen to it an in detail,' said Ray Matthews.

'You think you get over the worst by hearing the opening prosecution speech. You think it can't be any worse than because no one can prepare you for the graphic detail of what went on. When you hear that it totally throws you.

'I don't think anyone could suffer a death as bad as James did, yet in a sense hearing from the pathologist was a relief. There had been so many rumours flying around, but now we knew exactly what went on. It was not as bad as the rumours'.

On day eight of the trial the team from the forensic science laboratory at Chorley, Lancashire, gave their evidence. There was much technical information about the various blood and paint stains, and two particularly telling points emerged, one against Robert and one against Jon.

Scientist Graham Jackson gave a detailed and harrowing account of the evidence recovered from the railway track, and told of bloodstains found on the shoes of both boys. The blood was the same type as James's, but unfortunately 23 per cent of the population had the same blood type. However there was a large enough sample of blood from Jon's right toe cap to test the DNA profile successfully. This matched James Bulger's profile precisely, and Mr Jackson put the chances of such a match occurring randomly at one in a thousand million.

His colleague Phillip Rydeard told the court how he had matched the patterned injury on James's right cheek with the distinctive features of the uppers of Robert's black brogue right shoe. He produced an overlay picture showing how the raised stitching on the outer aspect of the shoe, the laces and the D-rings through which they were threaded all matched the marks on James's face. He also showed the jury a photograph of a mannequin doll, showing the angle from which Robert's shoe would have made contact with his head. 'In my view the bruising on James Bulger's face is entirely consistent with a kick or a blow with a shoe with the distinctive components which are found on Thompson's shoes,' he said.

A third expert, Andrew Mulley, gave evidence linking the paint stains on the stones, on James and his clothing and on the defendants' clothing with paint like that from the Humbrol modelling paint tin found at the scene. He held Jon's mustard jacket up for the jury to see and indicated a paint mark on the sleeve. He said James's hand had been heavily paint stained and added: 'I formed the opinion that that mark could well be a small hand print made by a small hand covered in blue paint'.

On the ninth day Ann Thompson came to court for the first time. She sat dabbing her face with a handkerchief, clearly deeply upset, as she heard the psychiatrist who the defence had appointed to examine her son called as a prosecution witness.

'Robert was very protective towards his mother,' a source close to him claimed. 'He had mixed feelings about her being in court because he didn't want her to hear things she might not know about'. The child had only seen his father once since he had left home, a brief meeting at his grandmother's funeral in 1992.

Consultant child and adolescent psychiatrist Dr Eileen Vizard had interviewed Robert on 16 October, a fortnight before the start of the trial. Now she told the court she was satisfied that Robert knew the difference between right and wrong and on the balance of probabilities would have known the difference on 12 February. She also testified that he would have known that it was wrong to take a child from the mother, wrong to cause a child injury and wrong to leave an injured child on a railway line.

Cross-examining Dr Vazard on Robert's behalf, Mr Turner referred her to a reference in her report to post-traumatic stress disorder and asked her to explain its relevance to her assessment. He asked: 'Post-traumatic stress symptoms could result from either direct participation in the events or witnessing the events that led to the death of James Bulger?'

'Yes,' replied the doctor. '

'So whether he took part or he witnessed it that could result in post-traumatic stress?'

'Yes'.

'Is it your opinion that the symptoms of post-traumatic stress are present in Robert Thompson?'

'It is my opinion that they are present'.

'That would involve a constant preoccupation with the crime scene events?'

'Yes'.

'Poor sleeping and eating patterns?'

'Yes'.

'And a lack of therapeutic help?'

'That is not a symptom of post-traumatic stress disorder but since in my opinion he does suffer from a lack of skilled therapeutic input it may relate'.

'If someone suffered from post-traumatic stress does that affect your assessment of their mental state at a previous time?'

'It may make it more difficult to assess but it doesn't preclude an opinion on the balance of probabilities such as the opinion I have just given'.

In his re-examination, Mr Henriques asked: 'Did you find that there was any abnormality of mind at the time of the alleged killing?'

She replied: There was no evidence in my opinion on the balance of probability of post-traumatic stress disorder being present before the killing. What I have indicated in my report was that on the balance of probabilities, this boy seemed to be suffering from two things - academic disorder and conduct disorder'.

She explained that academic disorder referred to difficulties a child might have at school in terms of attendance, which might include truanting, or achievement in terms of keeping up with lessons. Conduct disorder described disturbed behaviour unusual in a child of that age, such as telling lies, again playing truant, perhaps bullying of other children or initiating fights.

'Neither of those two descriptions indicates that a child's state of mind is psychiatrically disturbed to such a pitch that he could not distinguish right and wrong. It is possible to have both of those disorders and still distinguish between right and wrong as a child'.

Mr Henriques asked again: 'Was there in your assessment any evidence of abnormality of mind at the time of the killing?'

This time she replied with a simple: 'No'.

She said her view was that Robert was fit to stand trial but she had some concern about the post-traumatic stress symptoms he suffered from and how much they might affect his understanding of the procedures.

Mr Turner then put some further questions. He asked in what other respects the post-traumatic stress might affect Robert apart from affecting his understanding of procedures.

'My findings were that he was very preoccupied with thoughts, memories, nightmares, flashbacks to the crime scene,' said Dr Vizard. 'All of this is part of post-traumatic stress symptomology. It is really because of his preoccupation with what happened and his distress because of that that makes me concerned about his level of understanding of the court process'.

Mr Turner asked if Robert would be able to give evidence, and Dr Vizard said: 'It would cause some concern but I have to say that when we interviewed him he was, despite these symptoms, able to answer questions perfectly well. He was able to be spontaneous'.

The judge then asked her: 'Were the answers appropriate to the questions?'

'They were indeed appropriate to the questions so overall he presented as a boy of good, at least average intelligence'.

'Was that in relation to what happened on 12. February?' 'It was in relation to both the events of 12 February and a whole range of other matters'.

Consultant adolescent forensic psychiatrist Dr Susan Bailey was' called next, to give evidence about Jon Venables. Mr Henriques put to her the same initial set of questions he had asked Dr Vizard about Robert, and she confirmed that Jon too would have known it was wrong to take a child from his mother and leave him injured on a railway line. She said she found him clinically. and in other terms to be of average intelligence.

Mr Walsh, cross-examining for Jon, asked: 'You have seen Jon Venables on a number of occasions. Is it right that on each occasion that you have spoken to him, when you have asked him about the matter the court is inquiring into he has on each occasion burst into tears and, in your words, cried inconsolably?'

'He has cried inconsolably, that is correct,' replied Dr . Bailey.

'You have considered that and a number of matters, including the circumstances of his condition, the nightmares he ha and other things. In summary, is this right: that you have come to the opinion that for a number of good reasons at the current time he is not able to talk about the matters, the subject of this indictment, in any useful way?'

'That is correct,' said Dr Bailey.

The afternoon session began with the evidence of the boys' headmistress, who said children understood it was wrong to strike another child with a weapon when they entered school aged four or five. She confirmed that both boys would know it was wrong to take a child from his mother and to strike a three-year-old child with a brick.

Another teacher told the court that children at the school were specifically taught about right and wrong. He also confirmed that both boys would know it was wrong to take a three-year-old child from his mother and hit the child with a brick.

Next it was the turn of Detective Sergeant Roberts to go into the witness box. He gave brief evidence about the arrest of Robert Thompson, and then the judge, jury and lawyers donned special headphones to listen to the full tapes of the interviews. They were to spend several days listening to all eleven interviews with Robert and then all nine with Jon, a total of some 12 hours 23 minutes of tapes. For the rest of us the recordings were played through loudspeakers. It was an uncanny effect. The high-pitched Liverpool accents of the boys reverberated around the court as they sat in silence in the dock. It was as close as we were to come to seeing and hearing them tell their story from their own mouths.

Ray Matthews and the others were visibly shocked by much of what they heard from their seats in the public gallery. 'It was a child's voice that we were listening to but it was grown up actions that he was speaking about,' recalled Ray. 'You can't imagine a ten-year-old doing anything like that.

'Another thing that got to us was the amount of lies. They lied from day one. They were even telling lies now. Out of the two of them

Venables is the more honest one because in the end he did break down, but Thompson has denied everything. He showed no emotion whatever. When anyone caught his eye he tried to stare them out.

'One day Thompson looked round, stared at me and he had this cold stare. He looked for a few seconds and then looked away. Then he said something to his social worker. The social worker looked across to the other social worker and said something. Then Venables looked directly at me as well. He must have realized then that we were the family. After that Venables would have a quick look round and back again'.

By the Friday morning, the novelty of listening to the tapes was clearly wearing very thin for both boys. One reporter on the press benches close to me was certain that he heard Robert whisper to his social worker the words: 'I'm bored'. Sometimes Robert stared hard at me and colleagues on the press bench when he caught us looking at him, as if defying us to look away.

At one point he knotted the four corners of a white handkerchief and rested it like a tent on the back of his hand. Jon looked down at Robert's handiwork and then copied it with his own green handkerchief. He then glanced past the social worker sitting between them and briefly caught Robert's eye. A momentary shared smile flashed across their faces. It was as close as they had come to making any meaningful contact with each other in court. Jon's early tears and distress had given way to an uncomfortable resignation, as he sat in court, fingers twitching as if playing one of his video games. 'He was like an animal in the circus by now,' said Mr Lee. 'He had become habitualized. I think that's why there were no tears. He got very tired and wanted to go home. He just wanted the whole thing ending'. Between sessions in court Jon spent his time in the women prison officers' room under the court, playing with toys and games he had brought with him. His teddy bear 'Coach', resplendent in American-style baseball cap, came with him to court each day. He also had, a dartboard in the room and would play darts with his legal team.

Robert chatted to social workers in another prison officers' office nearby, often playing a computer platform game called 'Jill of the Jungle' on a solicitor's lap-top machine.

Mr Justice Morland had other court business to attend to on the, Friday afternoon and the following Monday, giving everyone else involved in the case a much needed break from the claustrophobic atmosphere of the courtroom. On the following Tuesday, the eleventh day of the trial, Robert appeared with a new haircut. His hair had been cropped close to his head, as it had been in February. It was a startling transformation. Suddenly we were looking at the boy in the video pictures again.

There were almost three more days worth of tapes to listen to, including some of the most harrowing passages of Jon's confessions. When they finally concluded on the Thursday afternoon, the prosecution dealt with a few loose ends but called no further witnesses. After 13 days, the case for the prosecution closed.

The case for each defendant took less than thirteen seconds. First Mr Turner and then Mr Walsh formally called no witnesses. It confirmed what we had already suspected, that neither of the boys was to be called to give evidence in his own defence.

Everything now rested on the closing speeches. First, on the Friday morning, it was the turn of Mr Henriques to speak for the prosecution. In twenty-six years at the bar, it was probably the most significant speech the fifty-year-old lawyer had ever had to make, and he did not disappoint. As is the convention when the defence has called no witnesses, he kept his closing address short and to the point. It was a masterpiece of incisive commentary, distilling the key elements of the prosecution case and anticipating the likely ploys of the defence, arguing persuasively against each one in turn.

He said a manslaughter verdict in either case would not be appropriate, understanding by some distance the gravity of the crime. 'This was, in law, a murderous attack on a small child'. He listed the sequence of events they had carried out together over a 20-hour period from playing truant in the morning to being apprehended in the video shop.

Mr Henriques said the thirty-eight witnesses who saw the boys on the route from the Strand to the railway would have asked themselves a thousand times why they had not intervened. They had not associated murder with ten-year-olds. 'Many were shaken to the core by the realization that their intervention would have saved James. I trust they will find comfort in the fact that each made the reasonable assumption that this was a family group'.

He added: 'If ever a crime was committed jointly and together, then this was that crime. Could one boy seriously have committed this crime while the other was present and innocent?'

He said children might play on that railway line at weekends but getting there on a school day at dusk with a toddler was no game'. 'Did one build a platform of bricks to assist James's destruction by a passing train without the help of the other? Did one rain thirty or more blows on James's body while the other looked on with no active encouragement?'

He reminded them of Jon's words in one of his interviews when he said it was a very bad thing to do. Said Mr Henriques: 'This was a very bad thing to do. Both these boys did it and both these boys certainly knew it. We submit that their guilt is proved on all three counts'.

The trial was then adjourned until Monday, 22 November. It was the fifteenth day of the trial, and at last we were to hear from the defence".

Mr Turner rose first, to make his closing speech on behalf of Robert Thompson. A youthful-looking forty-six, Mr Turner had taken silk only in 1991. Married with two sons and a daughter, his first few words left little doubt of the impression the case had left on him.

'The sorrow and the pain of Denise Bolger and her husband dominate this trial,' he told the jury, in a grave, deliberate tone. 'Those of us who have children must find the depth of their grief unimaginable. As I address you I can only hope to reflect the dignity that has been shown by the Bulger family in this harrowing trial.

'When the news of young James Bulger's death and, the manner of his death became known on St. Valentine's Day this year, the 'city of Liverpool missed a heartbeat and the nation was shrouded in grief. This case is not the tragedy of one family, but three families - a tragedy for the Bulger family, yes, but also for the families of Jon Venables and Robert Thompson.

'In this case there have been many tears shed, public tears and private tears, tears in the witness box, tears in the public gallery, tears in the dock but those who have been dry-eyed in this case may also be feeling pain and misery. No one who has been involved in this trial will ever be the same again. None of us will ever see a child separated from his or her mother in a shopping precinct without remembering James Bulger.

'You will appreciate from the measures taken to ensure the safety of these children that whatever the verdict their lives will never be the same again. Whatever your verdict they will never have a normal childhood.

'And what of you? Those of you with children will inevitably have identified yourselves and your children and your own experience with the facts that have occurred in this case. You will each take with you from this trial some terrible moment'.

He said the jury were hearing perhaps the most sensational case the ancient court had ever heard, covered in the full glare of the world's media. 'It is probably no surprise then to you that neither boy in this case was called to give evidence,' he added.

Mr Turner dismissed the Crown's allegation that the boys had planned deliberately to abduct James and cause him really serious harm. 'That children, whose only previous misdemeanours were no more than shoplifting and occasional truancy should conceive and execute such a diabolical plan is beyond belief,' he told the jury.

He painted a picture of the boys not knowing what to do with James, saddled by their own mischief with a little toddler who must have been tired out as they were themselves, after hanging around the Strand since school-time that morning. He suggested that they had not been able to abandon him or foist him off on a grown-up, and lacked the courage to take him to a police station in case they got in trouble -'a far more likely scenario than the planned evil put forward by the Crown'.

'They did get on the railway. What happened there was terrible and terrifying. You know that Robert's case is and always has been that the attack on little James was initiated and carried our by Jon Venables. It is no pleasant case for us to make that accusation against another, now eleven-year-old boy, but we say that for whatever-reason, petulant tiredness, a sudden swing of mood of the sort evident in the interviews, Jon Venables unhappily and tragically carried out a sudden but sustained attack on little James.

Mr Walsh began his speech late that morning. His assessment of Robert Thompson was blunt. 'The prosecution say he is a liar, a sophisticated liar who lied from beginning to end. I regret to say we agree. He lied to put the blame on Jon Venables and shuffle it off himself. He treated the police interview as a debate, a challenge match, a sparring match. He was confident and assertive, the sort of person who would only admit something if you caught him in the act or produced a film of him doing it. Was there a word of remorse, an expression of sympathy or shame for what had undoubtedly happened in his presence?'

Reviewing the evidence at length and in minute detail, Mr Walsh said Robert had used the 'imagination and guile at which he was adapt' in a 'persistent campaign of lies'.

He described him as 'a cool, calm, collected and brazen little rogue'. He said the evidence showed that Jon intended to take James to Walton Lane Police Station. When there was a dispute about the fact, it was Jon who had told the truth. 'This isn't a boy who is trying totally to absolve himself. He is not saying "I am whiter than white, as innocent as the day's long." '

He reminded the jury that Jon had told police he had deliberately missed James with bricks and only thrown small stones, not wanting to hurt him. He had given what for a child was about as good a description of the difference between manslaughter and murder as could be thought of.

'If he played a part in the causing of the death, it is the intention that he had in his mind only to hurt him with little things. If that is true, if it may be true, unless each and every one of you is sure that it can't be true and it isn't true, then he is not guilty of murder - manslaughter maybe - but murder clearly and undoubtedly not'.

The judge began his summing up on the morning of the sixteenth day of the trial. The Honorable Sir Michael Morland had been called to the bar in 1953, after an education at Stowe and Oxford, and service in Malaya as a second lieutenant in the Grenadier Guards. Married since 1961 with a son and a daughter, Sir Michael became the Honorable Mr Justice Morland, a judge of the Queen's Bench Division of the High Court of Justice in 1989. Rarely had the words of this vastly experienced judge been the focus of as much worldwide attention as they were that foggy November morning in Preston.

'All of those involved in this case will have been emotionally affected by the circumstances of James Bulger's death, but I am sure each of you will assess the evidence and reach your conclusions dispassionately and objectively and will not allow your emotions to cloud your judgement'.

He said many of the witnesses had been doing the humdrum things of everyday life on that Friday afternoon when, wholly unaware, they were caught up in the last few tragic hours of James Bulger's life. Many of them must have asked themselves 'if only', 'If only I had stopped them or questioned them more thoroughly and realized this was not a case of three brothers out together but a case of a little boy being taken away from his mother by two older boys, I would have gone to the police and James Bulger's life would have been saved'. He said the jury must consider if those natural, in some cases inevitable feelings had coloured their recollections, affecting the accuracy of what they said they saw. 'You will probably come to the conclusion that the witnesses gave their evidence honestly, doing their best to tell the truth. But the question for you is, have they been accurate? That is the all important question you must answer in assessing each witness'.

He then explained to the jury that between the ages of ten and fourteen years a child was exempt from criminal responsibility unless the prosecution could prove that the child knew when committing the offence that it was really seriously wrong.

He said that to convict them both the jury must be sure that they both took an active part in the offences. 'To put it simply, are you sure they were in it together?' he asked. 'It would not matter who inflicted the fatal injury if you were sure that both Robert Thompson and Jon Venables had decided to kill or inflict really serious injury to James Bulger. If both were agreed and had the common intention that James should be killed or suffer really serious injury and played their part in the assault on him, it would not matter which of the two inflicted the fatal injury. If you are left in any doubt in relation to any count that they were in it together you could only convict a particular defendant if you were sure that particular defendant had committed the offence'.

On the charge of abducting James, the judge told the jury 'You may think that the evidence is overwhelming that James Bulger was abducted and that both defendants were involved physically in taking James Bulger from the Strand precinct to the railway line. You may also think that by the conclusions of their separate interviews each defendant had admitted the abduction of James Bulger'.

He said that there was no dispute that the blows to James's skull that caused his death were inflicted unlawfully. 'You may think the evidence is overwhelming that the blows were struck by the bricks found on the railway line. You may think the evidence is overwhelming that James Bulger was unlawfully killed and whichever of the defendants it was who inflicted those injuries intended either to kill James Bulger or to do him really serious injury'.

To find both boys guilty the jury would have to be sure, which ever of them intended the blows to James's skull, that both intended at the time that James should either be killed or suffer really serious harm. It would not matter which part each of them played if both of them played an active part.

'The crucial question is not what was their intention when James Bulger was taken from the Strand or during the long walk of over two miles to the railway line, but what was the intention of each defendant on the railway line when the fatal injuries were inflicted'.

On the issue of ensuring that both boys knew what they were doing was wrong, the judge told the jury to take into account the number of blows, the weapons used, the kicking. If the jury was not sure that either defendant intended to kill or cause James really serious injury, but that he had played an active part, that defendant would be guilty of the lesser offence of manslaughter.

He reminded the jury of the evidence of the psychiatrists and teachers, and that the boys had no abnormality of mind, were of average intelligence, and attended a Church of England primary school where they were taught the difference between right and wrong.

'This was not a single throwing of a stone or brick but involved a number of blows to the skull of a two, nearly three-year-old little boy. You will consider why James Bulger was stripped of his shoes, socks, trousers and underpants when he was attacked, and why the body was moved from one part of the track near the wall to the other line. Was that to suggest that the child had been subject to some form of assault, possibly by an adult, and then run over by a train? Was that to conceal or attempt to conceal the true cause of death?'

Of the 'untruths' the boys had told police, the judge asked the jury: 'Did they lie because of the fear of being charged with the offence of murder, or because of their realization of their guilt and because they knew what they had done was really seriously wrong?'

The judge then turned to the detailed evidence of each witness in turn, and the accounts the boys had given to the police in their interviews, in a long and careful review of the entire prosecution case.

Denise Bulger came to Preston for the first time on the morning of the seventeenth day of the trial, Wednesday, 24 November. She was there to see the boys who had killed her son for the first time. Wearing a long white cardigan which helped to conceal her advanced pregnancy, she was ushered quickly into court along with Ralph, Ray and the other uncles. It had always been her plan to go just once, to see the boys for herself. She did not go into the court during the morning to hear the judge conclude summing up, preferring to wait for the moment in a room that had been allocated for her in a private area of the court complex.

Hundreds of journalists from all corners of the globe had gathered in Preston by now. The Press Association deployed four reporters, Peter Beal and myself who had covered the trial throughout, Stephen Guy from Manchester and Tello Colley from our London headquarters. Seconds count in the media business more than ever in these high-tech days, and PA takes a pride in coming first on the stories that matter. Few mattered more than the verdict in the James Bulger murder trial.

It was late morning when the jury retired to consider its verdicts, with a detailed list of twenty questions to consider. We all settled down for what was anticipated to be a long wait. The general consensus was that with so many questions to consider, so much evidence to digest, and three separate counts on which to rule against two defendants, the jury would be spending at least one night in a hotel before it finally reached it conclusions.

During the afternoon we returned to court with the jury still out deliberating, to hear an application by Mr Stuart Neale, a barrister acting for Associated Newspapers, asking for the order forbidding the naming of the two defendants to be dropped if they were convicted.

During the legal discussion that followed, the judge said he had no doubt that lifting the ban would be extremely distressing for the parents. 'On the other hand, this is not merely a question of ghoulish interest in the macabre,' he added. 'Whatever the verdict, this was a ghastly crime, and it is unbelievable that it could be perpetrated by one or two ten-year-old boys. It could be argued that it is in the public interest that the circumstances, the exposure of children today to film, radio, television and newspapers, videos and so on may have played their part'.

He said serious sections of the public could be genuinely interested in these issues and added: 'The bizarre and terrible circumstances of the killing put this case, so it could be argued, in a class by itself'.

Counsel for both boys spoke against lifting the restriction but Mr Henriques said both defendants and their families could change their names, which the Bulger family could never reasonably be expected to do. 'Publicity is in itself a deterrent to those who are minded to commit grave crimes. Young children hearing about this and seeing that others are simply known as A and B may themselves wonder if they commit crime whether they can do so under the shield of such anonymity'.

The judge said he would make a ruling only when the verdict was returned, and would not then express his reasons for making it, and the court adjourned again.

It was just after 5 p.m., and night had fallen in Preston, when the message came out to the public waiting area that the jury were going back into court. There was a rush towards the courtroom doors, where a bottleneck developed as a security man had to check off every journalist on his list as we filed back into court to our reserved seats. The consensus among those in the queue was that the judge had invited the jury back to send them to a hotel for the night. Then we noticed that Denise had been brought into court for the first time, and the faint possibility that something significant was about to occur began to dawn on us.

Robert Thompson and Jon Venables looked calm enough as they sat awaiting the return of the jury. If the rest of us remained tense, the atmosphere eased tangibly when the court clerk asked the jury foreman if they had reached a verdict on the first count of attempting to abduct Diane Power's son, and he replied 'No'.

Then the clerk asked: 'On count 2, have you reached a verdict on which you are all agreed?'

'Yes,' came the response from the grey-haired foreman. Suddenly the suspense became almost unbearable in the courtroom, and in the annexe where his words were being picked up on the audio link thanks to a microphone precariously perched atop a pile of legal tomes.

The clerk asked, in a voice so calm it was almost ridiculously at odds with the mood of the assembled company, if the jury found Robert Thompson guilty or not guilty of the abduction of James Bulger. 'Guilty,' said the foreman, in a gruff resolute tone, with a trace of a Lancashire accent. The same question was put about Jon Venables. 'Guilty,' the foreman answered again.

'And is that the verdict of you all?'

'It is'.

Thompson glanced sideways at the foreman not quite certain that he had understood what he had just heard. Venables looked bewildered.

The clerk moved on inexorably to the third count, the murder of James Bulger. When the foreman said the jury had a verdict, nobody in the room dared breathe.

The clerk formally asked him if they had found Robert Thompson guilty or not guilty. 'Guilty,' he replied firmly. Jon Venables?: 'Guilty'.

The second verdict brought a collective gasp from the public gallery. A distinct 'Yes!' hissed from the family section.

In the dock Thompson was glancing around apprehensively. Venables still looked uncertain at first. Slowly he started to realize what bad happened. He whispered urgently to his social worker, who replied quietly. Then Jon's eyes brimmed over with tears and he held a hand to his eyes. Neil Venables glanced anxiously up at him, and as the jury filed out to carry, on their deliberations on the attempted abduction charge he and Susan broke down and wept as inconsolably as their son. Ann Thompson was not in court for the most critical moment of her son's young life.

Denise Bulger sat and listened showing no obvious emotion, though the second 'guilty' to murder brought a sudden flush to her pale cheeks. Detective Superintendent Kirby moved to the barrier separating me well of me court from the public gallery, leaned over and kissed Denise softly on me cheek, before shaking Ralph Bulger's hand. His duty was done.

The boys were taken back downstairs to await further news from the jury. Jon Venables knew all about the legal significance of the sentence of detention at Her Majesty's pleasure that awaited him, and the lawyers' jargon term for it. 'Have I got HMP?' he asked through his sobs. When it was explained to him that he had not yet been sentenced, his thoughts turned to the Bulger family and he said to Mr Walsh: 'Would you please tell them I'm sorry?'

Susan was crying bitter tears in the little prison officers' room. Jon told her to stop crying. Mr Walsh then told him he would have to be brave in the future and start talking about what he had done for his own sake.

At 5.45 p.m., 5 hours 56 minutes after the jury had first retired, the judge brought them back into court. They had still not reached a unanimous or a 10-2 majority verdict on the attempted abduction charge, so the judge discharged them from returning a verdict. Next business was the judge's ruling on the anonymity order. He removed his original order banning reporting of their names, and replaced it with orders relating to information about their whereabouts and care since 18 February 1993 or photographs taken since that day. It meant that for the first time the world could officially be told the names of Robert Thompson and Jon Venables.

The judge next invited counsel for the defence to make any remarks they might have before he passed sentence. Mr Turner declined the offer. Mr Walsh rose briefly and reminded the judge of Jon's words to DC Dave Tanner all those months ago: 'What about his Mum? Will you tell her I'm sorry?' Added Mr Walsh: 'While to someone older these may seem pathetically inadequate words, for a child of his years they meant a great deal, and he wanted me to repeat them when I saw him a few minutes ago'. Mr Walsh resumed his seat.

Mr Justice Morland then focused his attention squarely on the two little boys in the dock. Jon was still crying, and Robert's face was crumpling as if he was fighting back tears. The judge spoke slowly and deliberately, so that the words might imprint themselves on their very souls.

'The killing of James Bulger was an act of unparalleled evil and barbarity,' he said. 'This child of two was taken from his mother on a journey of over two miles, and then on a railway line battered to death without mercy. Then his body was placed across the railway line so that it would be run over by a train, in an attempt to conceal the murder. In my judgement your conduct was both cunning and very wicked.

'The sentence that I pass upon you both is that you should be detained during Her Majesty's pleasure in such a place and under such conditions as the Secretary of State may now decide. You will be securely detained for very many years until the Home Secretary is satisfied that you have matured and are fully rehabilitated and are no longer a danger'.

Venables, in his dark jacket and school tie, continued to sob. Thompson, in a white open-necked shirt, showed real emotion for the first time. He clutched at his chest with his left hand as he sucked in huge gulps of air. The first hint of tears showed round the rims of those strange little eyes.

At the back of the court Ralph Bulger put a protective arm around Denise and hugged her to him as they listened together to the judge's words.

The boys were then taken down from the dock, moving quickly, hard on the heels of their social workers. Ray Matthews had been a model of restraint throughout. He could stand it no longer. As his nephew's killers briefly faced him he had his moment. 'How do you feel now, you little bastards?' he said.

When the boys had gone, the judge resumed his address to the court. 'How it came that two normal boys of average intelligence committed this terrible crime is very hard to comprehend. It is not for me to pass judgement on their upbringing, but I suspect that exposure to violent video may in part be an explanation. In fairness to Mrs Thompson and to Mr and Mrs Venables, it is very much to their credit that during the police interviews they used every effort to get their sons to tell the truth.

'The people of Bootle and Walton and all involved in this tragic case will never forget the tragic circumstances of James Bulger's murder. Everyone in court will especially wish Mrs Bulger well in the months ahead and hope that the new baby will bring her peace and happiness. I hope that all involved in this case, whether witness or otherwise, will find peace at Christmas time'.

A crowd of about four hundred people jeered outside the court as the boys were driven away in their separate police vans. Their shouts of 'murderers' mixed in the chill night air with the carols from a nativity tableau under the glow of Christmas lights in a nearby square. A few flakes of snow began to fall over Preston Crown Court.

Chapter Fourteen

Soft footsteps whispered across the bedroom carpet and a tiny figure clambered up the side of the double bed and burrowed under the bedclothes. The child was whimpering softly. His mother awoke instinctively at his arrival. This had happened before. Since all the publicity surrounding Jurassic Park, dinosaurs had dominated the troubled dreams of her six-year-old son.

'What's wrong, sweetheart?' she asked as the child cuddled up against her. 'I had a bad dreams,' he answered.

'What about?' 'I dreamed that two bad boys took me away and I never saw you or Daddy again'. The mother, a shop assistant at a local store, recounted this story to my wife as the renewed publicity surrounding the James Bulger case once again dominated the headlines during the trial at Preston Crown Court. She had not discussed the story with her son, and had been astonished to realize the extent to which he had become not just aware of the case but genuinely frightened by it.

The ripples and shockwaves from the tragedy that unfolded on Merseyside that bleak February afternoon have touched many of us in our different ways. Perhaps the saddest effect it has had is the way in which it has permanently altered perceptions of childhood. Where once the sight of a couple of scruffy ten-year-olds on the loose on a school day might have provoked suspicions of playing truant and possibly petty theft, in future there will always be a more sinister question mark. For me, and for many others, the James Bulger case has left a permanent scar on the innocent image of children.

Robert Thompson and Jon Venables are likely to spend a long time in institutions. They will remain in the kind of regime they have become used to in recent months in their separate secure units until they are old enough, at eighteen, to be sent to young offenders' institutions and ultimately to adult prisons when they are twenty-one.

There is a significant proviso. The psychiatrists said the boys were sane and as such fit to stand trial. Whether they will retain that state of mind it is impossible to say. It is certainly not beyond the bounds of possibility that one or both of them may develop into such disturbed characters that they will be transferred from the prison system into the care of one of the country's top security special hospitals.

The likely length of their sentence in years would be the subject of a private letter of recommendation from the judge to Home Secretary Michael Howard. Given his expressed view when sentencing, detention for anything up to twenty years does not seem an unreasonable estimate. The judge's 'tarrif' or minimum recommended sentence could be increased or lowered by the Lord Chief Justice, Lord Taylor, or Mr Howard. The first review of their sentence would come three years before that date or after seventeen years, whichever was sooner.

Mary Bell served eleven years and five months before her release on 'life licence'. On average, adult lifers released in 1992 spent thirteen years and two months in jail.

The sentence on Thompson and Venables attracted considerable criticism in Europe. In Germany children under fourteen cannot be brought before a court. Herr Walter Wilken, head of Germany's Child Protection Society, said: 'This barbarous judgement, condemning two children to an undetermined length of detention and imprisonment, should be brought before the European Human Rights Commission. In Germany a case like this would be handled by the local youth office, which would work out, in consultation with the parents, a programme to rehabilitate the offender'.

In Holland a senior judge, Mr Cornelius de Groot, said the sentences were inhuman. 'Young children who murder another child are social misfits,' he said. 'That almost always has to do with their background. They have no sympathy for pain and suffering. Through re-education, they can learn to have sympathy'.

Denise and Ralph Bulger were understandably more concerned about the risk for other children in the future than the welfare of the defendants. Lawyer Sean Sexton said on their behalf after the trial that the couple hoped that whichever Home Secretary eventually considered their release would bear in mind what they had endured and would not release them while there was any danger that they could put more parents through a similar ordeal.

Their parents and siblings face their own long-term ordeal in the years to come. No parent who has raised a child to commit' such a crime at the age of ten can avoid a sense of responsibility for what happened. It is a heavy burden that the parents of Robert and Jon will have to bear with fortitude for the sake of their other children. Some support is available to them through the counselling provided by the charity Aftermath, set up in September 1988 to offer long-term help to the families of very serious offenders. Jon's parents had counsellors from Aftermath with them in court throughout the trial. Clearly the families will also remain under the close scrutiny of local authority social services departments in whatever parts of the country they eventually settle. It must be unlikely that they will ever feel truly safe there again.

The boys were by now so terrified of the outside world that they had no wish for escape. They welcomed the sanctuary of the locked doors that kept them in.

Laurence Lee said Jon had put on over two stone while he was in his unit because he got so little exercise, as social workers were worried he might run off. 'He has no intention of running off. He wants to remain in the safety of that sanctuary,' said Me Lee. 'Jon now gets three square meals a day and is getting very well educated but he has no freedom. He is used to it now. He is so traumatized that he looks on it as his sanctuary. I think he is scared of the outside world now'.

Sources close to Robert told a similar story. 'He is frightened of the outside world. When the paperwork didn't come through for his fortnightly detention order he thought they would have to turn him out. He was terrified. He is quite happy to stay where he is. He has trouble sleeping'.

It is difficult to imagine the likely impact of the crime and its aftermath on its two perpetrators as they develop into teenagers and then young adults. Jon could not even bring himself to discuss the events of that day - events which were still giving him nightmares. The lawyers in his defence team came up against the same problem as Dr Susan Bailey when she tried to talk it through with him. He would simply dissolve into a flood of tears.

The Liverpool Echo managed to gain access to Dr Bailey's report on Jon Venables, and revealed that it told of the boy's dreams, including one in which he turned back the clock and became a hero, rescuing James from death and carrying him back to his parents. It said he loved watching videos but recoiled from violent scenes. He dreamed of living for ever in good health and wished the world could be turned into a giant chocolate factory, according to the Echo's report of the document.

Said Mr Lee: 'We still haven't got a full story of what happened on the railway and may never get from him the truth of who did what. He does express remorse to his mother. He has told me he wishes he could put the clock back. He has nightmares, flashbacks to the incident. He has never explained why. The psychiatrists say there is extreme trauma. We don't know if it is because of what happened or if it existed before. He is a very emotional boy, shy and timid'.

He said Jon did not like Robert one bit, referring to him by a rude nickname.

Mr Lee says of Neil and Susan: 'His parents have been extremely dignified. They are now back together, though that is scant consolation. Jon gets on very well with his brother and sister. There has never been a policeman over the door of that house'. Social services have been involved with the family but only in relation to learning difficulties, mainly with the brother and sister.

'With hindsight people say that is the kind of family that can result in crime, but they were a perfectly happy family. Although split, they were together for the sake of the children and made a lot of joint decisions. There is nothing in their houses that is a reason for what happened. I don't believe that the most deprived house in Liverpool is sufficient reason for what happened. It is a tragedy that could have happened anywhere'.

Susan and Neil Venables spoke after the trial of their shame at what Jon had done. 'It is just a nightmare,' said Susan. 'You look at him and you say to yourself, "How could you be involved with anything like this?" On the other hand you are looking at him and you are saying "Well, I know why", because he is so weak. He did like to be liked and loved to have friends, and he has got involved with the wrong person'.

They denied recognizing Jon when they saw the video pictures from the Strand until he was arrested. 'It never crossed our minds at all,' said Neil. "

'We watched every bulletin, every news that came on,' said Susan. 'We read the papers, everything, because we were very concerned ourselves for the safety of the little boy. We were very upset on the Sunday when they had found him'.

The couple asked Jon about the killing after his arrest, but he told them little about it. 'All he said when we asked why didn't you run away was that he was frightened,' said Susan. 'He said he was frightened of Robert's older brother. Robert said, "If you tell anybody I'll get my big brother to batter you up". He mentions James, not all the time, but now and again. He gets upset. He says, "I know, Mum". He is broken-hearted over it'.

They are resigned to his long-term incarceration. She said Jon was upset at being parted from his family and wanted to come home, but she would just tell him, 'Well, you can't. We are still there for you. We can try and visit you as much as possible and try and support you in that way but you just can't come home because of what's happened'.

Neil Venables said: 'He was brought up right. He had everything we could give him. His Mum was more strict. I was the softie but I still kept him in if he was naughty or anything like that'.

Susan said their other son knew what Jon had done and was very upset. 'I don't think he can take it in,' she said. 'I don't think he fully understands anyway with him having learning difficulties, but he just wants Jon back home like we all do. But it's not going to happen, is it?'

They denied that there had been any violence in their home, and said Jon and his brother and sister were very close. They also insisted that Jon had never watched horror videos.

Neil Venables was a film buff who enjoyed watching horror films from the video library. A suggestion grew up behind the scenes during the trial that his son had seen the video Child's Play 3, which Neil had hired out less than a month before the day of the crime. This mainstream Universal Pictures film depicted a toddler-sized doll being possessed by the soul of a killer and terrorizing children at a military school. In one sequence the doll, dressed in a child's clothes, is hit by a paint ball fired by young cadets during a field exercise, and his face is splashed with blue paint. The doll is destroyed later in a final showdown with the film's child hero on a fairground ghost train.

The police checked the video hiring patterns of both families and found nothing they considered significant. Having viewed this particular film myself I concluded that while the coincidences sound strong on paper they look rather less convincing on screen.

The couple said their son's crime had had a 'devastating' effect on them. 'My life at this present time…I don't know if I'll ever get it back together again completely,' said Neil. 'I suppose I am still in shock. I don't know'.

'It will never go away,' said Susan. 'You feel a bit guilty if you laugh or something like that, and you say what am I laughing at?" and people say you have to smile and laugh or you will never go on. We just try and take it day by day and just try and help Jon as much as we can and support him all the way and just try and be a normal family, which at the moment isn't happening. But we just want to try and get our lives together again and concentrate on bringing our other two-children up'.

To hear Ann Thompson tell it, the problem was that the whole world was against her and her family. In an interview with a journalist published at the conclusion of the trial, she continued to protest that Robert was no murderer. She blamed the headmistress, the social workers, the police, her neighbours, Jon Venables, everyone except Robert and herself. 'He's a little liar, he's devious, he's a scally, he robs, he plays truant. He's not a murderer,' she said defiantly.

'They always blame' the parents. It's a very difficult situation when you are getting no support as a family, you're alone and you face the world alone as I'm 'doing now…We look over our shoulders. We don't go out'.

She confirmed that the 'older of her two sons who remained at home had not been to school since the murder. 'I won't let them go,' she said. 'I am not sending my kids to school for another one to end up in prison. 'The teachers can't do their jobs properly. You send a tutor to me and I know where my kids are.

She blamed the school headmistress for not notifying her of Robert's disappearance on the day of the killing, and for not keeping him in school. 'I was fed up going to the school and being told "You're son is not here", she said. 'That was from September up to Christmas. I don't know on how many occasions I went up and shouted at the headmistress for not keeping him in there'. She claimed her son was playing truant because he did not like the headmistress and there had been victimization.

'All my children have gone to that school and she has never liked any of them,' said Mrs Thompson.

She agreed that Robert might have been a bit cheeky, and said: 'I think that's part of me coming out in him really'. She claimed that Robert had told her he felt like crying in court. Asked why he didn't, he had told her 'Because all those people are looking and they would call me a baby'.

She told of her regular visits to Walton Lane Police Station, just round the corner from their home in Walton Village. She would ask them to throw him in a cell but they would say: 'Take him home, he's your son'. Asked if she thought that the murder could have been prevented if the police had done something about it, she said: 'Yes'.

By her account Jon Venables had bribed her son with £2 to go with him that day. 'I don't know why he was with that baby from the beginning. I want to find out. What I really think is he's frightened of Jon Venables'. She claimed Robert's truancy problems started when Jon came on to the scene. 'Jon Venables has some strange ways about him. Why did he have a ruler around another kid's neck? Because he's never harmed anyone in his life before?'

She painted a lurid picture of the neighbourhood of Walton, claiming: 'You have to be tough or else you don't survive' and that near neighbours dealt with drugs and threatened to blow her kneecaps off. Her children were a marked family. 'They are scallies, little scallies, but they are not fucking murderers!' she insisted. 'Name one family in the area who would have a good word for us. If things went missing from washing lines, people would say, "It's the Thompsons". I am not saying they are innocent, but they got blamed for things they did not do'.

Mrs Thompson agreed that her son played on the railway. 'Every kid in Walton played on the railway. All they were short of up there was swings and slides. So why would my son go on the Strand, take a baby, walk it all the way home past people that know him? Why would he do it? He swears blind he hasn't done it…he hasn't killed the baby, and I believe him'.

Robert was left with an obsessive preoccupation with that remote railway line and the scene of horror that helped to create upon it. His 'post-traumatic stress' left him, in Dr Eileen Vizard's words, with thoughts, memories, nightmares and flashbacks to the crime scene. Another of her observations was particularly worrying. She was concerned that Robert was suffering from 'a lack of skilled therapeutic input'. 'He has not accepted at all that he did it,' a source said of Robert. 'He has convinced himself that he played no part in the killing. That is what he firmly believes. He will talk quite easily about it all. Sometimes he does cry but there is no remorse because he doesn't accept he has done anything he has to be sorry for'.

He claimed that children at the boys' school had said they were being invited to join Thompson and Venables's gang 'because were going to kill someone'. 'It may have started out as a bravado about wanting to kill someone but then things got out of hand and they found it really was happening'.

It is to be hoped, with the trial behind them, that Robert and Jon will get the kind of in-depth therapy that will confront and bring out the dark fantasies that almost certainly led to their crime. That is likely to be a long and painful process, but it must be carried through for their own sakes and for the safety of others.

Forensic psychologist David Glasgow said in June: 'Because they have done what they have, they will never be the same again and they must be put away for a good long time. I say that without any sense of retribution at all. It has to be that way because they will be so profoundly changed by what they have done and how they came to do it that they need to be contained separately. My anxieties are that the system for doing that is feeble. It doesn't often correct what happened to people.

'Certainly one of the boys, and possibly the other too, will turn into very worrying teenagers. There is nothing more likely to fit in with their sense of rejection, isolation and uniqueness than to be put in a special unit and treated as a sub-unit in that unit. That can be quite pathological in itself. They don the mantle or status that goes with being apart and different, not being part of humanity, not being touched by hurting other people or feeling the empathy other people feel'.

Psychiatric nurse Professor Ann Burgess works closely with the FBI in trying to identify behaviour traits likely to recur in killers. Her team studied eighty-five juveniles who committed murders in the USA, using techniques like getting the young killers to draw pictures of the crime scenes. These images alone often provided clues to the inner motivations of the youngsters involved.

She cautions that the boys will go to great lengths to cover the fantasy that led to the crime. Something that one of the boys had witnessed would have excited him to set the fantasy into motion. 'He sees something enough and he is probably a bright little child and he begins to use his mind in a very deviant way rather than to achieve positive goals. He spends his time planning. My hunch is that the lead boy will be brighter. Something he witnessed sets the kernel of the plan,' she said.

She then summed up in stark terms just why it is vital that this strange fantasy world is opened up. 'Men will go away for fifteen years and come out and commit the exact same crime,' she said. 'It is very serious. If you don't get in and expose that thinking it will continue. They should not be thinking about how to kill. It is a very dangerous way to think. They have got to channel that thinking into the way normal people think'.

Clearly these boys will need long-term investigation by the best psychiatrists. Their tender age suggests that it may not be too late to alter their patterns of thinking. One day, given their age and such precedents at the Mary Bell case, there must be the possibility that they will be released into society once more. If that day comes it will be deeply controversial. Society will neither forgive nor forget what happened to James Bulger. The very least it has the right to expect is that we can be certain that whatever malevolent instincts drove these boys to their crime have by then been expunged for ever.

The wider impact of the James Bulger case on the law and order issue in Britain was emphasized again in the run up to the Queen's Speech, in which the government traditionally lays out its plans for legislation during the new session of Parliament.

The Queen's Speech for 1993 with its emphasis on the campaign against crime took place while the trial was on, and a few days earlier Prime Minister John Major spoke of the need for parents to instill the difference between right and wrong in their children. He could not make reference to the trial for fear of prejudicing its outcome, but the inference was clear enough.

For Ralph and Denise Bulger the damage had been done. No amount of reform or legislation would ever bring back their beautiful little boy. The trial was an important hurdle for them. All summer their lives had been in a kind of limbo. Their natural grieving process was made all the more painful because there remained on the horizon this final part of their son's story.

To begin with they could hardly bear to face the outside world. After the funeral they returned to the cocoon of family protection that was Eileen's cosy little house in Scoter Road.

Said Denise: 'I remember Ralph's brother James would come and say 'Come out. You can't stay in here all the time. You are looking terrible.

It isn't all bad here. Kirkby is a nice place to live in. But all I remember thinking was I would like to be up there where James is. That's all I wanted. I remember someone asking my feelings and I just said: "I want to be with me two kids again." '

'I still think about Kirsty now. I always think, "I wonder what she would look like and how big she would be". It is just so hard to believe that we've lost two'.

Father Michael O'Connell -'Mick the priest' to Ralph - played a major roll in easing them back into their community.

'It was Mick the priest who got us out first. He helped us a lot,' said Ralph.

'Only for him I would still be stuck in that bedroom,' recalled Denise. 'After the funeral he would take us out in the car. One day he said: "Where's your walking boots?" and said to go and put them on. He took us to a big park and we walked up a hill'.

Said Father Michael: 'The trip to the park was a conscious effort on my part to try and get them some space, to take them out to give them a chance to look at things again. People kept asking me how Denise and Ralph were. It was best to say they were coping and to give a bland, non-commital answer. You can meet someone on a day and they can be up and 10 minutes later someone may say something and it pulls them back down into the depths of grief.

'Someone dies and you take them to the crematorium. If you arrange to go back in a week or a fortnight to collect their ashes, until you have buried those ashes it still isn't finished, that aspect of it. If you had made a decision that you weren't going to collect the ashes it would finish at the crematorium. I felt that this hadn't finished yet for Denise and Ralph. November was approaching and that would bring things. There was still unfinished business.

'The case didn't shake my faith but I found it frightening that two ten-year-old boys could do that. I didn't want to believe that two boys could have done this, two little children'.

I asked Father Michael if he thought the Bulgers would ever be able to forgive these two boys for what they had done. He thought for a long moment before replying: 'Anything is possible. But I think that before forgiveness can enter in the ground has to be prepared. You have to be able to reach peace and freedom to be able to contemplate forgiveness. Forgiveness is more about self than the others. We are saying forgive them so we are not bound by hatred or upset. It doesn't matter to the other person whether he is forgiven or not. It is the person who is hurt who is still caught" up, and that is a long way down the road yet'.

After my conversation with Father Michael, in the lounge of Ray Matthews' home, he had some news to break to the family. He was being transferred to a parish at Tamsworth, in the Midlands, and would soon be leaving Kirkby. Ray was visibly shaken. Father Michael promised that he would stay in close contact, and be available for Denise, Ralph and the others whenever they needed him.

He was to prove as good as his word, but you could tell at once that they would still miss him terribly.

Another 'outsider' to the immediate family who was to be an enormous help to them was solicitor Sean Sexton. A 34-year-old Walton-based lawyer, Sean was actually distantly related to the family by marriage. Ray's wife's mother and Sean's grandmother had been sisters. They had met a few times at family gatherings, and Sean's name had also made national headlines the previous year when be exposed a loophole in police procedures relating to drinking and driving prosecutions.

'The police were getting thousands of letters, cards and gifts and money were pouring in and the case had obviously attracted immense media attention,' said Sean. 'The police advised them to get a solicitor and I got a call on the Saturday lunchtime –the day the boys were charged - to say I was wanted in Kirkby about the Bulger case. I had not realized that Ray's sister was Denise Bulger, and my initial reaction was horror because I thought I was wanted by one of the two boys. I had only recently been talking about it with colleagues at a legal dinner and we were saying we would not want to be involved in it at all.

Sean took on he role of legal adviser to the family, and went to Marsh Lane Police Station. 'I was shown a room with three or four police officers just going through hundreds of cards and letters and sorting money. I had never seen anything like it and neither had they'.

The family kept some of the toys, which they plan to put in a special room for James, but most were donated to children's hospitals or flown out to Romania.

As to the money, they wanted no part of it. Their first impulse was to donate it all to charity in James's name. Sean had to look to their future and give them practical advice.

'I thought it was all very well them giving it away to charity, but where were they going to be in a year's time?' he recalled. 'I suggested a compromise solution. I said: "People want to help you. Let's do what we can for you, but also for young people in Merseyside and in Kirkby in particular. That will be a memorial to James". I wanted to ensure that Denise and Ralph would have some security on which they would build. It was going to be immensely difficult for them anyway'.

The result was the launch by Mayor of Knowsley Cllr Harold Campbell on 25 February of the James Bulger Memorial Appeal. Sean was to be one of the three trustees, along with Knowsley Council chief executive David Henshaw and Mike Reddington, who was vastly experienced in such matters as the administrator of the Hillsborough Disaster Appeal. By the time of the trial over £161,000 had been gathered for this fund.

A series of projects were to benefit from the fund. All sixteen primary schools in Kirkby were asked to submit proposals for practical schemes in the schools which would benefit the pupils and provide a suitable memorial. The response was described as 'splendid' by the trustees, who announced that all of them would be helped to put their ideas into practice. Among them was a delightful little project at Sacred

Heart RC Primary School, alongside the church where James's funeral was held. It was Ralph's old school and several of James's cousins went there. A special corner was to be furnished with little tables and chairs of different sizes for different age groups, and landscaped with trees, plants and a pergola. It was to be a quiet corner where children who did not feel like playing games could sit and chat with their friends or read at breaktimes. It was to be called, simply, James's corner. The Trustees also decided to help provide facilities for physically disabled children at a special school in the town.

Amongst the many offers of support and help that came in were many from holiday companies. They could literally have flown around the world, but Denise and Ralph had never flown in an aircraft in their lives. Home and its familiar protection was what they wanted most. They were finally persuaded to take a short break in Jersey, with Ray Matthews travelling with them to provide any support they needed. Everyone connected with the family held their breath, worrying that they might fall apart outside their circle of love. Happily the trip was a success, giving them the opportunity to relax for a few days in an environment where they were not surrounded by their new-found and deeply unwanted fame.

But the brightest spot in Denise and Ralph's long and difficult summer was undoubtedly the news that Denise was pregnant again. They bad hoped to keep it a secret, but news leaked out thanks to a chance remark, and Sean issued a statement on 13 May confirming: 'Denise has known for approximately two weeks that she was pregnant and the baby is due in December. After all that Ralph and Denise have been through in the last three months this is wonderful news and they are both delighted'.

Sean Sexton saw the news of Denise's pregnancy as giving them the focus their lives needed so badly at that point. 'They will have something to build on, where back in February and March there seemed to be nothing left'.

Father Michael said he had a twofold reaction to Denise's news. 'One was joy and delight and happiness that it would give hope and provide a future and something to look forward to. But there was also a question mark. Sometimes we can escape from grief by getting absorbed in something else. I wondered whether it would be a postponement of coming through it. But my main reaction was that if Denise and Ralph were happy that was the important thing really'.

For a long time, Ralph and Denise, like the rest of us were largely in the dark about the full details of what had happened to their son. Albert Kirby was prepared to brief them in full when they were ready, but they kept putting off the moment. Eventually, with the trial drawing close, they had to be told. Albert met Ralph and went through the details of the attack, slowly and patiently. Afterwards it was expected that Ralph would pass on the information to the others. He could not bring himself to talk about it, and Albert had to have another meeting to explain the situation to some of James's uncles. Much of the information was shielded from Denise at least for the moment, because of her by then advanced pregnancy.

James Bulger, who had identified the body, knew what to expect better than most. 'Ralph was not facing it,' he recalled. 'Till he does, he isn't going to move on. I think when Denise has the baby it might be the one thing that triggers them back into life. Denise will be all right. She is very strong. She has lapses when she breaks down but that is only normal and it strengthens her for the next time round. Ralph should be stronger than he is by now. I think he was scared to know the truth'.

James will carry the thought of the sight of his little nephew on a mortuary slab to his grave. The anger still eats into his soul. 'I blame the whole of their families. Someone must have shielded them for all those days. They must have had a lot of blood on them,' he said.

Ray Matthews had looked grey and haggard during the long courtroom ordeal, the strain of enduring day after day as his sister's eyes and ears in the court clearly telling on him. 'The trial was like losing James all over again,' he said afterwards. 'It felt as though James had just been taken.

'I watched their parents in court. I never saw Mrs Thompson smile or laugh in court. None of my family did. But Venables's mother actually laughed when she walked past us. I don't think she was aware who we were, and she was talking to someone else; but she found something funny in that court, and in that atmosphere'.

He, too, finds it hard to believe that none of the parents rang the police after seeing the security video pictures. Even if they could not believe their children were involved, they must have noticed the clothing similarities, he believes. 'They just let it go on till the police came to the door five or six days later. They could at least have picked up the phone and said "I don't believe it's my son but it looks like him". They didn't even do that.

'When we were in court people passed us letters. One in particular was from a woman with two children who said she was now frightened for the time when these two come out because she believes they will do something again. It can never happen again to us, but we feel now for the people out there. If they are released while they are still young they will be putting more kids in danger, and it is them we are frightened for now'.

Ralph did his best to endure what he was told by Albert Kirby, and what he was hearing in court that first week of the trial. 'It is something we wouldn't believe possible,' said Ralph. 'Their parents couldn't have loved them. The wickedness is in those two'.

Denise sums up her feelings for Robert Thompson and Jon Venables in one word: 'Hate'.

'I look at my own nephews of ten and you wouldn't think it possible. It is hard to believe.

'I blame the parents, but it is them mainly. The parents didn't tell them to bunk off school. They didn't tell them to go out and kill someone. Broken homes are no excuse. There are lots of kids stuck in homes that come out at sixteen and they get on with their lives. They don't go and do anything like that.

'They had every intention of going out to do it. They knew what they were doing. I blame the parents, but I blame them more'.

Sean Sexton knows that the end of the trial is far from the end of the pain for Denise and Ralph Bulger. 'In the early years there will be the anniversaries of when he went missing, and his birthday. There will always be reminders and difficult times to get through. They don't want the whole thing swept under the carpet. They don't want people to forget about what happened. They know about Mary Bell and how long she served. They are genuinely concerned that these children could be back out in society at twenty-one or twenty-two living next door to ordinary people, maybe with families, and maybe the same thing could happen again.

'I have defended young people on serious charges including attempted murder and had no qualms about it, but I would be reluctant to do it in future having seen the devastation it has caused the family. I am no longer the bleeding heart liberal that I was. It has made me think about whether there is such a thing as evil and there are some things you can't explain except by accepting that there is evil in the world. Once I would have been talking about boys like this needing a lot of work and counselling but that nobody is irredeemable. Now I would take an awful lot of persuading that they could ever be released - and I wouldn't have said that nine months ago'.

While the trial was coming to an end, one of the major building bricks in a new future for Ralph and Denise fell into place. Some of the money from the trust has been used to buy them a modest three-bedroomed house in Northwood, Kirkby, only a three-minute walk from Scoter Road. During the trial Denise and Ralph tried to occupy their thoughts hunting for furniture and planning its layout, anything to take their minds off the events in Preston for a few hours. One of their first tasks was to prepare a bedroom for the new baby. 'We can't wait to move in,' Ralph said. 'It is small but it has three bedrooms, and it's less than five minutes from Scoter Road'.

Sean Sexton remained optimistic that an employer would at last find a use for Ralph's considerable manual abilities.

In the meantime, Ralph had occupied his mind for much of the summer tinkering with a second-hand Ford Escort car. He did all his own maintenance on the car, while Denise took driving lessons so that she too would eventually be able to drive it. It would mean a lot more freedom for them both. The new baby could look forward to many a happy outing in the family car with Mum and Dad. James would have liked that.

Postscript

Robert Thompson and Jon Venables were set free on Friday, June 22, 2001, after serving eight years and four months in custody for the murder of James Bulger. Their release was hugely controversial, bringing to an end a legal battle that began almost from the moment the jury returned its guilty verdict at Preston Crown Court.

The trial judge, Mr. Justice Morland, gave a recommendation a few weeks after the case that the minimum sentence that the boys should serve would be eight years. Britain's most senior judge, The Lord Chief Justice, recommended that 10 years should be their minimum sentence. The final decision, though, lay with a politician, Home Secretary Michael Howard, who imposed a 15-year minimum sentence upon them.

This was not enough for Ralph and Denise Bulger, who were firmly and understandably of the view that life, in their case, should mean exactly that. Most people accepted, however, that even the perpetrators of such a wicked crime as the murder of James Bulger at the age of 10 should have the opportunity at some stage in the future of being rehabilitated into society.

The nature of the trial itself became the subject of a legal challenge which was eventually taken to the European Court of Human Rights. The lawyers argued that it had been inappropriate to try such young children in the intimidating surroundings of the adult courtroom in Preston. The European court accepted that the boys were, as the British court had established, criminally responsible for their actions, but nonetheless decided that the manner of their trial had been inhumane.

In a second legal challenge, lawyers representing the boys sought to overturn Mr Howard's 15-year minimum sentence. This challenge, too, was to prove ultimately successful. First the British Law Lords ruled that the 15-year minimum was illegal, and then the European courts intervened once again to declare that the final decision on sentences should sit with the judges, and not with politicians like the Home Secretary.

That put the decision on the fate of Thompson and Venables back in the hands of the judiciary, and specifically those of a progressive new Lord Chief Justice, Lord Woolf. He decided that the boys should be eligible for parole before they reached their 19th birthdays.

Throughout their time in custody, before and after their trials, Thompson and Venables had been held at secure local authority units in the north west of England, just a few miles from James's Kirkby home. Only now, after their release, are the British media legally allowed to reveal details of where they were held.

Thompson was an inmate at Barton Moss, an installation run by Salford council on the outskirts of Eccles, Greater Manchester. It is known officially as the Eccles and Irlam Children's Resource Centre, and unofficially to locals as the "bad lads' home". It is hidden away down Barton Moss Lane, a narrow country lane, next door to a Manchester School of Engineering research laboratory. With its sandy red brick buildings, Barton Moss could be a smart modern secondary school - until you notice the high, prison-style security fences penning in the unit's open areas.

Venables did not even leave Merseyside. He was locked up in the secure Vardy House wing of Red Bank, run by St. Helens council at Newton-le-Willows. This unit had been home, many years before, to another notorious British child who turned killer, Mary Bell. She was jailed in 1968 at the age of 11 for killing two toddlers and served 12 years before her release. Red Bank is set back down a short private road, shrouded by trees to obscure it from view from the busy main A47 road. Like Barton Moss it is a modern institutional brick building, its open areas enclosed by high security fences and monitored by security cameras.

Perhaps one of the greatest ironies of this case is that the education and life-training both boys received in these institutions was significantly superior to what they could have expected had they never been arrested but continued their feckless lives of truancy and petty criminality on the back streets of Liverpool.

However, at the age of 19 Thompson and Venables would have become too old to stay in these units, and would have had to transfer to young offenders institutions and eventually, at 21, to adult prisons. Many who have followed the case feel that at least a taste of these tougher regimes would have been appropriate, both as a punishment for their crimes and a deterrent to others.

This was not a view shared by Lord Chief Justice Woolf. He declared that exposing the two boys to young offenders institutions, surrounded by hardened young criminals and drug abusers, would have had a corrosive effect and destroyed much of the good work done at Barton Moss and Red Bank in terms of their rehabilitation. To the huge consternation of the people of Merseyside, he ordered, in October 2000, that the boys had completed their minimum sentences and were eligible to seek parole. Lord Woolf made his ruling based on information from social workers that Thompson and Venables had made good progress in custody and neither of them had shown any propensity for violence.

Ralph Bulger mounted a legal challenge against Lord Woolf's decision, which he took to the High Court in London, but it was to no avail. Public opinion, particularly in Merseyside, was overwhelmingly against the boys being released so soon. The Liverpool Echo newspaper ran a telephone and Internet poll which received 42,000 votes, concluding by 5 votes to 1 that the time was not yet right to let them go. But a process had begun, and it was already clear that nothing was now likely to halt it.

In June 2001, parole hearings were held, and both boys were granted their freedom. The decision was announced to Parliament by Home secretary David Blunkett.

Denise and Ralph Bulger's marriage did not survive the ordeal of living through the murder of their first son in such dreadful circumstances. They eventually divorced, and Denise is now remarried, with children by her new husband. But it is fair to say one common bond still unites them, and that is that they will both carry the emotional scars of James's death with them for the rest of their lives.

Lawyer Sean Sexton, who continued to represent Denise, said when the decision to release the boys was announced: "Denise will be devastated. She has just received a life sentence-a life of looking over her shoulder all the time when she leaves home, a life where she will be afraid to send her children to school. Denise still believes that they remain a danger to the public. She doesn't want any other family to go through what she has had to go through. We submitted expert evidence which suggested that at least one, if not both of them, might be suffering from a psychopathic personality disorder. I pray to God that we are wrong and the Parole Board have got it right".

Like all convicted murderers granted parole under British law, Thompson and Venables are on life licence. That means that if they commit any further offence, at any time for the rest of their lives, they will be automatically recalled to prison to resume serving their life sentences for murder.

They enjoy the protection of new identities, and draconian legal restrictions on the British media which make it illegal not just to report on their lives or whereabouts, but even to make enquiries about them.

Inevitably rumors surface from time to time, from the credible to the utterly far-fetched, about their current whereabouts and behaviour. Given the legal shackles placed upon British journalists, we have to take it on trust that the authorities are monitoring them properly, and will not allow a situation to develop where they can become a threat to others.

Even Venables's former lawyer, Lawrence Lee, expressed concern at the decision to set them free. He said he believed the killers were "emotionally incapable" of coping with their new secret identities, adding: "Physically they may be free, but mentally they will be incarcerated for ever".

-Mark Thomas, October 2005

For sales, editorial information, subsidiary rights information
or a catalog, please write or phone or e-mail

iBooks
1230 Park Avenue, 9a
New York, New York 10128, US
Sales: 1-800-68-BRICK
Tel: 212-427-7139
www.BrickTowerPress.com
email: bricktower@aol.com.

www.ingram.com

www.ingramcontent.com/pod-product-compliance
Lightning Source LLC
Chambersburg PA
CBHW030530100426
42813CB00001B/209